A LEARNING COMPANION

Your guide to practising
independent learning

LORRAINE MARSHALL

PEARSON
Longman

© 2006 Pearson Education Australia (a division of Pearson Australia Group Pty Ltd)

Pearson Education Australia
Unit 4, Level 3
14 Aquatic Drive
Frenchs Forest, Sydney NSW 2086
Ph: 02 9454 2200
www.pearsoned.com.au

Associate Editor: Jill Gillies
Project Editor: Chris Richardson

Printed in Malaysia (CTP - GPS)

4 5 10 09 08 07

ISBN 10   0 7339 6977 1
ISBN 13   978 0 7339 6977 5

An imprint of Pearson Education Australia

Contents

Acknowledgements

It is impossible for a book of this nature that has grown and developed over many years to be the work of one person. My thinking and ideas were enriched by many people, while others have contributed directly. Where exercises or information are based on other people's ideas or work, their contribution has been acknowledged.

I thank my daughter, Suzannah, who when she was 9 was responsible for the title of the book. When explaining my struggles for a title with her fresh, unencumbered insight she spontaneously said 'this book is a sort of friend, a companion to those who use it, and a companion to *A guide to learning independently*.' Thank you also to Joan for providing a room at her homestead in eastern Victoria where I completed the substantive work on this book. And a special thank you to Jim with whom I developed many of the original lesson plans that formed the basis of this text.

Acknowledgements for this edition

For this Pearson Education edition I thank Claire Pickering for her detailed proof reading of the manuscript and Bonnie McBride for her expert word processing. A special thank you to Jill Gillies and the staff in the Sydney office of Pearson Education for their patience as they waited for the finished product while I nursed my elderly mother and coped with her death. Jill's understanding at this time made it possible for me to complete the final draft in time for it to be available to students.

Acknowledgements for Murdoch University editions

In 1997 when the book was compiled in its current form Sally Knowles, Colin Beasley, Ann Firth, Marian Kemp and David Lake contributed extensively. Several others, including Liana Christensen, Frances Rowland and Jim Macbeth, read earlier editions, Anne McBride put in many creative hours on the computer, and Allison Brown made suggestions on layout and design.

The material on learning logs has been adapted from work written and used by David Tripp. The exercises on numeracy have developed and been influenced by people who have held the numeracy position in Student Learning at Murdoch University: Marian Kemp, Mary Dale, Marilys Guillemin, and Anne Chapman. The material on plagiarism and collusion was developed in the School of Education, and has been used and adapted by various people at Murdoch.

Thank you all.

Introduction

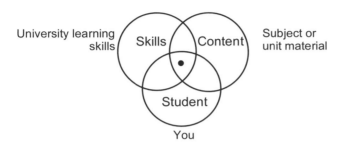

The graphic above is a venn diagram. One circle represents the **student** (you), another the **learning skills** that you require at university, and another the **content** (subject matter or material) that you are learning. The intersection of these three areas is the focus of this book. *A learning companion* is a collection of exercises that consider and discuss who you are as a student and the skills that you need at university. Although the content or subject matter that you are studying is not directly covered, the exercises can be systematically integrated with the content and requirements in most disciplines and units of study.

The exercises are designed to develop study, literacy and critical thinking skills:

- study skills, include:
    - organising and planning your time;
    - concentrating;
    - remembering information;
    - preparing for exams.

- literacy skills, include:
    - listening to lectures and making notes from lecture;
    - participating in academic discussions and debates;
    - preparing and giving oral presentations;
    - reading (including the reading of numerical information);
    - preparing and writing essays;
    - researching.

- critical thinking skills, include:
  - recognising and evaluating arguments presented verbally and in writing;
  - developing your own arguments, verbally and in writing.

All of these skills will continue to develop throughout your university studies and beyond. This book is designed to help you embark on this lifelong voyage of learning.

Using the exercises

You may be studying a unit in which the coordinator links the relevant exercises to the content and requirements, or where you apply the exercises to the unit independently of your teacher. The exercises can be used in on-campus units, perhaps with supporting classes to discuss the issues raised with a tutor or other students. They can be applied within distance or open learning units where you are working alone, perhaps with limited opportunities for discussion with either a tutor or with other students in online discussion groups. They also lend themselves to online collaboration between students with support from a tutor.

If you are using these exercises independently, select a unit or part of a unit that you are currently studying or about to study and apply the exercises to the content and requirements. It is not necessary to complete the exercises in the order they are presented, nor to complete all of them. There are several exercises that deal with study tasks, so select those that are most appropriate to your needs. The exercises can also be applied to informal or non-study learning tasks.

The skills that you develop by applying these exercises to one unit can help in subsequent units when similar tasks are required. The exercises relating to a particular skill or task are grouped together, which enables you to go back and apply them to a different unit, or to spend more time developing a skill or an aspect of your study.

This book is divided into chapters, and each chapter into exercises. Each exercise includes:

- an **introduction** explaining the rationale behind the exercise, that is, its place in your overall study;

- the objectives or **what you can expect to gain** from completing each exercise is explained in terms of what each exercise encourages and enables you to achieve;

- the approximate **time** it should take to complete the exercise (This estimate is an average, and spending longer on an exercise might suit your needs.);

- a list of **log entries** to guide your writing;

- a list of the **materials** required to complete the exercise (Some of these are provided and some you need to supply, such as your unit materials.);

- a list of **worksheets** for each exercise;

- any required **reading** (Most exercises are based on, support and extend the material in Marshall and Rowland, 2006, *A guide to learning independently*. As this book is a companion to *A guide to learning independently*, it should be used in conjunction with it. Some exercises refer to other books but can be completed without them.);

- a series of **learning activities** to complete (Each of these has a bold heading which makes previewing the exercises easier.).

The following symbols are used as follows:

Log entries

Worksheets

Additional materials

Answer sheet

Beginning this book

First, preview this book to gain an idea of what it contains. You have already started previewing by reading this introduction. Also carefully read the table of contents and look through the book to find out how it relates to your learning goals and objectives and to your unit content and requirements. Note that each chapter contains a detailed summary as an explosion chart or patterned notes. Now before you proceed any further, refer to Exercise 15, 'Previewing a book', for tips on previewing.

If this book is a main text in your unit of study, your learning guide or your lecturer will explain which exercises, log entries and/or worksheets to complete, and how to do these. You may be required to complete more exercises at the beginning of a unit than at the end, as you can then refine these skills in tasks that are required later. If you are working through this book on your own, you can choose those exercises that are most relevant and useful to you. Nevertheless, the exercises and information in this book will be especially useful if you are commencing or are early in your study of a unit.

You may use the exercises in the following ways.

- The first chapter of this book, 'Getting started', is intended to set you on the right track, both with your studies and with this book. This chapter will help you begin a learning log, assess your current learning strengths and skills, and start your studies by leading you through a preview of your study materials.

- The first exercise, 'Keeping a learning log', explains the importance of strategies for keeping a learning log. Please begin with this exercise, as a learning log can help you reflect on your learning. Each exercise includes suggestions for log entries to stimulate and give structure to your reflections. Aim to keep your log in a loose-leaf format so you can add your completed worksheets to it. If these exercises form part of a unit, you may be required to submit the worksheets and/or your learning log to your tutor and they may be assessed. Note the symbols used for log entries and worksheets.

When you have completed Chapter 1, decide which exercises are most appropriate to your needs.

- Work through the second chapter, 'Learning about your learning', if you are interested in increasing your awareness of how you learn.

- At the beginning of your study you may need to develop a study timetable, which allows time for your formal learning as well as for the other priorities in your life. Work through Exercise 5, 'Organising and planning study', if you need to organise and plan your study time more effectively. However, make sure that you return to this exercise later as it can be difficult to realistically allocate time to different tasks at the beginning of a semester or study period.

- Work through Exercise 15, 'Previewing a book', if you wish to preview your unit texts, or work through Exercise 16, 'Previewing edited books', if your text is a book of readings.

Principles, methods and outcomes of the exercises

In order to help you develop the necessary skills, these exercises are based on two key principles: that learning is a lifelong activity and that learning to learn is a developmental process. The methods used include the integration of skills with content, reflecting on learning and sharing learning with others. Some of these methods are applied in all exercises, while others are encouraged where appropriate. In addition to the development of skills, the exercises aim to help you develop certain attitudes and approaches to learning that can further enhance your skills and their future development.

The intended outcomes or what you can expect to gain from completing these exercises include:

- empowering you to function successfully in the university system;
- helping you transfer your learning skills from one context to another;
- focusing on your learning goals and objectives;
- encouraging you to reflect on your learning;
- helping you become a more independent and autonomous learner, while still learning from and with others;
- helping you become a more effective and efficient learner;
- fostering the attitude that learning to learn is a lifelong activity;
- increasing your awareness of how you learn, of other approaches to your learning and of learning expectations at university;
- continuing to use the strategies presented to further develop your learning.

Limitations of the exercises

The written exercises have certain limitations as they are designed to be completed by yourself.

- Providing or receiving immediate **feedback** is not always possible. However, feedback in the form of answers to the numeracy exercises is available in the appendices. Lectures or tutors who use this book are urged to give feedback on, but not assess, your log entries and worksheets.

- **Working with other students**, either in pairs or groups, is not always possible but is encouraged where it is appropriate to the skill being developed. In several exercises you are asked to discuss your approach to learning with other students and receive feedback from them.

- Students have **different skill levels** and these are difficult to accommodate in one set of materials however carefully planned. However, you can decide on which activities to focus by previewing the introductory statements outlining what you should gain from each exercise. In most exercises you are asked to reflect on and self-assess your ability in each skill before working on it, and in this way you are more likely to be able to judge your developmental needs in relation to each skill.

- Instruction in **grammar and punctuation** is not provided. Students who have difficulty with these skills should seek help from a learning adviser or an appropriate text. As university assessment is mostly in the form of writing, grammar and punctuation skills are important.

CHAPTER 1

Getting started

This chapter is designed to help you start using this book and applying the exercises within it to your unit(s) of study.

This chapter begins with an exercise on keeping a learning log. Learning logs provide a systematic way to reflect on your learning, and can be used in various contexts during university study. The second exercise encourages you to reflect on your previous learning experiences, which is a theme followed throughout the book. It asks you to identify your learning strengths and weaknesses in order to identify those skills you need to develop. The third exercise examines and explores the materials that you will be using in a unit of study.

1. Keeping a learning log

- Previous experiences with keeping a journal, diary or learning log
- Value of keeping a learning log
- Types of learning logs
  - type of log to keep
  - necessary equipment
- Ground rules for keeping a learning log
- Making log entries
  - what to write about
  - make a log entry
  - continue to write

2. Transferring learning strengths into university study

- Previous learning experiences
- Conditions that enhance your learning
- Your learning strengths
- Gaps in your learning experiences
- Lifelong learning
- Transferring reading skills
- Evaluating your learning

Getting started

3. Planning your approach to study

- Previous formal learning experiences
- Preview your unit study guide
- What is expected in your unit
- Skills you need for effective learning
- Planning your study for the next few weeks
- Questions for your tutor

1.   Keeping a learning log[1]

Introduction

Reading and writing are vital activities in university study. An effective and organised way of keeping track and recording your learning from reading, discussion, writing and other study tasks involves documenting what you are learning as you progress through a unit of study. Your development as a student can be enhanced and can be more satisfying if you reflect on your learning by regularly writing about it.

A learning log can be used to reflect on your learning and any transformations in your thinking. Reflection is a key process in integrating what you learn with your existing knowledge. Throughout this book you are invited to stop and reflect on a task or problem, and to write about these reflections in your learning log. It is hoped that this will guide and help transform your learning. At the end of most exercises there are suggestions for log entries that provide stimulus and structure for making entries on a computer, as a web log (blog) or with pen and paper.

This exercise encourages you

- to develop a method of keeping a learning log;

- to comment on the various strategies outlined in this book;

- to write regularly in your log;

- to use your log to explore your ideas, issues and questions and to document your reflections on your learning;

- to be aware that the process of writing informally in a log, on a regular basis, can have an impact on your formal academic writing.

Approximate time

60 minutes

Reading

Marshall & Rowland, 2006, Chapter 12, pp. 200–203

---

[1]   Adapted from materials written by Dr David Tripp, School of Education, Murdoch University. See also David Tripp, 1993, *Critical incidents in teaching: the development of professional judgement*, Routledge, London & New York.

Learning activities

Activity 1 Previous experiences with keeping a journal, diary or learning log

Reflect on previous experiences you have had with keeping a journal, diary or log and make notes about the actual experience.

Was it positive? Why?

Was it negative? Why?

If your previous experiences were positive, you may not have any difficulty with the idea of keeping a learning log.

If your previous experiences were negative, outline what you need to do to make keeping a learning log more positive. You may need to persevere more with your log and think about it as one that can be more satisfying for you. You may need to put in more effort or talk to someone about this (preferably your tutor).

Consider any alternatives to keeping a log that are acceptable to you.

It might be helpful to talk to someone who is also keeping a learning log and perhaps share log entries by email, as a blog or by telephone. This can help motivate you to keep going.

Activity 2 Value of keeping a learning log

Think of your log as a place where you, the student, can spend time noting your reflections. Relate the information from your reading, lectures and other study activities to yourself and to those life experiences that impinge on and influence your learning.

You will find that the thoughts and ideas you express in your log can be invaluable in developing your thinking about formal assignments. It can save time if you put ideas and concepts into words that you will use later in your writing. As always, how much you get out of your study depends on how much you put into it.

It is not usual practice to formally assess a learning log, as it is for your own use. However, in some units you might be required to submit your log or some of your entries. By using a loose-leaf format (see Activity 3), you can easily remove those entries that are personal or that you don't want anyone else to read.

Activity 3   Types of learning logs

It is important to made decisions about the type of learning log you would like to keep.

Type of log to keep

First, consider whether you will use a word processor, pen and paper or a combination of these to make your log entries. Consider whether you will use a bound notebook or a loose-leaf format. By using a computer you will be able to revise, copy and move text more freely than on paper. However, by using a loose-leaf folder you can still be flexible in how you organise your log. Using both a computer and loose-leaf format will enable you to intersperse hand written or typed material, carry a few sheets of paper and write when the inspiration strikes and insert material jotted on scraps of paper. You might prefer to use a standard notebook that restricts your flexibility but is more attractive to you.

Necessary equipment

If you decide to use a loose-leaf format, purchase a file and file dividers, and create a cover for your log. If you decide to use a notebook, purchase a book that you find attractive and easy to hold and write in. If you decide to use a computer set up separate folders and documents.

Activity 4   Ground rules for keeping a learning log

Aim to use the following ground rules for keeping your log.

1. Date each entry in your log.

2. Divide your log into different sections or categories.

- Clearly distinguish entries about your self and your life from entries about your study. For example, you might write about your family life but keep it in a separate section from your reflections on your study. You might choose to use different coloured paper (background) or pens (text) to separate these.

- Separate lecture and reading summaries and notes from your opinions, comments and reflections on these. If working on a computer, use a different font or format to distinguish these. Or if using a book, write your summaries and notes on the left-hand pages and write your opinions, comments and reflections about these on the right-hand pages.

Read Marshall and Rowland, 2006, Chapter 12, 'Keeping a personal journal/diary' pp. 200-203, which discusses the method and rationale for keeping a journal or diary. This is about keeping a personal journal but there are many similarities between this and keep a learning log.

Then read the entire chapter 'Developing your writing', pp. 193-207, which details the benefits of regularly making learning log entries. Writing is both a means of recording information and transforming information into your own knowledge.

Activity 5   Making log entries

What to write about

Keeping a learning log can help you understand yourself as a learner and your learning (both formal and informal). Throughout this book you are given suggestions on making log entries. At times you are asked about your 'self' and at other times you are asked to link who you are as a learner with the content you are learning. When writing about your learning you might like to consider and discuss the following points in your log:

- your history as a learner;
- any memories of learning as a child, and any significant learning experiences in your life;
- your experiences of learning in school;
- the most common type of learning in which you are currently engaged;
- the type of learning you most enjoy;
- your study goals and objectives;
- your study expectations, what you are expecting to learn and what you think each unit you study will (or should) cover.

Make a log entry

When you have organised your log, make your first entry. Refer to the questions asked in Activity 1 and describe your previous experiences with keeping a journal, diary or log.

If you have trouble writing about yourself or your previous writing experiences, begin by making notes about your day. You might use a patterned noted format[2]. For example, think about your day and pick out one feature or theme that represents what this day meant to you. Your day might have been ordinary or perhaps something happened in the morning that made you feel happy all day. Write this in the middle of the page and put a circle around it. On spokes coming from this circle, list aspects about the day that relate to this central feature or theme.

Read the following extract, 'Keeping the daily log', by Ira Progoff[3] to guide your first entry.

Keeping the daily log

Think back to how you felt when you awakened in the morning.

Describe the mood, the sensations – physical, mental.

Do you have the feeling that you were dreaming during the night? What was the general atmosphere of those dreams? How much of them can you remember and write down?

What was your mood as the day started? How did the morning unfold?

What thoughts kept coming into your mind without your deliberately thinking them? Worries, hopes, fantasies? What emotions? Angers, loves?

What events took place with people, works, groups?

Did unusual situations occur, situations of intensity, crisis, joy?

How does the day proceed? Note the rhythms of the day as you move from the morning to the afternoon, into the evening. Does the quality of your feelings, your mood, your emotions change?

---

[2]   Examples of patterned notes are used throughout this book. For further information on using mind maps for self-analysis, see Tony Buzan, 1993, *The mind map book*. BBC Books, London, pp 176-182.

[3]   Marshall & Rowland, 2006, pp. 200–201.

> Recapitulate your experiences of the day – all the occurrences that you can perceive both within your mind and on the outside of your life.
>
> Write these without judgement: nothing to be proud of, nothing to be ashamed of; no praise, no blame.
>
> Now feel the day as a whole. Write a few adjectives and a metaphor for how the day feels to you.
>
> Ira Progoff

Allow yourself about 30 minutes to complete your first entry, but make sure you have enough time for thinking and writing. It can be useful to jot down ideas quickly in point form that capture an important thought.

Continue to write

In your learning log continue to write your reflections on your learning as requested throughout this book.

Keeping a learning log

1. Previous experiences with a journal, diary or log

Describe your previous experiences with keeping a journal, diary or learning log.

Explain why you found this experience positive or negative.

If your previous experiences were negative, outline what you need to do to make keeping a learning log more positive. You may need to persevere more with your log and think about it as one that can be more satisfying for you. Consider any alternatives to keeping a log that are acceptable to you.

If your previous experiences with keeping a log were positive, write about any changes you need to make to follow the approach explained in this exercise.

2. Transferring learning strengths into university study

Introduction

Usually when considering the transfer of knowledge and skills, we think about the process of transfer from an educational to a non-educational context. However, it is also possible to transfer skills and knowledge from a non-academic to an academic setting. You are constantly involved in the learning process, in learning new information or skills, but you probably rarely consider your prior learning or how you use your new learning. This exercise encourages you to transfer your learning to new situations by asking you to consider your learning strengths so that you can adapt and apply those that are appropriate to your study.

Many of the exercises in this book require that you consider if any of your previous learning experiences are relevant to the academic skills being developed. The following exercise asks you to reflect on your prior learning in formal situations, such as secondary school, and apply your knowledge of this learning to what is expected in university study. If possible complete this exercise with another student, friend or family member. Write your log entries on your own and then discuss what you have written with your partner or in a group. It is preferable if both or all of you complete the exercise.

This exercise encourages you

- to reflect on the skills and abilities you bring to university study;

- to transfer learning from one situation to another.

Materials

2.1   Profile of the lifelong learner

2.2   Reading with transfer in mind

Approximate time

60 minutes

Reading

Marshall & Rowland, 2006, pp. 82–83.

Learning activities

Activity 1   Previous learning experiences

Reflect on your previous learning experiences – perhaps at home, in a job, for a hobby or at school. Select a project in which you were involved and interested, where you learnt a lot and that was enjoyable and successful. In your learning log, briefly describe the project, what you learned and the skills involved.

Examples of informal learning projects include choosing a new car, negotiating a contract, learning to play tennis, fixing your car, raising a child, learning to scuba dive and so on.

A further example of an informal learning project might be learning to care for an aged relative. This could have involved you actually deciding what you needed to learn about caring for the aged, setting goals that you hoped to achieve for your relative, seeking information on health and other associated issues, and learning how to listen sympathetically.

Activity 2   Conditions that enhance your learning

In your learning log, re-read your description of a past project and describe the conditions that helped you to learn. Try to be as specific as you can.

Consider and then describe how you can transfer your knowledge of how you learn into your study. Write about this and then share it with another person.

Activity 3   Your learning strengths

In your learning log, draw up two columns. In the first column, list those learning skills that you consider to be your strengths. Don't restrict yourself here. Your strengths might be reading, planning parties, organising other people, working for extended times on topics of interest, using your hands, visualising, rote learning, parenting, following recipes, writing letters to the editor and so on.

In the second column, describe the origin of this skill and where it has been fostered.

Using an asterisk, identify those skills that you think might be useful in your university study. Which skills do you need to adapt, change or refine to fulfil the expectations of study at university?

If you are beginning tertiary study, you may find this question challenging. Remember that the formal learning environment of a tertiary institution may require that you modify present skills or develop new abilities.

Activity 4   Gaps in your learning experiences

Reflect on your life and in your learning log write about any gaps in your life experiences that may have influenced your repertoire of skills. For example, perhaps you are an expert plumber and handy with your hands, but have little experience with book learning. Perhaps you were raised in a household with few books. Perhaps you spent a lot of time alone and are uncomfortable talking in groups. Perhaps you grew up in a family where listening to others was not the norm.

Discuss with a study partner(s) what you will do to overcome these gaps. For example, perhaps you can attend special classes, seek out appropriate material or work through the appropriate chapters in this book.

Activity 5   Lifelong learning

2.1

Read the attached information, 'Profile of the lifelong learner', and note the following about this profile[4].

- The attribute will be embodied in different people in varying degrees and combinations, according not only to their individual backgrounds and fields of study, but also according to their construction of the demands of each particular learning situation. Thus there is no such thing as a 'one size fits all' profile of the lifelong learner; these characteristics are only generic or context-free to a limited extent.

- Overarching all these various attributes is the ability to act strategically as learning needs and opportunities arise.

---

[4]   Phillip C. Candy et al., 1994, *Developing lifelong learners through undergraduate education*, NBEET, Australian Government Publishing Service, Canberra, pp.43-44.

- Learning competence cannot be achieved in isolation, nor can it meaningfully be lifted out of the total context of the educational outcomes desired from any particular course of study, or for that matter from undergraduate education as a whole.

In your learning log, describe the qualities and characteristics of a lifelong learner and compare these with your skills and knowledge.

If you are beginning university study, you may feel that you have a long way to go before reaching this level. This book aims to support your learning as outlined in the profile. However, it cannot help you with the two points under the heading 'helicopter vision'.

Activity 6   Transferring reading skills

Reading is one skill that you need to transfer from your everyday life to your tertiary study. Examine the attached material, 'Reading with transfer in mind', which contrasts reading a newspaper (an informal environment) with reading an academic text. Read these and consider the skills you have that are appropriate for university reading, and any skills that you may need to refine or develop.

In your learning log, arrange a response under the following headings.

- Reading skills I have that are appropriate for university study.
- Reading skills I need to refine or develop.

Make other entries in your log on any skills you will need to adapt or modify that can be transferred into your university study. How will you these skills?

Activity 7   Evaluating your learning

Refer to these log entries as you progress through your study as they can serve as a useful checklist when you complete these exercises and evaluate your learning. They can also provide a benchmark of your learning strengths at the beginning of your study. See also Exercise 9, 'Evaluating your learning'.

You will be referred back to this exercise when you complete this book.

Transferring learning strengths into university study

1. Previous learning experiences

Reflect on your previous learning experiences – perhaps at home, in a job, for a hobby or at school. Select a project in which you were involved and interested, where you learnt a lot and that was enjoyable and successful. Briefly describe the project, what you learned and the skills involved.

2. Conditions that enhance your learning

Describe the conditions that help you to learn. Try to be as specific as you can.

Describe how you transfer your knowledge of how you learn into your study.

3. Your learning strengths

Draw up two columns. In the first column, list those learning skills that you consider to be your strengths. Don't restrict yourself here. In the second column, describe the origin of this skill and where it has been fostered.

Using an asterisk, identify those skills that you think might be useful in your university study. Which skills do you need to adapt, change or refine to fulfil the expectations of study at university?

4. Gaps in your learning

Write about any gaps in your life experiences that may have influenced your repertoire of skills.

5. Lifelong learning

Describe the qualities and characteristics of a lifelong learner and compare these to your skills and knowledge.

6. Transferring reading skills

Which reading skills do you already have that are appropriate for university study? Which reading skills do you need to refine or develop? How will you do this?

Profile of the lifelong learner[5]

The report *Developing lifelong learners through undergraduate education* suggests that lifelong learners exhibit the following qualities or characteristics to some degree.

An inquiring mind

- love of learning;
- a sense of curiosity and question asking;
- a critical spirit;
- comprehension-monitoring and self evaluation.

Helicopter vision

- a sense of the interconnectedness of fields;
- an awareness of how knowledge is created in at least one field of study; and an understanding of the methodological and substantive limitations of that field.

Information literacy

- knowledge of major current resources available in at least one field of study;
- ability to frame researchable questions in at least one field of study;
- ability to locate, evaluate, manage and use information in a range of contexts;
- ability to retrieve information using a variety of media;
- ability to decode information in a variety of forms; written, statistical, graphs, charts, diagrams and tables;
- critical evaluation of information.

A sense of personal agency

- a positive concept of oneself as capable and autonomous;
- self-organisation skills (time management, goal setting etc).

A repertoire of learning skills

- knowledge of one's own strengths, weaknesses and preferred learning style;
- range of strategies for learning in whatever context one finds oneself;
- an understanding of the differences between surface and deep level learning.

---

[5] Phillip C. Candy et al., 1994, pp.43-44.

2.2

Activity 6

Reading with transfer in mind[6]

Check where it's from. Is it likely to be relevant?

Catchy title skim to see if you want to read on.

Home filled ceiling-high with rubbish

ADELAIDE: An Adelaide family lived for 10 years in a house so filled with rubbish that the owner and her three sons had to sleep in the attic.

Cleaners ordered in to tidy the house last week were shocked by what they found, filling a 10-tonne tipper bin with rubbish from the kitchen alone.

The four cleaners, wearing masks because of the stench, had to crouch beneath the ceiling as they shovelled rubbish into bags.

So much rubbish was piled against doors that they could not be opened or closed, and doors to the toilet and bathroom were jammed so tight they had to be removed.

The toilet bowl had disappeared under debris and after several hours the cleaners had not seen any furniture.

Cleaners were confronted by cats and kittens crawling out of the mess.

"There are cats popping up everywhere," one cleaner said.

The stench from rotting garbage could be smelled in the street.

Putrid food and the remains of meals from years ago formed a knee-deep layer in some rooms.

Cleaners estimated there were thousands of empty baked beans tins inside.

Three fridges contained the remains of food, some in containers which had use-by dates of three and four years ago.

The cleaners used shovels, garden forks and picks to get into the mess.

The house was so full of rubbish that the family had converted the carport into a lounge.

The Department for Family and Community Services called in the cleaners because of the health risks.

A FACS spokesman said the department had been counselling the woman and boys — aged 12, 14 and 16 — for about two months to help them resolve family problems.

She said FACS had only become aware of the extent of the rubbish problem after seeing photographs given to them by the local council two weeks ago.

Cleaners said the big bin would be filled at least three more times before the house was finally emptied of rubbish.

"The family started to live outside and I even saw them using a broken front window to get in and out at the front because they couldn't open the front door," a neighbour said.

Perhaps just read first and last paragraphs.

National Beacon signals

One sentence paragraphs — easy to read – each contains a single point or issue. May scan the article looking for interesting points.

Little need to retain the information.

---

6   Jill Barrett, Linda Butcher & Lorraine Marshall, 1995, *From life to learning: transferable skills for independent learning*, Gripping Films, Murdoch University.

Note source

Agriculture & Recycling, Vol 2, pp 269 - 271.
Pergamon Press Ltd., 1979 Printed in Great Britain

NEW PROCESS FOR RECYCLING AGRICULTURAL WASTE AS A SLOW RELEASE FERTILISER

Ask yourself questions about title

J. WATSON
Bailieboro Co-Operative Group, Ireland.
and
J. O'SHEA, T. A. SPILLANE, J. F. CONNOLLY
Agricultural Institute, Dunsinea Research Centre, Ireland.

Note authors – check to see what else they have written.

Abstract — The trends towards intensive livestock farming and intensive fertilisation of agriculture, and, to counter increased food demand, has led to an upsurge in research aimed at efficiently recycling nutrients present in animal wastes. This has been stimulated further, in many countries, by recent anti-pollution laws that restrict present disposal methods.

A new process is presently being developed in Ireland to convert organic waste to a high premium slow release fertiliser. The process includes anaerobic digestion of the waste and subsequent chemical treatment with urea and formaldehyde. The product formed is similar to others commercially available for horticultural purposes.

Introduction – read carefully as provides background. Then skip to conclusion.

INTRODUCTION

The purpose of this paper is to outline development work, currently in progress in Ireland, which involves the recycling of animal waste in a unique manner and, as a consequence, eliminates the potential pollution associated with the disposal of waste from agricultural sources.

Material divided into distinct sections – preview all headings in article

PRESENT NUTRIENT RECYCLING METHODS

It has been estimated from figures produced by the E.E.C. Ministry of Agriculture and Fisheries[10] that in 1974 the total waste obtained from cattle, pigs and poultry in the community was 859 million tonnes (Table 1). Of this total about 80% will have been deposited

Make notes on purpose of paper

Table 1. Animal waste production (1974)

Item		E.E.C.	U.S.	Total
Waste Tonne × 10⁶/year	Cattle	720	1,168	1,888
	Pigs	115	100	215
	Poultry	24	14	38
	Total	859	1,282	2,141

Read table carefully and relate it to text.

directly onto the land and the nutrients were thereby recycled naturally to the soil. The remaining 172 million tonnes of waste was obtained from housed animals and had to be disposed of by the best means available. In recent years, as growing economic pressures have encouraged the development of intensive farming and as more stringent anti-pollution legislation was enacted, the problem of animal waste disposal has increased greatly.

The treatment of livestock waste is being studied extensively and emphasis is being placed on utilization of slurry rather than disposal. The processes which are currently being investigated include: solids separation[1]; biological treatment — both aerobic[12] and anaerobic[5]; flocculation, heat drying; incineration[3]; conversion into feedstuffs and usage as a basis for the production of protein[4].

Text dense so read slowly to determine main points. Underline key sentences to reduce density.

269

Aim to relate content to what you already know.

16

3. Planning your approach to study
Introduction

This exercise is designed to get you started on your study materials. In this exercise you will apply your previous learning experiences in formal learning situations (perhaps in secondary school) to what is expected of you in your university study. You are also asked to consider the skills that you will need in your current study.

This exercise builds on the previous exercise where you examined your learning strengths.

This exercise encourages you

- to reflect on your previous formal learning experiences in relation to your current university study;

- to consider your learning in a unit to which you will apply these exercises;

- to plan systematically for your study.

Approximate time

30 minutes

Reading

Marshall & Rowland, 2006, Chapter 1, pp. 1–18 & Chapter 3, pp. 37–59.

Learning activities

Activity 1 Previous formal learning experiences

 Consider how you learned in your school subjects or in other formal learning environments. In your learning log, list the activities and skills that were involved. Think about how these combined, and which you found most useful, easy or difficult.

Activity 2 Preview your unit study guide

Select a unit to which you will apply the following activities.

Preview your unit study materials to remind yourself of the overall unit requirements, including the unit aims and objectives, lecture programme, required reading and submission deadlines for assignment. Refer to the exercise on previewing in Chapter 4, 'Reading', to help you here.

 In your learning log describe what you think is expected of you in this unit.

Activity 3 What is expected in your unit

Compare what you are expected to do in the unit with what was expected in your previous school science and/or humanities subjects.

In most university units you will be expected to do some or all of the following:

- use the unit aims and objectives to guide your learning;
- use different mediums (lectures, written material, experimental observation) to gain information;
- use a range of information sources;
- preview material to identify the main points;
- read widely for assignments;
- read for understanding;
- analyse and evaluate arguments;
- sift evidence when reading and listening to lectures;
- express your arguments clearly in discussions and writing.

Activity 4 Skills you need for effective learning

In your learning log, reflect on your answers in the previous activities and describe the skills you will need to develop in order to learn effectively in the unit.

Activity 5 Planning your study for the next few weeks

Begin to take charge of your learning by planning what you are going to do for the unit and when. List the unit requirements.

Develop a temporary timetable for the next few weeks or until you work through Exercise 5, 'Organising and planning study'. Allow plenty of time to research and read before writing. Display your timetable in an obvious place, such as on the front of your workbook or file or on a noticeboard by your desk. This is your plan. When you have a clearer idea of what is expected, you can make a more definitive timetable. If you do change your timetable, do so consciously and keep in mind your reasons for study. Where possible, make sure that you remain in charge of your learning.

Activity 6 Questions for your tutor

In your learning log, list any questions about the unit to ask your tutor. You might find it useful to set aside a section in your learning log for such questions.

Make a habit of noting any questions that you may have about particular readings or sources, as well as about administration and assessment. Attach these to each assignment, or email or telephone your tutor if this is more convenient. Asking questions can help you gain what you want from a unit.

Planning your approach to study

1   Previous formal learning experiences

List the activities and skills that were involved in learning in school subjects or in other formal learning environments. Which activities and skills did you find most useful, easy or difficult?

2.   Preview your unit study guide

Describe what you think is expected of you in the unit.

3.   Skills you need to develop to learn effectively

What skills do you need to develop in order to learn effectively in the unit?

4.   Questions for your tutor

List any questions about the unit to ask your tutor.

CHAPTER 2

Learning about your learning

Many students are unaccustomed to reflecting on how they learn, or on the conditions required to learn effectively. The exercises in this chapter are designed to increase your awareness of your own learning by encouraging you to reflect on this through discussion and writing.

Some exercises in the chapter use material from research studies to enhance your reflection, while other exercises ask for an analysis of particular learning tasks and an evaluation of learning in relation to goals.

All of the exercises in this chapter take into account that each student learns differently. The exercises emphasise the importance of:

- being aware of your study goals and objectives;

- the role of reflection in transforming and transferring learning;

- being aware of your own learning processes and strengths and weaknesses;

- experimenting with different learning techniques;

- being systematic, that is, organising and planning;

- deciding on and setting goals and objectives for study tasks.

You have your own individual learning style and it is your responsibility to take charge of your learning and decide how to approach your university study.

5. Organising and planning study
- Previous experiences with organising and planning your time
- How you spend your time
  - collect and summarise data
  - analyse data
  - attitudes to keeping track of your time
  - importance of a study space
- Relationship between goals and planning
- Deciding on your priorities
- Planning your time
  - long-term tasks to accomplish
  - short-term tasks to accomplish
  - map out a week's study
- Time expected on study
- Reflection on organising and planning

4. Examining reasons for studying
- Your reasons for studying
  - your highest hopes
  - why you are studying
  - why study particular units
- Orientations and approaches to study
  - apply research data
  - orientations in relation to your long-term goals
- Your mode of study

Learning about your learning 2

9. Evaluating your learning
- Previous experiences with self evaluation
- Value of self evaluation
- Evaluating learning skills development
  - identify what to evaluate
  - evaluate the development of a learning skill
  - write a self evaluation
  - continue to evaluate your learning
- Evaluate overall learning skills development
  - review the learning skills covered
  - evaluate your learning skills
  - write a self evaluation
- Self evaluation in other contexts

6. Concentrating
- Previous experiences with concentrating
  - concentrating well
  - concentration problems
- Concentration levels during study sessions
- Techniques for longer study sessions
- Graphing your concentration levels
- Reflection on improving your concentration

8. Preparing for examinations
- Your attitude towards exams
- Information on the exam
  - what is expected
  - types of exam
  - types of questions
  - what is being tested
- The revision process
  - the rocket model of revision
- Effective exam study techniques
- Effective time management for exams
- Exam simulation
  - exam techniques
  - an exam situation
  - reflection on exam simulation
- Reflection on time management following an exam

7. Remembering information
- Techniques you use to remember information
- List of techniques for remembering
- Techniques to improve remembering

4. Examining reasons for studying

Introduction

Some students have clear reasons for studying, others don't. Students' reasons for enrolling in particular units of study can vary from one unit to another, as can their approach to studying them. By analysing your reasons for studying you can come to understand your approach to learning. This exercise uses research data on the orientations of one group of students to study to help you analyse your reasons for studying[1].

This exercise encourages you

- to analyse, reflect on and articulate your reasons for and approach to studying, using research findings on why students study;

- to articulate your reasons for studying in a particular mode (on campus, distance education or open learning).

Materials

4.1   Why students study: student orientations to study

4.2   Summary of students' orientations to study

Approximate time

30 minutes

Reading

Marshall & Rowland, 2006, Chapter 3, pp. 45–50.

---

[1] Elizabeth Taylor, et al., 1980, *The orientations of students studying the social science foundation course*. Study Methods Group Report. No. 7. Institute of Educational Technology, The Open University, Milton Keynes.

Learning activities

Activity 1   Your reasons for studying

Your highest hopes for university

In your learning log, answer the following question.

If your university study fulfilled your highest hopes, what would you gain from your study when it is completed?

Why you are studying

In order to articulate your reasons for studying take a few moments to reflect on why you have enrolled at university. This can help you clarify your ideas.

In your learning log, answer the following questions.

- What are your life goals for the next five years?
- Why you are studying?
- How does studying at university relate to your life goals?

Why study particular units

Select a unit that you are currently studying, and in your learning log answer the following questions about it.

- Why are you taking this particular unit?

- Why did you choose to enrol in this unit as opposed to other units offered?

- What do you hope to gain from this particular unit?

- What do you expect to learn from this unit?

Your reasons for doing a degree may differ from your reasons for taking a particular unit, and your reasons for enrolling in different units may vary.

Activity 2 Orientations and approaches to study

Read the attached information, 'Why students study: student orientations to study'. This reading is a summary of a research study on Open University students in the United Kingdom. It explains that students' reasons for studying influence how they study[2].

Apply research data

Refer to the attached material, 'Summary of student orientations to study', and work through the following points.

- Using the first column, decide whether your main *orientation* to study is vocational, academic, personal, social or a combination of these.

- Is there an overlap in your reasons for studying? For example, vocational and academic as well as social.

- Using the second column, decide whether your *interests* are intrinsic or extrinsic.

- Using the third column, consider whether your *aims* coincide with those listed. If not, how are your aims different?

- Using the fourth column, examine whether your *concerns* coincide with those expressed. If not, how are your concerns different?

Orientations in relation to your long-term goals

In your learning log, reflect on the above activities. Consider your orientations to study in relation to your highest hopes for university study and your long-term life goals.

- It is important to set and articulate long-term and short-term goals. (This skill is discussed in Exercise 5, 'Organising and planning study'.)

- The skill of setting study goals is one of the first steps in becoming an independent and effective student.

---

[2] Elizabeth Taylor, et al., 1980.

In your learning log, describe whether your approach to study is negatively or positively affected by your orientations to study.

Activity 3   Your mode of study

 Consider different modes of study – internal (on-campus), distance education (external) or open learning. If you could choose your mode of study, in your learning log, reflect on which mode you would choose. Consider why you would make that choice.

Describe the advantages and disadvantages of that particular mode of study.

Examining reasons for studying[3]

1. Your reasons for studying

If your university study fulfilled your highest hopes what would you gain from your study when it is completed?[4]

- What are your life goals for the next five years?
- Why are you studying?
- How does studying at university relate to your life goals?

- Why are you taking this particular unit?
- Why did you choose to enrol in this unit as opposed to the other units offered? (Your answer to this and the following question may not have anything to do with the subject matter of the unit.)
- What do you hope to gain from this particular unit?
- What do you expect to learn from this unit?

2. Orientations and approaches to study

Consider your orientations in relation to your highest hopes for university study and your long-term life goals.

Is your approach to study negatively or positively affected by your orientations to study?

3. Your mode of study

If you could choose your mode of study, internal (or on-campus), distance education (external) or open learning, explain why you would make that choice. Describe the advantages and disadvantages of that particular mode of study.

---

[3] The questions asked here parallel or are adapted from the questions used in the research.
[4] Elizabeth Taylor, et al., 1980, p. 27.

Why students study:
student orientations to study[5]

Activity 2

Students have different reasons for studying, and for taking a particular unit or course of study. They also have different orientations to study. Being aware of and articulating your reasons can provide insights into how you approach your studies.

A study at the Open University in England examined 'The orientations of students studying for the social science foundation unit'. This study defined orientation as 'all those attitudes and aims that express the student's individual relationship with a unit and the university. It is a collection of purposes that orientates the student to a unit in a particular way. Orientation, unlike the concept of motivation, does not assume any psychological trait or state of belonging to the student. It is a quality of the relationship between student and unit rather than a quality inherent in the student' (p. 3).

A study of two units (The Hotel and Catering Administration Degree unit and the Philosophy, Psychology and Sociology Degree unit) at Surrey University (Beaty, 1978)[6] identified four types of orientation: 'vocational which is to do with concern to get future jobs; academic which is to do with continuing education; personal which is to do with developing as a person; and social which is to do with enjoying the freedom of university life. These main types have sub-groups that discriminate between intrinsic and extrinsic interest in a unit. Intrinsic interest is where the student is interested in studying a unit for its own sake. Extrinsic interest is where the student is studying the unit as a means to an end' (p. 3).

How does orientation affect how you will study?

Beaty found that students whose orientation is vocational and who are intrinsically interested will seek training and tend to emphasise the practical aspects of their units and criticise parts that seem irrelevant to their future careers (p. 4). On the other hand, students who are vocationally oriented but extrinsically interested focus on the value of the unit or degree to their future employers. If, for example, grades are important to a prospective employer, a student might only care about passing. If employment depends on high grades, the student will work hard towards receiving these.

A student academically oriented and intrinsically interested in a unit will aim to follow his or her particular interests. Thus, some areas of a unit or degree will be more important, and at times the syllabus and assessment will hinder this aim. Students who are academically oriented but extrinsically interested 'tend to be syllabus bound and in some ways 'model' students in that their essays will be on time and the work will be

---

[5]   Summarised from Elizabeth Taylor, et al., 1980.
[6]   Elizabeth Taylor (née Beaty).

done evenly over all subjects involved. These students are concerned to get to the next activity in the academic ladder' (p. 6).

The student who is personally oriented and intrinsically interested is concerned with self-improvement and with using the university for personal change. 'Extrinsic personal orientation is where the student is doing the unit to test his (or her) own capability' (p. 7). This student wants to get the highest possible grades, and tends to be more concerned with this than the content of the unit.

Students who are socially oriented all tend to have extrinsic aims. These students are primarily interested in the sporting and social activities offered at the university and choose to allocate only a percentage of their available time to their studies.

Summary of students' orientations to study

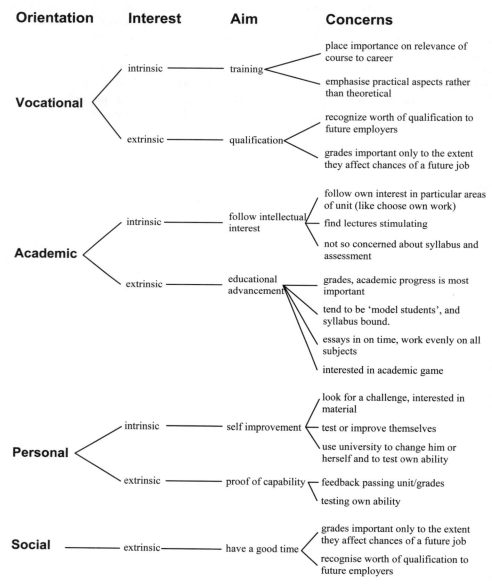

Orientation	Interest	Aim	Concerns

Vocational

intrinsic ——— training
- place importance on relevance of course to career
- emphasise practical aspects rather than theoretical

extrinsic ——— qualification
- recognize worth of qualification to future employers
- grades important only to the extent they affect chances of a future job

Academic

intrinsic ——— follow intellectual interest
- follow own interest in particular areas of unit (like choose own work)
- find lectures stimulating
- not so concerned about syllabus and assessment

extrinsic ——— educational advancement
- grades, academic progress is most important
- tend to be 'model students', and syllabus bound.
- essays in on time, work evenly on all subjects
- interested in academic game

Personal

intrinsic ——— self improvement
- look for a challenge, interested in material
- test or improve themselves
- use university to change him or herself and to test own ability

extrinsic ——— proof of capability
- feedback passing unit/grades
- testing own ability

Social ——— extrinsic ——— have a good time
- grades important only to the extent they affect chances of a future job
- recognise worth of qualification to future employers

5.   Organising and planning study

Introduction

Some people are naturally more organised than others; others don't like to be so structured. It is important to be aware of your propensities and preferences, and to be able to draw on time scheduling skills when you need to use your time more effectively and efficiently. By analysing how you spend your time, you can begin to make changes in line with your goals, objectives and priorities, and to suit your life style, personality, and your study demands. It is important to provide honest responses throughout this exercise, as this will increase the likelihood of a more meaningful integration of study into your life in a way that suits you. This exercise includes a worksheet with a numeracy task to help you see more clearly how you spend your time.

This exercise encourages you

- to be aware of how you spend time and how to use you study time effectively;

- to organise a study schedule to maximise your efficiency;

- to organise and plan your time according to your priorities and study goals.

Materials

5.1	Instructions on completing the time schedule
5.1	Time schedule: record of time spent during a week
5.2	Summary of information from the time schedule
5.3	Bar graph to show time spent on different activities
5.4	Analysis of time record: questions to ask
5.5	Priorities
5.6	List of things to accomplish next week
5.7	Time schedule: plans for next week's study

Approximate time

50–60 minutes (completed over a week)

Reading

Marshall & Rowland, 2006, Chapter 2, pp. 19–31.

Learning activities

Activity 1   Previous experiences with organising and planning your time

In your learning log, reflect on your previous experiences with organising and planning. Do you like to plan and organise your time? Why or why not?

- Some people like to plan and organise; others don't.

- Even if you don't, it can be useful to organise and plan when under pressure, for example, before exams or if you have a house full of visitors. Organising and planning at these times can make life seem more manageable and can help you through difficult times.

Activity 2   How you spend your time

Collect and summarise data
(begin a week before you intend doing this exercise)

5.1

- Read the attached instructions, 'Instructions on completing the time schedule'. Over a one-week period complete the attached data collection worksheet, 'Time schedule: record of time spent during a week'. You should collect this information on how you spend your time during a representative week, including class and study time. Be honest in your responses.

5.2

- At the end of the week following your data collection, complete the attached worksheet, 'Summary of information from the time schedule'. Calculate the amount of time you spent on each activity.

5.3

- Using this data, draw a bar graph using the attached worksheet, 'Bar graph to show time spent on different activities'. This numeracy task should help you see clearly how you spent your time during a representative week.

Analyse data

 5.4 Based on the above data and graph, consider your time schedule in relation to the questions below. Write your answers on the attached worksheet, 'Analysis of time record: questions to ask', or in your learning log[7]. Note any changes that you need to make.

- Did you have a particularly heavy workload during the representative week?
- Which activities were excessive time users, for example, TV, internet, partying, hobbies, family activities, travel, wasting time?
- Were there times when you studied more effectively, such as early in the morning or when you had the entire day to study? Why?
- Did you work more effectively in some places than others, for example, in the library or at home? Why?
- How did the amount of time you spent in class compare with the time spent on study out of class (independent or private study)?
- Did you work more effectively in short periods and then lose concentration, or did it take you time to settle into study so that you needed longer periods for serious work?
- Is your study connected to any of your other activities?
- Did you prepare yourself for long periods of serious study? How? Was this effective?
- Did you relax after a study session? How? Did you give yourself a reward for completing the work?

 Include the above worksheets 5.1, 5.2, 5.3, and 5.4 in your learning log.

Attitudes to keeping track of your time

 Keeping track of your time and analysing how you spend it may generate questions about how you organise and plan time. In your learning log, consider and answer the following questions.

- Did you enjoy keeping track of and analysing your time?
- What did you find out about yourself in relation to organising and planning time?

---

[7] Adapted from Marshall and Rowland, 1998, p. 21.

Keep in mind the following points.

- There are different levels of planning:

    - structuring each week and day over a lengthy period (a month or semester) and following a timetable that you stick to (long-term planning);
    - planning study for a week at the beginning of each week (short-term planning);
    - studying when you feel like it without a plan (non-planning!).

- When you are following a plan, don't be too distressed if you lose a day or more. Take time to reassess your plan, think about why it did not go as intended and start again.

Importance of a study space

Having a study space where you can concentrate will help you use your time more effectively and efficiently.

In your learning log, consider and answer the following questions.

- Do you have a space (or spaces) where you regularly study? Describe this space. Does this space include objects that prompt you to study? Why do these spaces and objects motivate you to study?

- Does your study space affect your concentration and thus the quality of work that you produce? Why?

- If you don't have a study space can you arrange one?

Activity 3   Relationship between goals and planning

Exercise 4, 'Examining reasons for studying', asked you to consider your reasons for studying. Refer to your learning log entries for this exercise and consider whether your organising and planning level will help or hinder your achievement of your study goals and objectives.

- It is important to set long-term and short-term goals.
- Setting goals is the first step in becoming an independent and effective student.

- It is important to identify and articulate your objectives for both long-term and short-term tasks.

- Setting clear long-term goals will help you identify short-term objectives and clarify your priorities

Activity 4 Deciding on your priorities

 5.5

Using the time schedule and the bar graph, complete the attached worksheet 'Priorities'. This requires you to order information mathematically.

Column 1: list the activities on which you spent your time.

Column 2: rank the activities according to the amount of time spent on each (1 = most time; 10 = least time).

Column 3: rank the activities according to how you would like to spend your time (1 = most prefer; 10 = least prefer).

Column 4: rank the activities according to how you think you should spend your time to succeed in your study (1 = most time; 10 = least time).

In relation to your priorities, answer the following questions and briefly note any discrepancies. Be honest in your responses.

- Are your priorities clear? In your goals, does study have a high priority? Is this reflected in how you spend your time? Can you manage study and your other priorities? If your study is not a high priority, should you be studying at all?

- Is there a difference between how you actually use your time for study and how you would prefer to use your time for study?

- In order to achieve your goals, on what aspects of study should you spend more time?

- In order to achieve your goals, on what aspects of study should you spend less time? Can you delegate some tasks to other family members or get help from a friend?

- Is study more important than your other commitments? What can you change in your life? For example, if study is a priority, but your job and/or children consume so much time that there's none left for study, what can you change?

Activity 5   Planning your time

Long-term tasks to accomplish

Find a year-long or semester-long calendar and note your large commitments. (There are excellent online and computer calendars available.) For example:

- end of semester exams (include starting and finishing dates);
- assignment due dates;
- large non-study commitments, such as holidays, guests, school holidays.

Keep this calendar close at hand so you can refer to it frequently. Use it to guide your short-term planning.

Short-term tasks to accomplish

 5.6

On the attached worksheet, 'List of things to accomplish next week', list what you want to accomplish during the next week. List both study and non-study objectives and any special commitments or tasks that you need to complete.

- Does this list take into account your long-term goals and plans?
- Does this list coincide with your priorities?

Map out a week's study

 5.7

- Using the above information, complete the attached worksheet, 'Time schedule: plans for next week's study'. Record time allocated to:

  - long-term commitments;
  - formal classes;
  - independent or private study;
  - informal appointments, such as with your tutor;
  - other study commitments;
  - paid employment;
  - travel;
  - relaxation/exercise;

- domestic duties and family activities;
- food preparation and eating.

- Block out fixed commitments, such as classes, travel, social functions.

- Note any special tasks that need to be completed.

Activity 6   Time expected on study

The above activities may have generated questions about the number of hours per week that students are expected to study.

- The time each week that students spend studying will vary between part-time and full-time students, and will depend on:

  - ability;
  - interest;
  - reasons for studying;
  - the grade aimed for.

- There can be a difference between perceived and actual study load. There are extremes: some students want to complete everything set (for example, all reading listed for every lecture), while other students only want to complete what is required to pass their units. How much you do is your choice and will depend on what you want to achieve from your study.

- The 38 to 40 hour week is a useful guideline for how many hours to spend studying. For internal students, this includes class time and independent study. For distance education or open learning students this includes reading, lectures, online discussions and any required work.

  If you have a full-time load and spend 40 effective hours studying each week, and you do this consistently over a semester or term, you should be able to successfully complete the required work and pass your units (unless they are unusually challenging).

  If you have a part-time load, work out the proportions accordingly. For example, an Open Universities Australia student studying one unit would need to spend an average of 10 effective hours a week on work related to that unit.

Activity 7   Reflection on organising and planning

In your learning log, reflect of this exercise and discuss any changes you think you need to make in relation to organising and planning your time. Decide on one or two changes that you will implement straight away.

Include the worksheets from this exercise in your learning log.

Organising and planning study

1. Previous experiences with organising and planning

Do you like to plan and organise your time? Why or why not?

2. How you spend your time

Answer the following questions.

- Did you enjoy keeping track of and analysing your time?
- What did you find out about yourself in relation to organising and planning time?

- Do your have a space (or spaces) where you regularly study? Describe this space. Does this space include objects that prompt you to study? Why do these spaces and objects motivate you to study?
- Does you study space affect your concentration and thus the quality of work that you produce? Why?

3. Reflection on organising and planning

Discuss any changes you think that you need to make in relation to organising and planning your time. Decide on one or two changes that you will implement straight away.

Include the worksheet from this exercise in you learning log.

Instructions on completing the time schedule

5.1

Activity 2

You cannot realistically think about planning or organising your time until you have a precise idea about how you actually spend your time.

Completely document how you spend your time over one week. It is important to do this carefully and honestly.

Note how much time you spend:

- in formal classes or completing required commitments (C)

- on private or independent study, including working on assignments (PS)

- in paid employment (E)

- relaxing and socialising (R&R)

- on exercise and active recreation (E&R)

- domestic duties and family activities (DD)

- food preparation and eating (F&E)

- travelling (T)

- sleeping (ZZ)

- other codes as necessary.

Use the codes as indicated.

Note the times your study was most effective with an asterisk. Use a different symbol for less effective or unproductive study times

Name: ....

Date: From ....to ....

5.1

Time schedule: record of time spent during a week

	Monday	Tuesday	Wednesday	Thursday	Friday	Saturday	Sunday
6-7 am							
7-8							
8-9							
9-10							
10-11							
11-12							
12-1 pm							
1-2							
2-3							
3-4							
4-5							
5-6							
6-7							
7-8							
8-9							
9-10							
10-11							
11-12							
12-1 am							
1-2							
2-6							

Name: --

Date: From ------------------to --------------------

5.2

Activity 2

Summary of information from the time schedule

Are you studying full-time or part-time?

What percentage of a full-time student work-load
are you studying?

Time spent

In class (C)

On private study or doing additional study (PS)

Total amount of time spent on study

In employment (E)

Relaxing and/or socialising (R&R)

On exercise and active recreation (E&R)

On domestic duties and family activities (DD)

Travelling (T)

Sleeping – average hours per night (ZZZ)

Other

Study

Most effective study times

Total number of effective hours

Average length of effective study sessions

Time of day --

Place(s) --

Other comments on most effective study times -----------------------------------

----

Least effective study times

Total number of ineffective hours

Time(s) of day ---

Place(s) --

Bar graph to show time spent on different activities

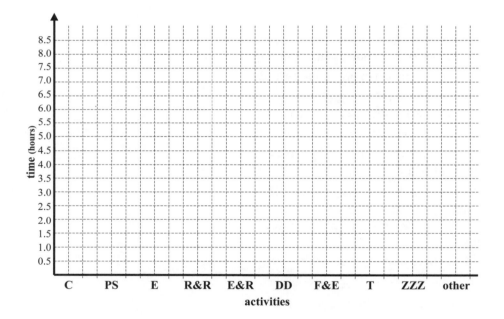

Analysis of time record: questions to ask[8]

5.4

Activity 2

Did you have a particularly heavy workload during the representative week?

Which activities were excessive time users, for example, TV, internet, partying, hobbies, family activities, travel, wasting time?

Were there times when you studied more effectively, such as early in the morning or when you had the entire day to study? Why?

Did you work more effectively in some places than others, for example, in the library or at home? Why?

How did the amount of time you spent in class compare with the time you spent on study out of class (independent or private study)?

Did you work more effectively in short periods and then lose concentration, or did it take you time to settle into study so that you needed longer periods for serious work?

Is your study connected to any of your other activities?

Did you prepare yourself for long periods of serious study? How? Was this effective?

Did you relax after a study session? How? Did you give yourself a reward for completing the work?

---

[8] Adapted from Marshall and Rowland, 1998, 3rd edn, p. 21.

Priorities

Activities on which you spent your time	Ranked (1-10) according to…		
	Amount of time spent on each activiey (1 = most time)	How you would **like** to spend your time (1 = most prefer)	How you **should** spend your time to succeed in study (1 = most time)
1.			
2.			
3.			
4.			
5.			
6.			
7.			
8.			
9.			
10.			

Note discrepancies

List of things to accomplish next week

5.6

Activity 5

List of things I need to do **(both study and non study)**	Order of importance	Time each will take
1.		
2.		
3.		
4.		
5.		
6.		
7.		
8.		
9.		
10.		
11.		
12.		
13.		
14.		
15.		

Comment on any special commitments or tasks

Time schedule: plans for next week's study

5.7

Activity 5

	Monday	Tuesday	Wednesday	Thursday	Friday	Saturday	Sunday
6-7 am							
7-8							
8-9							
9-10							
10-11							
11-12							
12-1 pm							
1-2							
2-3							
3-4							
4-5							
5-6							
6-7							
7-8							
8-9							
9-10							
10-11							
11-12							
12-1 am							
1-2							
2-6							

6.   Concentrating

This exercise encourages you

- to examine any problems you encounter with concentration;

- to develop strategies to concentrate more effectively.

Materials

 6.1   Concentration levels during a study session

 6.2   Graphing your concentration levels

Approximate time

30 minutes

Reading

Marshall & Rowland, 2006, Chapter 2, pp. 32–36.

Learning activities

Activity 1   Previous experiences with concentrating

Concentrating well

In your learning log, reflect on and describe an instance when you concentrated well. List the conditions that made it possible to concentrate well.

Concentration problems

Now reflect on and describe an instance when you found it difficult to concentrate. List the conditions that made it difficult to concentrate.

Activity 2   Concentration levels during study sessions

6.1

Examine the attached graph, 'Concentration levels during a study session'. This represents a three hour session for the 'ideal' student. Note how the student's concentration varied during the three hours.

Also note the following information.

- Concentration spans vary between students and from one task to another.

- Shorter study sessions, for example, an hour during your lunch break, are most useful for study that requires less concentration (such as looking for books in the library) or that can be completed in less time (such as reviewing a lecture).

- Longer study sessions are most useful for work that requires more intense concentration.

Activity 3   Techniques for longer study sessions

- **Warm up** before starting to study.

  - Mental preparation before starting study can make it easier to begin concentrating.
  - Consider how you feel. (Are you in the mood for study or do you need willpower to get going?)

- Make sure you are comfortable.
- Set time limits for the study session.
- Decide what to study.
- Decide on your objectives. Think about what you want to accomplish in this session.
- Decide whether to start with the easiest or most difficult material.
- Use deliberate warm-up techniques, for example, previewing, revising information.
- Plan a reward to give yourself when the task is finished.

- Work for as long as you can. When concentration begins to wane, push yourself a little. Don't give up immediately. Take a break when you cannot concentrate any longer.

- Take short breaks of 5–10 minutes. Don't do anything too distracting during breaks. For example, instead of 'phoning a friend who you know will talk for ages, make a drink, read the paper, bring in the washing or physically loosen up. If you take a long break you will have to warm-up again.

- Give yourself a planned reward at the end of the session. Just completing the task may be reward enough, but try to do something you enjoy.

Activity 4   Graphing your concentration levels

For an extended study session (approximately three hours) record your levels of concentration. Note how long you concentrated for and when you took breaks. Do this using the attached worksheet, 'Graphing your concentration levels'. This is a numeracy task. Using the axes provided draw your own line graph and reflect on any changes in your level of concentration.

Compare the two graphs.

Activity 5   Reflection on improving your concentration

In your learning log, reflect on this exercise and discuss any changes you need to make to improve your concentration. Remember it is up to you to implement these changes.

Concentrating

1. **Previous experiences with concentrating**

   Describe an instance when you concentrated well.

   List the conditions that made it possible to concentrate well.

   Describe an instance when you found it difficult to concentrate.

   List the conditions that made it difficult to concentrate.

2. **Reflection on improving your concentration**

   Discuss any changes you need to make to improve your concentration.

Concentration levels during a study session

Activity 2

THREE HOUR STUDY SESSION

How to maximise your concentration

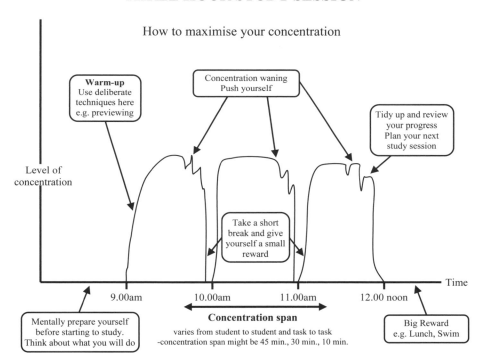

Level of concentration

Warm-up
Use deliberate techniques here e.g. previewing

Concentration waning
Push yourself

Tidy up and review your progress
Plan your next study session

Take a short break and give yourself a small reward

Time

9.00am   10.00am   11.00am   12.00 noon

←——— **Concentration span** ———→
varies from student to student and task to task
-concentration span might be 45 min., 30 min., 10 min.

Mentally prepare yourself before starting to study. Think about what you will do

Big Reward
e.g. Lunch, Swim

Graphing your concentration levels

6.2

Activity 4

Line graph to show your concentration levels
on different activities during a 3 hour study session

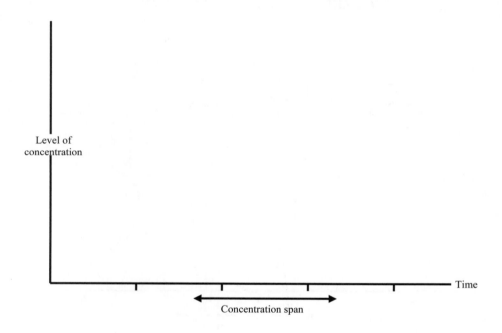

Level of
concentration

Time

Concentration span

54

7.   Remembering information
Introduction

It is important to develop strategies to remember information that you learn. You will find that the learning and remembering techniques you develop in this exercise can be applied in a range of contexts, including examinations. This exercise is designed to reinforce many of the ideas explored in other exercises and can be used in combination with Exercise 8, 'Preparing for examinations', as the two overlap. The exercises have been separated here because you need to remember information in situations other than for examinations.

This exercise encourages you

- to develop techniques for remembering information throughout your learning and for examinations;

- to understand a rationale behind the learning strategies and ideas developed in other exercises, such as using linear and non linear (patterned) note making, setting learning objectives, and consistently using effective study strategies;

- to share with others the techniques you use for revising information.

Approximate time

30 minutes

Reading

Marshall & Rowland, 2006, pp. 71–85.

Learning activities

Activity 1   Techniques you use to remember information

Reflect on previous informal learning situations where you have recalled information, such as someone's name or a story or joke you enjoyed. Now reflect on previous formal learning situations, such as recalling information for an oral presentation or an exam.

What techniques did you use to remember?

Did you learn information in the same way in all situations? Are there differences and/or similarities?

Share the techniques you use to remember information with another student or person.

 In your learning log, list the techniques that you use to remember information. Do you use different techniques in informal and formal learning situations?

Activity 2   List of techniques for remembering

 Read the following techniques for remembering and, in your learning log, add any to your list that are not already included.

1. Set learning objectives for all large and small learning tasks. (This is encouraged in all exercises in this book.)

2. Use linear and non-linear processes. Non linear processes include pictures, diagrams, patterned notes and flow charts. (Patterned note making is outlined in Marshall and Rowland, 2006, pp. 165–168. Also see Exercise 17,'Notemaking from reading'.)

3. Learn actively

    –   don't waste time reading and then re-reading;
    –   preview all material before reading it;
    –   break down material into manageable chunks;
    –   ask yourself questions and look for answers as you study;
    –   translate information into your own words;

- relate what you are learning to your own experiences;
- summarise material into linear and non linear notes;
- use patterns, diagrams, flow charts and other visual aids;
- repeat material at spaced intervals and in different ways;
- share what you are learning with others.

4. Use your strongest learning senses.

Humans learn through their senses. Sight, hearing and touch are those most used in academic learning. For many people one sense is stronger than the others. For example, do you learn best from listening or reading? Consider how you can use your strongest sense in learning, for example:

- listening and writing during lectures;
- reading information, writing about it, speaking it out loud and/or discussing it with others;
- using patterns, diagrams and different coloured pens in your notes;
- using imagery to enhance recall.

5. Use memory aids, such as:

- mnemonic techniques to encode information and as cues for recall;
- imagery to aid recall;
- breaking material into small chunks.

6. Before, during and after learning strategies.

Prepare yourself before learning, be active during learning, and revise and self test at regular intervals after learning.

- Learning is more effective if you warm up before starting a study session. This was discussed in Exercise 6, 'Concentrating'. Refer to this exercise for strategies on warming up and concentrating during learning.
- Use the techniques outlined above to learn actively during a study session.

- New information is initially stored in the short-term memory part of the brain. By reviewing information at intervals it becomes part of your long-term memory.

Tip: ☺ Work smarter. Not harder.

Read Marshall and Rowland, 2006, Chapter 5, 'Learning and remembering', pp. 71–85.

As you read, add any new techniques for remembering to your list.

Activity 3   Techniques to improve remembering

In addition to those techniques you already use to remember information, consider other techniques that might improve your ability to remember. In your learning log, describe these techniques and explain how they will enhance your memory.

Remembering information

1. Techniques you use to remember information

List the techniques that you use to remember information. Do you use different techniques in informal and formal learning situations?

2. List of techniques for remembering

Add any techniques to your list that are not already included and continue to do this as you work through the exercise.

3. Changes to improve remembering

Describe other techniques that might improve your ability to remember information and explain how they will enhance your memory.

---

8. Preparing for examinations

Introduction

Examinations are a significant part of assessment at university. It is important that all students develop their exam skills, so that examination results properly reflect their understanding and knowledge. This exercise deals with what, how and when you should prepare for exams. It is closely linked with Exercise 7, 'Remembering information' and refers to Exercise 5, 'Organising and planning study', Exercise 6, 'Concentrating', and Exercise 17, 'Notemaking from reading'.

This exercise encourages you

- to develop strategies to help you determine what is expected of you and the type of information included in an exam;

- to prepare for exams, which involves a revision process and effective study strategies;

- to organise your study timetable before an exam;

- to participate in a simulated exam experience, in order to evaluate the exam techniques you use when actually sitting exams;

- to reflect on your attitude towards exams, and learn to deal positively with negative feelings.

Materials

Sample final examination papers for your unit of study (if available).

8.1	A process for revision
8.2	Exam techniques
8.3	How to perform poorly in exams

Approximate time

50 minutes

Reading

Marshall & Rowland, 2006, p. 53 & pp. 83–85.

Learning activities

Activity 1   Your attitude towards exams

Do you suffer from exam anxiety or exam arrogance? If you have a history of being anxious prior to or during exams, deal with this problem by:

–   studying for the exam well in advance so that you are well prepared (See Exercise 5, 'Organising and planning study');

–   practising relaxation techniques;

–   seeing a counsellor or learning adviser.

 In your learning log, describe your feelings about exams. Explore any anxiety you have about exams.

Activity 2   Information on the exam

What is expected

▪   Find out what percentage of the overall grade is allocated to the exam.

▪   Read any regulations and conventions relating to the exam.

▪   Consider specific aspects of the exam:
    –   format;
    –   duration;
    –   length of answers;
    –   number of questions and answers.

Types of exam

Different units have different types of exams and you should prepare accordingly. Identify the type of exam you will be sitting.

▪   Some science and mathematics exams are based on **problem solving**, and you should prepare for this by practising questions from past exam papers.

- Some units require you to provide a large amount of factual information linked with concepts. Preparation for this often requires memorisation, but also requires more understanding and synthesis than simple recall questions.

- Some units are based on **open book** exams and you can take books or papers into the exam and refer to them. However, you will not be asked simple recall questions and you will be expected to have a good understanding of the concepts and ideas. The material you take can aid your confidence in answering questions. You will not fail an 'open book' exam because of a memory block, but you should still study as thoroughly as you would for a 'closed book' exam so that you have the answers at your fingertips.

Types of questions

Examinations can include a range of questions. It is important to know whether the questions in your exam will be multiple choice, short answer or essays. Some of the features of these question types are outlined below.

Type of question	Features
Essay	These require careful analysis of the question and planning of the overall approach. You will usually be given a choice of options.
Multiple choice	These are usually answered by ticking or nominating an answer. These are used to test understanding and retention of the subject matter, especially when there is a large body of factual information involved.
Short answer	These can include a request for information, a short problem, a test of comprehension or a combination of these. Sometimes there is a choice of questions. Students are required to provide answers that can vary in length from single words to phrases, sentences or paragraphs. This will usually depend on the marks allocated to a question.

- Find out the type and length of questions that will be asked in the exam by:

  - consulting your study guide or your teachers;

  - consulting previous exam papers.

- If you are required to answer an essay type question, review Exercise 24, 'Analysing an essay question', and Exercise 26, 'Writing the first draft'. Consider how you can apply these strategies to exam essay questions.

- Take time during your revision to write sample answers to questions under time restrictions.

What is being tested

- Read any information on the exam that is included in unit handouts or study guides.

- Briefly look at some recent previous exam papers for your unit. Note the type of questions covered. Don't try answering the questions at this stage. Previous exam papers are usually available in the library.

Answer the following questions to discover what is being tested.

- Can you see any patterns in the type of questions asked that relate to the overall aims and goals of the unit?

- Can you relate the questions asked to the list of topics for lectures and tutorials?

- Can you use this information to guide your study and revision for the exams?

- Can you make judgements on what the examiners will be looking for in your answers?

- If possible, reflect on the topics covered in your unit and outlined in your study guide. Consider the type of information you are required to know and remember, and how it could be usefully organised for your exam.

- Aim to use patterned notes to develop your understanding of the links between topics in the unit.

Activity 3   The revision process

The rocket model of revision

8.1   Refer to the attached rocket model, 'A process for revision', and apply the suggested strategies in your revision.

Revise Exercise 7, 'Remembering information', and consider the techniques you use to remember information.

Begin your revision and continue it.

Think positively.

Good **luck** with your exam!

Activity 4   Effective exam study techniques

Evaluate the effectiveness of your study techniques in the following ways.

Refer to Exercise 25, 'Researching information', and evaluate your method of recording and filing material. Is this method appropriate for recording and filing the information that you are revising?

Refer to Exercise 17, 'Notemaking from reading', and make sure that you are using both linear and nonlinear note making methods.

Review Exercise 6, 'Concentrating', and evaluate how effectively you are concentrating when studying.

Activity 5   Effective time management for exams

Review Exercise 5, 'Organising and planning study', and reconsider any time management techniques you should apply to ensure that you complete your revision in time for the exam.

- Plan your revision.

- List and prioritise the tasks to be completed and the material or topics you need to revise.

- Set objectives and establish deadlines. (Don't over-estimate the time available.)

- Prepare a study timetable setting out deadlines for tasks and material to be revised.

- Define boundaries for your revision so that you can manage the time available effectively.

- Be realistic and modify your plan when necessary.

Activity 6 Exam simulation

Exam techniques

Read Marshall and Rowland, 2006, p. 53 and pp. 83–85, and apply the suggested techniques for coping with exams.

Read the attached exam hints ('Exam techniques', 'How to perform poorly in exams').

An exam situation

Imagine that you are sitting the exam and that you are in the exam room.

Using a previous final exam paper for your unit give yourself ten minutes reading time, exactly as if you were really doing the exam.

Stop. Re-read the first two exam hints in 'Exam techniques'.

Did you follow these? Were they useful?

Again imagine you are in an exam. Now start working on a question. Give yourself ten minutes.

Stop! Refer back to the hints in 'Exam techniques'.

Did you follow the hints? Were they useful? What methods of revision would best suit this type of question?

Continue working on the exam paper. Aim to apply the techniques suggested and complete the exam paper in the time allowed.

Reflection on exam simulation

In your learning log, describe your exam simulation experience.

- What techniques do you need to develop before sitting the actual exam?

- Did this simulation help you overcome any exam anxiety? How?

Activity 7 Reflection on time management following an exam

After sitting an exam, in your learning log discuss your time management before and during the exam.

- Did you manage your time well in the lead up to the exam?

- How well did you manage your time during the exam?

List any changes you need to make to your time management before and during the exam.

Preparing for examinations

1. Your attitude towards exams

Describe your feelings about exams. Explore any anxiety you have about exams.

2. Exam simulation

Describe your exam simulation experience

- What techniques do you need to develop before sitting the actual exam?

- Did this simulation help you overcome any exam anxiety? How?

3. Reflection on time management following an exam

After sitting your exam, discuss your time management before and during the exam.

- Did you manage your time well in the lead up to the exam?

- How well did you manage your time during the exam? Explain.

List any changes you need to make to your time management before and during the exam.

A process for revision[9]

8.1

Activity 3

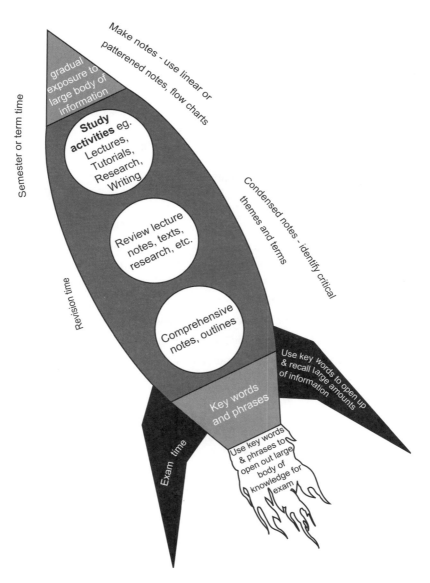

9 Adapted from materials developed by Sari Hosie, 1995.

Effective revision and study is an active and strategic process. Use the following learning activities and strategies: condense your notes, organise, classify, think of associations and try to understand the underlying logic of your work. Connect material in large chunks, with cues which connect the sections.

In the rocket model for revision note that:

–   the amount of knowledge you are taking in increases;
–   you need to condense notes down until you end up with key words and phrases to remember;
–   you use the key words and phrases during the exam to help you recall the large amount of information you have learned;
–   the act of shortening notes is an active form of learning.

Make use of any of the following techniques to help your revision:

–   write down only key ideas and phrases;
–   concentrate on the bigger issues, the key ideas and frameworks;
–   re-read your notes and re-learn material you do not understand;
–   test yourself by closing your notes and writing down the structure or main points of material you are learning;
–   check your answers against your notes;
–   compile lists of questions and locate the answers;
–   solve problems to test your understanding;
–   don't waste time revising material you understand.

Exam techniques[10]

8.2

Activity 6

1. If you feel uptight before an exam, try to relax.

2. When you are given the exam paper and before you start writing, take the following steps.

    ▪   Carefully read the instructions, which should tell you how to answer the paper, how many questions you should answer and the value of each question.

    ▪   Read through all of the questions.

    ▪   If you have a choice, decide which questions you'll answer or which questions you'll do first.

    ▪   Decide how much time you'll need to spend on each question according to its value and how thoroughly you can answer it.

    ▪   Decide on the order in which to answer the questions. Answer first the questions you know most about and which earn higher marks. Then, if you run out of time, it is likely to be on a question that will earn you fewer marks.

3. When you're allowed to start writing, jot down any thoughts or ideas you have about each question you'll answer. These jottings can be useful memory triggers when you actually come to answer the question.

4. For essay-type questions, analyse the wording of the question and plan your essay. Include you plan in your exam booklet.

5. Write as quickly and as clearly as you can.

6. For multiple-choice questions, don't waste time on questions you can't answer. Be careful about guessing answers if points are deducted for incorrect responses.

7. When answering mathematical problems, include all of your calculations. Even if your answer is incorrect, the examiner can see where you went wrong and you may gain some points for your method.

8. If you have a memory lapse in the middle of a question, leave a few pages, go to another question, and return to it later.

9. Answer as many questions as you can. If you only answer the questions you know well, you're unlikely to make up enough marks to pass.

10. If you run out of time, jot down the main points you were going to make.

11. Aim to leave time at the end of the exam to read over your answers. Correcting poor expression or spelling, or checking your calculations can make an important difference.

---

[10]   Adapted from Marshall & Rowland, 2006, p. 85.

How to perform poorly in exams[11]

- Turn up late and flustered – and thus lose time.

- Don't follow the exam instructions that detail which and how many questions to answer, and answer the questions that don't count and miss questions that do count.

- Budget your time poorly, so that not enough questions are answered.

- Misread or misunderstand questions and spend too little time deciding what is being asked– and so answer a question that has not been asked.

- Read all questions (whether 'Discuss ...', 'Compare and contrast ...', 'Evaluate ...' and so on) as 'List whatever you can think of about this topic in whichever order you can think of it'. Make no attempt to organise an answer and include disconnected facts.

- Write illegibly so that the examiner needs to read slowly, and is unable to work out what your answer is saying. (This is very common.)

- Use opinions and personal experience as a substitute for well-supported arguments. Abandon all logic and intellectual rigour.

- Believe that sheer quantity gains marks, and lose your good points and arguments in irrelevant detail.

- Forget that the first 50% of marks for an answer are relatively easy to obtain, the next 25% are reasonably difficult and the last 25% are very difficult. Waste time elaborating on already good or adequate answers, instead of improving poor and inadequate answers.

- Simultaneously try to remember what you know about a topic, select what is relevant to a question, organise it into an answer and formulate sentences to express that answer instead of in separate stages – and so produce partly irrelevant, disorganised, incomplete and incoherent answers.

- Fail to read through finished answers for incoherent and incorrect passages.

- Panic.

---

[11] Adapted from G. Gibbs, 1981, *Teaching students to learn: a student centred approach*, Open University Press, Milton Keynes, p. 43.

9. Evaluating your learning

Introduction

Becoming an independent learner involves the ability to evaluate your own work. Self evaluation or self assessment is not about giving yourself a grade or assessing your work. Rather it is about deciding whether or not you have achieved your goals and objectives. You need to evaluate your learning for both small and large tasks. This exercise will help you evaluate what you gain from a unit and from your overall studies. Remember that a balanced self assessment includes both positive and negative points.

Learning to evaluate your own work is a skill that will be invaluable in your future studies and is rated highly in graduates. However, you will not always receive immediate feedback from your tutors or an employer, and there are circumstances where an employee is required to produce a self evaluation for promotion.

This exercise requires you to evaluate your learning in a unit that you are currently studying.

This exercise encourages you

- to develop an understanding of the concept of self evaluation (or assessment);

- to write a self evaluation;

- to appreciate the relationship between reflecting on and evaluating your learning;

- to evaluate your learning as you work through these exercises;

- to reflect on your learning skills strengths and weaknesses when you commenced these exercises and how you have improved;

- to evaluate the development of your own learning skills

- to transfer the self-evaluation skills developed in this book to other study contexts and learning experiences.

Materials

9.1   Implementing student self assessment, (Extract from David Boud, 1986 HERDSA Green Guide, No 5.)

9.2   Using learning skills in your studies

Approximate time

30 minutes

Reading

Marshall & Rowland, 2006, Chapter 15, pp. 261–275.

Learning activities

Activity 1   Previous experiences with self evaluation

Reflect on previous learning situations where you were required to evaluate your own learning. These might have been in an educational context or in your everyday life. In your learning log, describe these situations and explain how self evaluation helped your learning.

Activity 2   The value of self evaluation

The ability to formulate learning objectives and then evaluate or assess whether you have achieved them is integral to being an independent and effective student. The process of self evaluation requires that you reflect on your learning.

9.1   Read the attached information, 'Implementing student self assessment'.

Read Marshall and Rowland, 2006, Chapter 15, pp. 261–275.

Activity 3   Evaluating learning skills development

Identify what to evaluate

When you evaluate something you carefully study its good and bad features and decide on its significance, value or quality[12].

In this exercise you are asked to evaluate the *development of your learning skills* in relation to the exercises that you have completed in this book.

It is important to remember your skill level before you began the exercises so that you can assess your skill level when you finish. You also need to decide which learning skills you consider most important to develop. Re-read the aims listed at the beginning of the exercise.

---

[12] J. Sinclair, (ed.), 1987, *Collins Cobuild English language dictionary,* Collins, London, Glasgow.

Evaluate the development of a learning skill

Revise any log entries or worksheets from the exercises you are evaluating. This can help you remember what you needed at the beginning of the unit.

Answer the following questions.

- How does your skill level before you began the exercises compare with your learning skills now? Has your skill level improved, fluctuated or remained static?
- What criteria are you using in your evaluation? Why are you using these and not others?
- How will you continue to develop these skills within a unit and beyond? What links can you identify between the exercises and the unit (or units) that you are studying?
- What aspects of the exercises were particularly helpful in undertaking the requirements in the unit(s) you are studying or in your study generally?

Write a self evaluation

Using the answers to the questions above, and any other ideas you consider relevant, in your learning log write a short evaluation. Discuss a specific learning skill that you have developed by working through an exercise (or chapter) in this book.

Continue to evaluate your learning

Continue to evaluate your learning as you complete each exercise and each chapter in this book. When you have completed the exercises that you consider relevant to your needs (or the whole book) and have applied them to your study, commence the following activity.

Activity 4 Evaluate overall learning skills development

Evaluate the impact that the total package of exercises in this book has on your learning.

Review the learning skills covered

To revise the skills that have been covered in this book, re-read the contents page and the introduction.

To remember the skills that you have developed for use in your study, review your log entries or worksheets. Pay particular attention to the first log entries you made when you began using these materials.

 9.2   Examine the attached worksheet, 'Using learning skills in your studies', and draw lines to link each skill with the content in the unit you are studying. Note the central place of these skills in all of your learning. Write in the content requirements for other units you are studying and link each skill to these. Draw lines on the worksheet to show how you will transfer these skills to these other units.

Evaluate your learning skills

Use the activities you have completed to evaluate individual exercises and your overall skill development. Answer the following questions.

- How does your skill level when you began your unit(s) compare with your skill level now? Has your skill level improved, fluctuated or remained static? You might discuss the following skills: self management, organisation, writing, reading, researching and study skills.

- How will you continue to develop these skills in the next units you take and beyond?

- Which learning skills did you find particularly helpful in the requirements for your unit(s)? Which skills were useful for any other units you took concurrently? Which skills were especially useful for your learning generally? Which skills were not useful?

Write a self evaluation

 Using the answers you provided to the questions above and any other ideas you consider relevant, in your learning log write a short evaluation. Discuss the overall development of your learning skills in relation to the unit(s) you are studying.

Activity 5   Self evaluation in other contexts

 Evaluate your work in the units you are studying. You might try some of the following.

- Write a self evaluation of an essay or project before you submit it and perhaps include the evaluation with your work. How does your tutor's assessment compare with your assessment of your work?

- At the end of a semester write a self evaluation outlining what you have learned in a unit. Try using the guidelines in Table 16.1, 'A self evaluation', in Marshall and Rowland, 2006, p. 267.

- Share your self evaluations with other students or a friend or family member.

Evaluating your learning

1. Previous experiences with self evaluation

Describe previous learning situations when you were required to evaluate your own learning. Explain how self evaluation helped your learning.

2. Evaluating learning skills development

Write a short evaluation in which you discuss a specific learning skill that you have developed by working through an exercise (or chapter) in this book.

3. Evaluate overall learning skills development

Write a short evaluation in which you discuss the overall development of your learning skills in relation to the unit(s) you are studying.

Implementing student self assessment [13]

Activity 2

Self assessment involves students taking responsibility for monitoring and making judgements about aspects of their own learning. Some students are effective in making self assessment and engage in this activity as part of their normal study patterns. Other students are less naturally self-reflective or have not developed the appropriate skills earlier in their career. All students, whether they are familiar with self assessment or not, need to consider how they can monitor their own performance when confronted with new types of knowledge and skills.

Self assessment requires students to think critically about what they are learning, to identify appropriate standards of performance and to apply them to their own work. Self assessment encourages students to look to themselves and to other sources to determine what criteria should be used in judging their work rather than being dependent solely on their teachers. The development of skills in self assessment lies at the core of higher education, and many teachers seek every opportunity to promote self assessment in their courses.

Self assessment is much more than the allocation of grades. Indeed, in many cases it is entirely separate from the formal assessment of students. It may take place as an exercise alongside other requirements or it may be linked to formal assessment procedures.

What is self assessment?

The defining characteristic of self assessment is the involvement of students in:

identifying standards and/or criteria to apply to their work, and

making judgements about the extent to which they have met these criteria and standards.

Students should be involved in making decisions on the basis of various kinds of information. Some of this they may generate themselves, other data may derive from teachers, practitioners and peers. Self assessment does not imply that students work in isolation from the views and judgements of others.

Self assessment is commonly a supplement to teacher assessment of students, although in some cases it may replace it. Teachers have an important part to play in student

---

[13] Extract from David Boud, 1986, 'Implementing Student Self-Assessment', *HERDSA Green Guide No, 5*. pp. 1-3; 5-6; 8-9.

assessment; however, if they see themselves as the only assessors they can limit the achievement of many of the central goals of higher education. Many existing assessment practices can encourage an inappropriate dependency by students on staff. The danger of an excessive reliance on teacher assessment is that students learn to look to their teachers and distrust their own assessments. They may be inhibited in becoming independent learners who can exercise their own critical judgement.

Self assessment is not just another technique for testing student performance; it is a way for students to become involved in assessing their own performance. In this process they may use quite familiar and routine techniques which differ little at all from those regularly used by teachers for testing achievement. The ends to which these methods are put characterise self assessment.

Self assessment means more than students grading their own work; it means involving them in the process of determining what is good work in any given situation. They are required to consider what are the characteristics of, say, a good essay or practical report and to apply this to their own work.

Can students be effectively involved in both stages of the assessment process: determining criteria and making judgements? The answer to this important question seems to be both 'yes' and 'no'. There do exist some subjects of either a highly technical or conceptually sophisticated nature in which it may not be practically possible at introductory levels to involve students in the specification of criteria. However, while students may not be able to articulate criteria as such at this stage, they can often recognise the applicability of criteria provided by others.

In such cases as these, where students use only the criteria provided by staff the term 'self marking' or 'self testing is used rather than 'self assessment'. ...

Premises

The theory and practice of self assessment is based on several premises about the intellectual development of students.

1. Self assessment is a necessary skill which should be developed by all students.

    It is important for students to develop the ability to be realistic judges of their performance and to effectively monitor their own learning. Graduates who develop the skill are more likely to:

    - wish to continue their learning,
    - know how to do so,
    - monitor their own performance without constant reference to fellow professionals, and
    - expect to take full responsibility for their actions and judgements.

2. Self assessment needs to be developed in undergraduate courses.

    It is appropriate to develop this skill as part of tertiary courses. Its development represents one of the most important processes that can occur in undergraduate education. If students are to be able to continue learning effectively after graduation and make a significant contribution to their own professional work, they must develop skills of appraising their own achievements during their student years. The foundation for this should occur at the undergraduate level if not earlier.

    Self assessment is not an isolated activity which can be practised independently of the courses which students study. It should find its way, to a greater or lesser extent, into all courses: the requirements for monitoring performance in one area of knowledge may not be the same as in others.

3. Self assessment is necessary for effective learning.

    The third premise is even broader and is one which forms a particularly important part of the thinking of those who are committed to such goals as autonomy or independence in learning. It is that for effective learning of any kind to take place at any stage, learners – whoever they may be – must develop the capability of monitoring what they do and modifying their learning strategy appropriately. Effective learning also involves learners being able to influence their own learning rather than waiting for others to do so. Those who require the impetus of others, be they teachers or supervisors, to develop and assess their knowledge and skills are severely handicapped in their learning.

Using learning skills in your studies

9.2

Activity 4

Skills

Study skills

planning and organising
concentrating
note making
remembering
preparing for exams
evaluating

Reading

previewing
reading in depth
numerical information

Writing essays and reports

objectives/expectations
creating
editing

Researching

reading
experimental

Communicating orally

presenting and participating

Unit content

study materials

lectures

tutorials

workshops

laboratories

essays

reports

tests

exams

Other units

Future learning

Effective
Independent
Powerful

CHAPTER 3

Learning from lectures and discussions

The exercises in this chapter are designed to help you develop listening and note making skills for lectures, and oral communication skills for tutorials. Exercise 10 aims to help you identify the argument[1] (thesis and supporting premises) or the main point and supporting details presented in a lecture. (This is also the focus of Exercise 18, 'Reading in depth'.) In this exercise you are asked to summarise information using both linear and patterned note making forms (which incorporates the ideas and methods of Tony Buzan). Exercise 11 aims to help you participate fully in discussions, and Exercise 12 aims to help you prepare, give and evaluate oral presentations.

---

[1]   An argument is a form of thinking in which certain statements (premises [or reasons]) are offered in support of another statement (a conclusion [or thesis]). Definition adapted from John Chaffee, 1990, *Thinking critically*, Houghton Mifflin, Boston, p. 499.

10. Learning from lectures

- Summarising a lecture
  - listen and make notes
  - review lecture notes
  - summarise the lecture
  - evaluate your summary
  - the role of the lecture in the unit
- Presentation of information
  - the objectives of lectures
  - lecturer's methods of presentation
- Lecture note making techniques
- Patterned notes of the lecture
- Sharing summaries and notes
- Reflection

Learning from lectures and discussions

3

11. Learning from discussions

- The role of discussion in learning
  - informal discussions in learning
  - compare informal and formal discussions
  - the importance of tutorials in learning
- The objectives of formal discussions in learning
- Different tutorial groups
  - leadership styles
  - student and tutor responsibilities
- Participating in tutorials
  - how you participate in tutorials
  - positive and negative behaviours
- Improving tutorials
  - preparation
  - participation
  - after the tutorial
- Establishing ground rules
- Ground rules for critical thinking
- Other ways to discuss learning
- Reflection on enhancing learning in discussions

12. Preparing and giving an oral presentation

- Previous experiences with oral presentations
  - your feelings about giving presentations
- Evaluating oral presentations
  - characteristics of good presentations
  - criteria for evaluating presentations
- Preparing an oral presentation
  - structuring a presentation
  - preparing visual material
  - rehearsing a presentation
  - fielding questions
  - reviewing a presentation
- Evaluating performance
- Reflection on your oral presentation

10. Learning from lectures

Introduction

In your units of study much of the content and information will be provided in lectures, and the more effectively you use lectures, the more you will gain from your study. Although many students attend and listen to live lectures, an increasing number of students (especially those studying at a distance) access lectures and accompanying information via the web. If you access lectures electronically or on audio tape it is possible to listen to them more than once. However, this is time-consuming and you should be able to avoid this by making effective notes from the outset. When making lecture notes, it is not necessary to copy everything the lecturer says. It is more important to record the framework of the argument or ideas.

This exercise encourages you

- to practice summarising a lecture;

- to practice recording the structure of a lecture, separating the thesis from the supporting premises or the main point from the supporting details;

- to utilise patterned note making as a technique to summarise a lecture;

- to make lecture notes that incorporate the arguments or main ideas and the themes presented in a lecture.

Materials

A lecture from a unit you are studying

 10.1 Abbreviations

 10.2 Patterned notes of the lecture

Approximate time

90 minutes (includes listening to a lecture)

Reading

Marshall & Rowland, 2006, Chapter 9, pp. 161–172.

Learning activities

Activity 1   Summarising a lecture

Listen and make notes

Listen to a lecture from a unit you are studying and make notes as you listen. If the lecture is available online (or on audio tape) make sure that you print out any notes or PowerPoint slides and read any preliminary information before you listen.

When you have completed this continue working through this activity.

Review lecture notes

Review the content of your lecture notes for about five to ten minutes.

Summarise the lecture

 Put your notes away and in your learning log summarise the lecture in one or two paragraphs (no more than 200 words). This should encapsulate the argument (thesis and supporting premises) or the main and supporting details. Answering the following questions about the lecture can help you write your summary.

- What is the thesis (or the main point) being presented in the lecture? Write a sentence outlining the thesis (or the main point).

- What premises or reasons (or details) are presented to support the thesis (or the main point)? Write down the most important reasons.

- What assumptions has the lecturer made? What is the theoretical perspective or paradigm underlying the lecture material?

Evaluate your summary

Read over your summary and make sure that it:

- contains a statement of the argument (thesis and supporting premises) or the main point and supporting details;
- includes any crucial definitions or concepts;

– doesn't include any unnecessary examples or illustrations;

– doesn't include any unnecessary names, concepts, authors and/or books.

If possible share your summary with another student studying the unit.

The role of the lecture in the unit

In your learning log, consider and explain how the argument, main point or theme in this lecture relate to the unit as a whole.

Activity 2   Presentation of information in lectures

The objectives of lectures

Some objectives of lectures include:

– imparting information to a large number of people;
– providing a common ground for tutorial discussions on a subject;
– serving as a starting point for private study;
– drawing together the main ideas in a new research area;
– providing a preliminary map of difficult reading material;
– reviewing literature that is difficult to locate;
– adapting a subject to a particular audience in a way that a standard course text can't.

Relate these objectives to the lecture you summarised.

- What was the purpose of the lecture?
- Did the lecturer make this purpose clear?
- What techniques were used to indicate the purpose?

Lecturer's methods of presentation

Answer the following questions.

- How did the lecturer present the argument in the lecture?

- If there was no argument, how was the main point presented?

- What approach did the lecturer use in the lecture (for example, presentation of theories, expressing own opinions)?

- What transitions, connectives or pointers were used (for example, topic changes, summing up, digressions, instructions, rephrasing)? Refer to 'Transitional words and phrases' in Exercise 27, 'Editing the final draft'.)

- What cues (words, voice, body movements) alerted you to the structure or organisation of the lecture (for example: a change in voice, a meaningful pause, a movement away from the microphone)?

- What signalling words were used? For example:

  - Introducing the lecture: "*I want to start by ...*'
  - Introducing a main point: "*The next point is crucial.*"
  - Rephrasing the main point: "*The point I am making is ...*"
  - Introducing examples: "*Take the case of ...*"; "*An illustration ...*"
  - Changing the topic: "*I'd like to move on and look at ...*"
  - Summarising main points: "*To recapitulate ...*"

- Did the lecturer indicate the sources of information presented?

Understanding a lecturer's style can aid your note making. Pay particular attention to how the material is presented and how the argument or main point is emphasised.

Activity 3   Lecture note making techniques

Examine your lecture notes and consider whether these were useful in writing the summary.

Examine the different techniques you used in your note making. Answer the following questions.

- How have you separated the thesis from the supporting premises?
  or
  How have you separated the main point from the supporting details?

- Have you used full sentences, phrases or point form?

- Have you framed information by using headings and subheadings?

- Have you distinguished information by using different coloured pens?

- Have you left plenty of blank lines and space?

- Have you indented from the margin so that later you can add questions or comments about the information?

- Have you recorded any references to sources of information?

- What abbreviations have you used? (Refer to the attached list, 'Abbreviations'.)

Read Table 10.1 in Marshall and Rowland, 2006, pp. 166-167 and p. 169.

Answer the following questions.

- When making notes in a lecture, do you use a linear or non linear (patterned) technique?

- When summarising your lecture notes, do you use a linear or non linear (patterned) technique?

Activity 4 Patterned notes of the lecture

At the beginning of each chapter in this book a patterned summary outlining the content of the chapter is included.

Refer to Table 10.1 in Marshall and Rowland, 2006, pp. 166–167 for information on patterned note making. Using the attached worksheet, 'Patterned notes of the lecture', summarise the content of the lecture into patterned notes. You may want to turn the page sideways before writing the thesis or main point of the lecture in the ellipse in the middle of the page. See the beginning of each chapter in this book and Exercise 18, 'Reading in depth', for examples of patterned notes

Activity 5   Sharing summaries and notes

Share your lecture summary and patterned notes with another student
in your unit, or with a friend or family member. Ask for feedback and
reflect on how you could make your lecture notes more effective.
Think in terms of what you could do before, during and after the
lecture.

If possible, ask your tutor for an example of a patterned summary and
notes. Compare your summary and notes with these

Activity 6   Reflection

In your learning log, reflect on this exercise and discuss the note
making methods and techniques outlined. Will you use them or not?
Explain.

Describe any changes you need to make to enhance your learning
from lectures.

Learning from lectures

1. Summarising a lecture

Summarise the lecture in one or two paragraphs (no more than 200 words). This should encapsulate the argument (thesis and supporting premises) or the main point and supporting details.

- What is the thesis (or the main point) being presented in the lecture? Write a sentence outlining the thesis (or the main point).

- What premises or reasons (or details) are presented to support the thesis (or the main point)? Write down the most important reasons.

- What assumptions has the lecturer made? What is the theoretical perspective or paradigm underlying the lecture material?

Consider and explain how the argument, main point or theme in this lecture relate to the unit as a whole.

2. Reflection

Reflect on this exercise and discuss the note making methods and techniques outlined. Will you use them or not? Explain.

Describe any changes you need to make to enhance your learning from lectures.

Abbreviations

Commonly used abbreviations		Arrows	
c	with	↑	an increase
@	at	↓	a decrease
w	which	→	causes, leads to, results in
eg	example	↔	is caused by, is the result of
re	concerning		is related to
ca	about	**Mathematical symbols**	
am	before noon / morning	∴	therefore
pm	afternoon / evening	–	because
etc	and so on	=	is equal to or the same as
i.e.	that is	≠	is not equal to or not the same as
pa	per annum, each year	≤	is less than
NB	note well	≥	is greater than
C	century	×	times
c/f	compared with	+	**and**
b/f	before	%	percentage
et al.	and others		
viz	namely		
q.v.	refer to, see (cross referencing)	**Other symbols**	
#	number	✘	incorrect or wrong
Shorten suffixes		✔	correct or right
n	…tion or …sion		
g	…ing		

Patterned notes of the lecture

10.2

Activity 4

Write the thesis or main point of the lecture in the ellipse in the middle of the page and then construct your pattern around it.

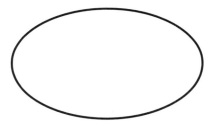

11. Learning from discussions

Introduction

This exercise is designed to be completed cooperatively in a group, preferably with other students who are studying your unit and with whom you discuss your learning. This group can consist of two people or a tutorial of 20 people. This exercise can also be completed with others as part of online discussions. Distance education or open learning students, who don't have the opportunity for face-to-face or online discussions about their learning with other students, can complete this exercise alone and apply it to other discussion situations. However, to get the most out of this exercise try to find a study partner or discussion group with whom you can share your learning, and if you cannot meet in person, establish contact by email or telephone.

This exercise encourages you

- to reflect on the place of informal and formal discussions in your learning;

- to evaluate the role you and others play in discussions;

- to evaluate the effectiveness of discussions as a learning experience;

- to take responsibility for discussions;

- to improve your discussion skills.

Approximate time

50 minutes

Reading

Marshall & Rowland, 2006, Chapter 10, pp. 174–192.

Learning activities

Activity 1   The role of discussion in learning

Informal discussions in learning

Identify a group discussion in which you learned something important. This may have been a heated discussion with friends at a dinner party, a long discussion with a travel companion, a club meeting, a meeting of school parents, a family meeting and so on.

In your learning log, answer the following questions.

- What did you learn in this discussion?

- What did you do during this discussion? How did you behave? How could you change your behaviour to improve this discussion?

Compare informal and formal discussions

Compare informal and formal (tutorials and seminars) discussion groups. One important difference is that tutorials and seminars are led by a tutor. How does this change the group? What other differences are there?

Are you involved in a group project with other students? How are these similar and dissimilar to informal or informal groups? How are they like or unlike tutorials?

Have you participated in online discussion groups? How do these groups differ from face-to-face discussions?

The importance of tutorials in learning

Refer to your log entries for Exercise 2, 'Transferring learning strengths into university study'. Did you list discussions and particularly formal discussions (tutorials and seminars) as important in your learning?

In your learning log, consider the importance of formal discussions in your learning by answering the following questions.

Is your learning in tutorials or in online discussions:

- Meaningful;
- relevant to your units of study;
- interesting?

Why or why not?

If you have participated in monitored, online discussions, compare these with face-to-face discussions.

Before you begin working with your discussion group, read Marshall and Rowland, 2006, pp. 173–192. Use the suggestions to guide you in the following activities.

Activity 2 The objectives of formal discussions in learning

Consider the objectives of formal discussions (tutorials and seminars).

Some objectives might be:

- to discuss lectures and reading;
- to clarify ideas;
- to apply 'new' ideas;
- to make 'mistakes' and to learn from the interchange of ideas that develops;
- to engage in a dialectical process with ideas and concepts;
- to discuss any problems you are having with your work;
- to practice communicating ideas;
- to verbalise ideas before writing them in an assignment;
- to integrate learning with other aspects of a unit;
- to develop your verbal and language skills.

The following list[2] includes many other possible content and process objectives of formal discussions in learning.

---

[2] Pat Bertola and Eamon Murphy, 1994, *Tutoring in the social sciences and humanities: a beginner's practical guide*, Curtin University, Western Australia, p. 8.

Content	Process
– discussing a controversial issue	– practising listening skills
– consolidating knowledge	– generating questions
– clarifying issues	– developing group skills
– identifying a major theme	– practising presentation skills
– solving a problem	– reviewing how to or how others structure arguments
– outlining an alternate perspective	– expressing thoughts, ideas, opinions and solutions verbally and in writing
– analysing an argument	– practising self criticism and evaluation
– assessing evidence	– working as part of a team
– planning an essay	– developing interpersonal skills
– evaluating writing	– developing positive attitudes: tolerance, empathy, respect for others and intellectual rigour

Activity 3   Different tutorial groups

You will notice that tutorial groups differ. Identify a group that functions well and one that doesn't. Try to determine the differences between these. Some tutorials work well due to the mix of students, and some don't. It is partly your responsibility to ensure that tutorials are effective.

Leadership styles

Discuss different leadership styles. Discuss the difference between tutoring styles.

Refer to Marshall and Rowland, 2006, pp. 188–191 for information on this.

Student and tutor responsibilities

Remember that tutorials are not only the tutor's responsibility.

Some student responsibilities include:

- to prepare before the tutorial;
- to participate during the tutorial, which includes expressing your knowledge and opinions;
- to review what you have learned after the tutorial.

Some tutor responsibilities include:

- to prepare before the tutorial;
- to provide guidance;
- to provide expertise.

Activity 4 Participating in tutorials

How you participate in tutorials

In your learning log, reflect on and explain how you participate in tutorials and seminars.

- Is your role in formal groups (tutorials and seminars) different from your role in informal groups? Compare the way you discuss something with your friends with the way you discuss something in a tutorial. What are the differences and similarities?

- List some of the different ways to participate in discussion groups.

- What role do you play in tutorials? What do you do during discussions?

- How do you behave? It is important to be aware of your behaviour and be willing to change it in order to make tutorials more meaningful in your learning.

Positive and negative behaviours

Make a list of positive and negative behaviours of participants in tutorials or seminars.

Compare your list with those outlined below. Add to your list any behaviours that you have observed.

Positive behaviours	Negative behaviours
– summarises information	– observes but never speaks
– seeks information	– talks much of the time
– gives information	– is uncooperative
– questions	– knows it all
– keeps to the topic	– is disruptive
– listens carefully to others	– interrupts others
– is open to new ideas and information	– is silent and watchful
	– is silent and downcast
– uses notes to raise issues	– interacts mainly with the tutor
– prepares for discussion	– interacts with the main talker
– affirms what others say	– is argumentative
– displays a sense of humour	– arrives late
	– prepares rarely
	– keeps changing the topic

Activity 5   Improving tutorials

Consider what you can do to improve tutorials. Consider any action you can take **before**, **during** and **after** tutorials.

Preparation

- Make sure you complete the set pre-reading to familiarise yourself with the topic.
- Make sure that you attempt any pre-tutorial problems or questions so that you are able to participate and ask questions about areas you don't understand.
- Consider how the information to be discussed relates to earlier material and the overall unit.

Participation

- Think of several questions/comments you would like to make, form them into sentences and practise them in your head and out loud.
- Be ready to speak at a relevant time. Look for pauses that enable you to enter the discussion and jump in quickly.
- Indicate that you wish to speak by gaining eye contact with the tutor, taking an alert body posture and moving in your seat.
- Be prepared to feel nervous with your first few contributions, but remember that you are not alone Accept that you are nervous, and don't be further upset by it.

After the tutorial

- Contact your tutor to clarify any information you didn't understand.
- Complete any unfinished work.
- Revise and consolidate what you have learned (particularly concepts).
- List any questions in your notebook and answer them.
- Check terms/jargon.
- Associate concepts to terms.
- Practise expressing concepts in your own words.

When participating in a discussion remember the following important points. [3]

- You are participating in a discussion:
  - to learn;
  - to help others learn.
- Always have a paper and pen/pencil handy during discussions.
- If you don't understand something, ask for further explanation.
- If two people have misunderstood each other, help them out.
- If someone has said something that you think is important, remind the group about it.

---

[3] Adapted from Michael Marland, 1977, *Language across the curriculum*, Heinemann, London, pp. 133-137.

- Always let others 'have their say', even if you are bursting to speak.
- Be prepared to change your mind if you have been proven wrong.
- Don't shout people down when you don't agree with them.
- Don't show off in a discussion.
- Participate in a discussion even if you feel shy.
- Listen carefully to what others say.
- Always have one person writing down the most important points discussed and any decisions that are made.

Activity 6   Establishing ground rules

As a group develop a list of at least five ground rules that are important in making tutorial discussions effective.

These ground rules might include, for example[4]:

- no put downs;
- all members of the group will be on time;
- it's okay to make mistakes;
- when somebody speaks, everybody listens;
- all members of the group will prepare.

Write out your list of the ground rules for each member of the group.

When you have finished developing a list of ground rules, discuss your willingness to operate according to these guidelines in all discussions. Try to reach agreement in order to improve your discussion group.

Also, make sure that any online discussion groups in which you participate establish ground rules.

---

[4]   Pat Bertola & Eamon Murphy, 1994, *Tutoring in the social sciences and humanities: a beginner's practical guide*, Curtin University, Western Australia, p. 15.

Activity 7   Ground rules for critical thinking

Consider whether your list of tutorial ground rules will help foster the attitudes necessary for critical thinking. What are these attitudes?

Below is a list of ground rules for critical thinking developed by a group of students for their tutorial group. [5]

- Avoid being dogmatic.
- We are all fallible. We can all make mistakes.
- Don't silence others.
- Don't be racist or sexist or ethnocentric.
- Don't use coercive methods to dominate and thus silence others.
- Respect everybody's opinion.
- Explain assumptions.
- All claims can be challenged and they must be defended with reasons that are themselves subject to further challenge.
- Establish the relevance of your evidence to your thesis.
- Treat the offerings of others seriously.
- Clarify your meaning – define your terms.
- Be prepared to explain your assumptions.

Activity 8   Other ways to discuss learning

It is important to be aware that even if you prefer to work alone, you can learn a lot from other students.

Many units now provide online discussion for students. Even if you don't actively participate in these groups, you can learn much from reading other views. Given some time you may feel sufficiently comfortable to participate.

If you are a distance education or open learning student and don't have the opportunity for online or face-to-face discussions with other students, work out ways that you can do this.

- Contact your Distance Education or Open Universities Centre for a list of students who are willing to share their name and email

---

[5]   Lorraine Marshall, John de Reuck & David Lake, 1996, *Critical thinking in context: A teacher's guide to the video*, Gripping Films Production, Academic Services Unit, Murdoch University.

address or phone number. If you find students who live nearby, try to meet with them.

- Phone other students to discuss mutual study concerns.

- Use email to share ideas and receive quick feedback on your questions, your concerns and even your writing.

- If you live a long way from other students and don't have email and find telephoning too expensive, find a student studying the same unit, with whom you can exchange CDs or audio tapes. Discuss/verbalise your ideas on tape and ask for a response or feedback.

- If you are unable to work with another student in any of the ways suggested, try to find someone (friend or family member) with whom to discuss your ideas and learning.

Activity 9 Reflection on enhancing learning in discussions

In your learning log, describe any changes you (and others) need to make to enhance your own (and other's) learning in discussions.

If you are in a discussion (face-to face or online) that isn't effective, explain what could be done to improve it. Discuss this with the group.

Learning from discussions

1. The role of discussions groups in learning

Identify a group discussion in which you learned something important.

- What did you learn in this discussion?
- What did you do during this discussion? How did you behave? How could you change your behaviour to improve this discussion?

Consider the importance of formal discussions in your learning by answering the following questions.

Is your learning in tutorials or in online discussions:
- – meaningful
- – relevant to your units of study
- – interesting?

Why or why not?

2. Participation in tutorials

- Is your role in formal groups (tutorials and seminars) different from your role in informal groups? Compare the way you discuss something with your friends with the way you discuss something in a tutorial. What are the differences and similarities?
- List some of the different ways to participate in discussion groups.
- What role do you play in tutorials? What do you do during discussions? How do you behave?
- Make a list of positive and negative behaviours of participants in tutorials or seminars.

3. Reflection on enhancing learning in discussions

Describe any changes you (and others) need to make to enhance your own (and other's) learning in tutorials.

If you are in a discussion (face-to face or online) that isn't effective, explain what could be done to improve it

12. Preparing and giving an oral presentation

Introduction

Giving an oral presentation in front of an audience is a stressful experience for many people. However, oral presentations are an important component of university learning, and you need to prepare for them in much the same way as you would for written assignments.

You will already know a great deal about the characteristics of presentations from the many good and bad presentations that you have listened to. This exercise encourages you to explore your knowledge of what constitutes a good presentation, and to use this to develop a set of criteria for evaluating your own and other students' presentations.

This exercise encourages you

- to develop criteria for evaluating your own and other students' oral presentations;

- to improve your oral presentation skills;

- to develop skills in preparing and delivering an oral presentation;

- to develop skills in preparing a handout, overhead transparency or PowerPoint slides for an oral presentation;

- to apply coping strategies when dealing with anxiety about making an oral presentation.

Materials

12.1	Evaluating oral presentations checklist
12.2	The structure of formal oral presentations
12.3	Preparation for an oral presentation: questions to consider
12.4	Guidelines for fielding questions

12.5	Evaluation of oral presentations

Approximate time

50 minutes.

Reading

Marshall & Rowland, 2006, Chapter 10, pp. 165–168; Chapter 11, pp. 173–192.

Learning activities

Activity 1 Previous experiences with oral presentations

Your feelings about giving presentations

Reflect on your feelings, both positive and negative, about giving oral presentations.

In your learning log, discuss your past experience (both positive and negative) with giving oral presentations, and explain any fears and anxieties or pleasures and excitements related to these experiences. If you feel overly anxious about giving oral presentations, discuss this with your tutor or with a trained counsellor. It is important to work towards overcoming any fears that you have.

The following activities aim to help you prepare fully and rehearse your presentation. Preparation and rehearsal reduce anxiety. However, there is evidence that a certain amount of stress can be positive.

Activity 2 Evaluating oral presentations

Characteristics of good presentations

Reflect on different oral presentations that you have experienced, such as university lectures, church sermons, political speeches, after-dinner talks, public lectures, seminar presentations and so on. In your learning log, list the characteristics of a good oral presentation under the following headings: structure, content and presentation.

12.1 This list might include some or all of the points outlined in the attached information, 'Evaluating oral presentations checklist'.

If your oral presentations are to be formally assessed, find out how this will be done. This exercise is designed for oral presentations that are assessed on structure, content and presentation.

Criteria for evaluating presentations

It is important to find out exactly what is expected of you in a formal oral presentation, for example, how much time you have for the presentation, who will be in your audience, what equipment is available and so on.

12.1 Use the list of characteristics of good presentations that you generated and also the attached material, 'Evaluating oral presentations checklist', to decide on the criteria that you think will be most important in evaluating your oral presentations. If you are working with another student or in a group compile the list together.

12.5 When you have decided on these criteria, complete the attached worksheet, 'Evaluation of oral presentations'. Use the list of criteria to complete this worksheet. Choose five criteria to place under each of the headings: structure, content and presentation. If possible, ask another student who will be listening to your presentation to evaluate it using the worksheet. It is important to obtain feedback.

Activity 3   Preparing an oral presentation

Structuring a presentation

12.2 Refer to the attached information, 'The structure of formal oral presentations' to help you decide how to organise your material so that you have a clear beginning, middle and end.

If your presentation is based on a written essay or report, consider which parts to include and which parts to omit, which sections to present fully and which sections to present briefly. As a general rule, you won't have to present too much detail. An oral presentation necessitates selecting and prioritising information to inspire interest and a basic understanding of the question/topic. Save some points you won't have time to address for the discussion time afterward.

Summarise the purpose of your presentation in a sentence. Consider your audience, their level of knowledge on the subject, and their needs and values. These considerations should determine the type of language and formality (tone) of your delivery.

Discuss with another student how you will structure your presentation.

Preparing visual material

It is important to prepare visual material that summarises the structure and content of the presentation. It is preferable to prepare PowerPoint slides or an overhead transparency and perhaps a handout for distribution. For shorter presentations a handout should comprise one page and can be in a linear or patterned form. Experiment with these or other visuals that can illustrate your presentation. Patterns and charts can provide an overview of what you intend to discuss. They can also help calm your nerves, as the audience has something else to look at besides you. Numerical representations can be useful for some topics. (See the Exercise 10, 'Learning from lectures', and Exercise 18, Reading in depth', for more on patterned notes.)

Rehearsing a presentation

A key element in giving an effective presentation is the rehearsal as this can give you confidence.

- It is particularly important to learn not to speak using written language and develop a conversational oral style. As a general rule don't attempt to memorise a text. Just remember to rehearse your entire presentation so that it is familiar.

- Find a convenient time to rehearse your presentation. You might find it useful to re-assess the evaluation sheet before you give the actual presentation.

- When rehearsing check that your presentation doesn't run over the time allowed, so that when you are delivering it you don't have to cut it short and leave out important points. Similarly, check that you have enough material (without padding), so that you don't finish much earlier than expected.

- Practise your opening sentences, so that you are clear about where you will start. This can help you feel and appear more confident.

- Practise using intonation to emphasise main points, to make statements, to ask questions or to make asides.

- Try to include connectives, so that your audience is informed about where the presentation is heading and how the ideas relate to each other and to the overall topic. (See Exercise 27, 'Transitional words and phrases'.)

Fielding questions

When promoting discussion and answering questions it is important to be prepared. This entails understanding why people ask questions and using strategies to answer them effectively. Refer to the attached information, 'Preparation for an oral presentation: Questions to consider' and 'Guidelines for fielding questions'.

Reviewing a presentation

Before giving your presentation, work through all of the materials provided in this exercise to make certain you have considered all of the important points.

Activity 4   Evaluating performance

After your presentation, request and collect any evaluations from other students. If appropriate, make an appointment to discuss your presentation with your tutor. If you feel you could improve, see a learning adviser for help. If possible, have a video made of a presentation, and have a trained person evaluate it and help you with your areas of weakness.

In your learning log, answer the following questions.

- What feedback did I get from the audience/tutor?
- How did I rate my delivery?
- In which areas do I need to improve?
- Was I too dependent on my notes?
- Did I read too much and alienate myself from the audience?

Activity 5   Reflection on your oral presentation

In your learning log, reflect on your performance. Explain any changes you need to make to improve your performance. Refer to the materials in this exercise as you write your reflections.

Preparing and giving an oral presentation

1. Previous experiences with oral presentations

Discuss your past experiences (both positive and negative) with giving oral presentations, and explain any fears and anxieties or pleasures and excitements related to these experiences.

2. Evaluating oral presentations

List the characteristics of a good oral presentation under the following headings: structure, content and presentation.

3. Evaluating your performance

After your presentation, answer the following questions.

- What feedback did I get from the audience/tutor?
- How did I rate my delivery?
- In which areas do I need to improve?
- Was I too dependent on my notes?
- Did I read too much and alienate myself from the audience?

4. Reflection on your oral presentation

Reflect on your performance. Refer to the materials in this exercise as you write your reflections.

Evaluating oral presentations checklist[6]

12.1

Activity 2

1. Structure
- ☐ logical
- ☐ identifiable beginning, middle and end
- ☐ indicated moves to new stages
- ☐ clear to audience
- ☐ important points emphasised
- ☐ didn't get bogged down with detail
- ☐ minimal repetition
- ☐ not too long

2. Content
- ☐ relevant
- ☐ fact versus opinion distinguished
- ☐ interesting
- ☐ focused on important points
- ☐ raised questions to think about
- ☐ answered questions
- ☐ provide useful information
- ☐ understandable to the audience

3. Presentation/Delivery

a. Audience
- ☐ awareness of the audience
- ☐ reaction to presenter's body language
- ☐ appropriate positioning of the audience and visual aids
- ☐ relationship between speaker and the audience
- ☐ enthusiastic?
- ☐ Were questions answered appropriately?
- ☐ Were answers related to the content?
- ☐ Were complex questions broken down into parts?
- ☐ Will the audience consider the presentation as a memorable event?

b. Language
- ☐ understandable language used
- ☐ written (like a report)
- ☐ oral (like a conversation)
- ☐ sentences long and complex/short and simple
- ☐ vocabulary over-technical or suitable for audience
- ☐ transition words appropriate

c. Voice
- ☐ fluent/hesitant?
- ☐ calm/nervous?
- ☐ audible/inaudible?
- ☐ too fast/too slow?
- ☐ monotonous/varied?
- ☐ clear/unclear?
- ☐ enthusiastic/dull?

d. Body language/non-verbal skills
- ☐ confident
- ☐ relaxed
- ☐ hand & body gestures
- ☐ posture
- ☐ eye contact with audience

e. Use of notes
- ☐ independent/over-dependent
- ☐ referred to/read

f. Timing
- ☐ too long/too short?

g. Visual aids
- ☐ clear/unclear?
- ☐ attractive/plain?
- ☐ explained well/glossed over?
- ☐ relevant/irrelevant?

---

[6]   Adapted from Sue Habeshaw and Di Steeds, 1993, 53 *Interesting communication exercises for science students*, Technical Education Services Ltd, Bristol, UK, pp. 213–214.

Evaluation of oral presentations

12.5

Activity 2

Presenter's name: _____ Date: _____

Tutor: _____

Presentation title: _____

_____

_____

Rating scale
(Rate student performance for each)

A. Structure or organisation   excellent 4   3   2   1   poor

1. _____? ☐ ☐ ☐ ☐

2. _____? ☐ ☐ ☐ ☐

3. _____? ☐ ☐ ☐ ☐

4. _____? ☐ ☐ ☐ ☐

5. _____? ☐ ☐ ☐ ☐

B. Content

1. _____? ☐ ☐ ☐ ☐

2. _____? ☐ ☐ ☐ ☐

3. _____? ☐ ☐ ☐ ☐

4. _____? ☐ ☐ ☐ ☐

5. _____? ☐ ☐ ☐ ☐

C. Presentation

1. _____? ☐ ☐ ☐ ☐

2. _____? ☐ ☐ ☐ ☐

3. _____? ☐ ☐ ☐ ☐

4. _____? ☐ ☐ ☐ ☐

5. _____? ☐ ☐ ☐ ☐

D. General comments

_____

_____

_____

_____

_____

The structure of formal oral presentations[7]

12.2

Activity 3

Most formal talks are structured. They have a beginning (the introduction) a middle (the body) and an end (the conclusion).

The beginning introduces the topic by:

- stating the aims of the presentation;
- defining the terms;
- outlining the scope of the presentation;
- giving a plan of the presentation;
- capturing the interest of the audience.

The middle or body develops the topic by:

- keeping to the topic;
- expanding the plan in a point-by-point logical sequence;
- explaining any data collected to support the aims;
- including audio-visual aids to help present more detailed information.

The end concludes the talk by:

- stating the main points again;
- evaluating the importance of the information;
- formulating some conclusions;
- reviewing the implications (if any).

You can talk about any topic following this basic plan. Common variations are:

---

[7] M. R. McEvedy et al., 1986, *Studying in Australia: speaking in academic settings,* Nelson, Melbourne, p. 35.

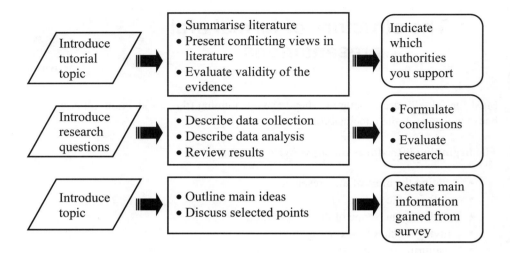

Preparation for an oral presentation: question to consider

12.3

Activity 3

Choosing, defining and analysing a topic

- How can I best choose, define and analyse my topic? (See Exercise 23, 'Choosing an essay question', and Exercise 24, 'Analysing an essay question'.
- What aspects of the content and format of my presentation are important?

Research

- Is there a specific tutorial question I should answer?
- How much background reading will I have to do?
- Will I use quotations in my presentation? Are they necessary or desirable?

Organisation of material/information

- How will I introduce my presentation?
- How will I capture the interest of the audience?
- Will I give an outline of the structure of my presentation?
- Which parts of my written material will I include? Which parts will I omit? Which parts will I present in detail and which parts only briefly?
- What will I use as a memory aid (for example, prompt cards, handout, overhead transparency)?
- Will I speak without notes or with full notes or from outline notes (with headings)?
- How will I show the relationship between ideas, concepts, facts etc. (for example, signalling words and phrases, graphics)?

Rehearsal

- How many times do I need to practise or rehearse the presentation?
- How will I calm my nerves?
- How will I use my memory aids in the presentation (for example, timing)?
- What aspects of my speech and presentation do I need to think about (for example, body language)?
- How will I vary my presentation to get my message across? How will I emphasise major points, ask questions, make asides and use humour?
- How will I keep to the time allowed (allocation of time to the introduction, body and conclusion)?

Guidelines for fielding questions[8]

Activity 3

For some presentations it is unlikely that you will have to answer questions following or during your presentation. However, if you do need to answer questions, if you do so effectively you will satisfy the questioner and create a good impression among the rest of the audience. In fact, the way you answer questions can affect the way your audience remembers your whole presentation.

When you are preparing your presentation it is wise to be prepared for likely questions from the audience. Be prepared to either:

- incorporate answers to questions in your presentation, or
- provide 'off-the-cuff' answers.

Why people ask questions

Knowing why people ask questions can help you give answers which satisfy the questioners. Most questions are an appeal for information. Other questions are asked to satisfy various needs, some of which you may have identified when analysing your audience. Some of the reasons people ask questions include:

- to gain attention
- to display their knowledge
- to gain approval
- to inform you
- to relieve their boredom
- to lead you on to another subject, or away from one
- to raise their own concerns
- to disrupt your speech.

Dealing with questions asked during your presentation

Avoid asking your audience for questions during your speech, unless you want to check that your audience understands what you have said. If you are interrupted with a question, stop to answer it and then return to your speech as soon as possible. Although you may lose the continuity of ideas, leaving a question unanswered until the end of your speech will sound like evasion and may distract the audience from listening.

---

[8]   From M.Stevens, 1987, *Improving your presentation skills: A complete action kit*, Kogan Page, London, pp. 84-86.

General guidelines for answering questions

The following **general guidelines** should help you answer questions:

- listen carefully to the question
- look at the questioner and try to decide from their manner and tone of voice why they are asking
- draw them out further if necessary
- repeat the question in your own words to ensure that you understand and everyone else has heard
- if it is a complex question, divide it into parts and state what each is before you answer
- relate your answers to points you have made in your speech. Don't raise new points
- answer briefly, keeping to the point
- if your answer must be more than a few sentences, give it structure - an introduction, middle and conclusion
- don't try to put questioners down, or ridicule them; answer reasonably
- if you don't have the information to answer a question, say so, and ask if anyone in the audience can help
- don't argue under any circumstances.

Responding to different types of questions

The way you answer depends on the specific question and the way it was asked, but the following ways are effective:

Type of question	How you would respond
▪ several questions in one	▪ ask what the main question is, and answer that
▪ one which includes incorrect information	▪ correct it, and then answer if it's still necessary
▪ hostile	▪ express understanding of the reason they feel as they do, but explain why you have said what they're reacting against
▪ rambling	▪ interrupt and ask what their question is
▪ argumentative	▪ answer in a way which reinforces what you've already said
▪ asking you to make a commitment	▪ don't make a promise you can't keep. If necessary, briefly explain why

CHAPTER 4

Reading

During your university study reading is the most important method of obtaining information. Everyone begins university study with a range of reading skills, but because of the extensive amount of reading required at university it is necessary to refine existing skills and develop new skills for selective, reflective and critical reading. The exercises in this chapter are designed to help you become a more effective and efficient reader, that is, to absorb more information in less time. The exercises emphasise that reading is an active thinking process, and developing your reading skills involves:

- **previewing** all study material;
- reading with a **purpose**;
- **'marking up'** the text and **making notes** as you read;
- adjusting your reading **rate/speed** according to your reading purpose and the difficulty of the material.

117

In this chapter there are six exercises on reading: one on understanding who you are as a reader, one on keeping a reading log, two on previewing books, one on note making, and one on reading in depth. These exercises can be applied numerous times to different material until you have successfully developed the necessary reading skills.

Each exercise emphasises the importance of previewing. Two exercises focus on previewing whole books. These exercises reinforce the strategic importance of previewing all study material regardless of length (chapter, article or book), before beginning to read in depth. Rather than reading and gathering everything that is vaguely relevant to a given topic, effective previewing can vastly improve the efficiency of your reading and research.

Each exercise aims to help you understand the content of the text you are reading. If you can understand the argument[1] (thesis and supporting premises or reasons) presented in a text, you will be in a better position to evaluate it critically. Evaluating what you read is not only an end-on process occurring after you read a text but should also occur as you read and make notes or 'mark-up' the text. Evidence of understanding and critical evaluation are expected of you in essays, reports, projects, discussions and exams.

Each exercise will also enable you to place what you are reading within a broader context, ask questions about the content, highlight information that you don't understand, draw connections between ideas presented and summarise the material.

Keep in mind that while the exercise on keeping a reading log can be applied to reading literary works, the other exercises specifically focus on reading academic material and are not appropriate for reading literature.

---

[1] An argument is a form of thinking in which certain statements (premises [or reasons]) are offered in support of another statement (a thesis [or conclusion]). Definition adapted from John Chaffee, 1990, *Thinking critically*, Houghton Mifflin, Boston, p. 499.

13. Understanding your reading habits and skills
- The role of reading in your life
  - you as a reader
- Reading skills
  - your reading skills
  - appropriate reading skills for university study
  - transferring reading skills to study
- Purposes for reading
  - identifying different reading purposes
  - articulating your reading purposes
- Reading rate or speed

14. Keeping a reading log
- The extent of required reading
- Objectives for keeping a log
  - what to include in a reading log
- Different systems for keeping a reading log
  - advantages and disadvantages of different systems
- Make reading log entries

15. Previewing a book
- Finding out what books are about
  - get to know the book quickly
  - analyse your method
- Previewing a book
  - when to preview
  - levels of previewing
- Previewing systematically
  - preview the book
  - think and write about the book
- Reflection on the process

18. Reading in depth
- Purposes for reading
  - identify and articulate reading purposes
- Previewing
  - your purposes for previewing
  - preview the text
- The introduction
  - examine the introduction
  - 'mark up' the introduction
- The conclusion
  - examine the conclusion
  - mark up' the conclusion
- Paragraph structure
  - read a section
  - examine each paragraph
  - identify the overall paragraph structure
- Transitions and links
  - identify transitions and links
- Making notes
  - make linear notes
  - make patterned notes
- Reviewing and summarising the text
  - evaluate your summary
- Share your notes and summary
- Reflection on this approach to reading
- Apply the techniques to another reading

Reading 4

16. Previewing edited books
- Previewing the edited book
- An interesting reading
- A familiar reading
- A difficult reading
- Reflection on the process

17. Note making from reading
- Objectives for 'marking up' and making notes
- 'Marking up' texts
  - your system
  - how to 'mark up' texts
- Making notes from reading
  - your system
  - linear and non linear techniques
- Organising your notes
- Reflection on the process

13. Understanding your reading habits and skills

Introduction

This exercise is designed to help you identify your reading habits and assess your reading skills. It considers the importance of setting purposes for reading, and highlights the relationship between your reading rate or speed, your purpose for reading and the complexity of the material.

This exercise encourages you

- to consider your reading strengths;

- to read for a purpose;

- to monitor your reading rate or speed;

- to transfer appropriate skills into your university study.

Materials

Exercise 2:

2.2   Reading with transfer in mind

Approximate time

30 minutes

Reading

Marshall & Rowland, 2006, Chapter 9, pp. 133-136, 137 and 145–152.

Activity 1   The role of reading in your life

You as a reader

In your learning log, write about your reading habits. Answer the following questions.

- If you like to read, why?

- If you don't like to read, why not?

- What types of material do you like to read? Do you read novels, magazines and so on? Do you prefer fiction or non-fiction?

- How much do you read? Do you read several books a week, one a year and so on?

- Do you like to read but find you never have the time for it? Why or why not?

- When and where do you read? Do you read in bed, in the bath, when eating breakfast, when commuting and so on?

- Do you discuss what you read with other people?

- Do you belong to a library from which you borrow books?

- Do you have a library of your own? Does it contain many books? What kinds of books does it contain?

Read Marshall and Rowland, 2006, Chapter 9, pp. 133–136.

Activity 2   Reading skills

Your reading skills

If you like to read and read a lot you will probably have developed many reading skills. Reading is a skill that consists of many different sub skills. Some reading skills include:

- recognising words;
- making sense of unfamiliar words by dividing the word into syllables using the context or a dictionary;
- using the features of a text (table of context, index and so on) to help you read;
- reading for a purpose;
- previewing or overviewing material before reading it;
- reading at a reasonable rate and varying this rate according to your purpose for reading and the complexity of the material;
- understanding what you read;
- making notes from what you read;
- 'marking up' or underlining the text;
- analysing or evaluating what your read;
- evaluating or criticising what you read;
- relating what you read to other material, ideas or contexts.

 Add any other skills to this list that you think are important. In your learning log, consider each skill and assess your reading strengths and weaknesses. Which skills do you need to develop or refine?

Remember that your competence with many of these reading skills will depend on your reason for reading, your familiarity with the material and its level of difficulty for you.

Appropriate reading skills for university study

In all university study reading is an essential skill and you need to consider which reading skills are appropriate for your study. For example, if you enjoy reading novels and are studying literature, then you will be well prepared to read the novels set in your study units. However, you may find that literary criticism demands different reading skills. If you have always enjoyed non-fiction and are required to read a novel, you may need to adapt and change your approach to reading.

 In your learning log, consider the type of study you are undertaking and write down the reading skills that are appropriate for you. Explain which reading skills are not appropriate.

Transferring reading skills to study

2.2 Refer to Exercise 2, 'Transferring learning strengths into university study', and read Activity 6, 'Transferring reading skills'. Re-examine the example 'Reading with transfer in mind', which contrasts reading a newspaper (reading in an informal environment) with reading an academic text. Re-read your log entry. Note the reading skills you already have that are appropriate for your university study and the reading skills that you may need to refine or learn.

Activity 3   Purposes for reading

Identifying different reading purposes

Identifying and articulating your different purposes for reading can help you determine what and how to read. Due to the extensive amounts of reading required at university, reading with a purpose can help you select the material that is most relevant to your task and ignore less relevant material. It is useful to identify five levels of reading that reflect different purposes.

(a) Reading for enjoyment	– light reading
(b) Reading for overview	– getting a general idea or the gist of a topic
(c) Search reading	– looking for specific information
(d) Reading for an in-depth understanding	– obtaining detailed information on a topic
(e) Critical reading	– reading to evaluate the argument.[2]

In your learning log, consider the reading you have done over the past few weeks. Identify and write about tasks where you have used each level of reading.

Articulating your reading purposes

In order to read more effectively, identify and articulate your purposes for reading a text before you begin. Use the list of purposes above to help you pinpoint your reading purpose.

---

[2] Adapted from Alex Main, 1980, *Encouraging effective learning*, Scottish Academic Press, Scotland, p. 40.

Activity 4   Reading rate or speed

Answer the following questions.

- Are you concerned about your reading rate or speed?

- Do you find it difficult to complete all of your reading?

- Have you ever timed the rate or speed at which you read?

Each exercise in this chapter is designed to make you a more effective and efficient reader, that is, to understand and absorb information faster. Reading rapidly is of little use if you don't understand what you read. However, you should not expect to read all material at the same rate and you should vary your reading rate (or speed) according to your purpose for reading and the complexity of the material. For example, if your purpose is to gain an in depth understanding of material for an essay or book review, you will need to allow more time and read the material slowly.

Previewing material before you begin reading it can help you decide on the appropriate reading rate. Previewing can also indicate how difficult or easy the material will be for you, which sections are difficult or easy and which are relevant to your purpose for reading. For example, if your preview indicates that the material is familiar or easy then it is possible to increase the rate at which you read. Developing a mental map of the material by previewing can improve your reading efficiency. This chapter contains two exercises on previewing and an exercise on reading in depth, which emphasise the importance of previewing.

Understanding your reading habits and skills

1. The role of reading in your life

Write about your reading habits. Answer the following questions.

- If you like to read, why?
- If you don't like to read, why not?
- What types of material do you like to read? Do you read novels, magazines, and so on? Do you prefer fiction or non fiction?
- How much do you read? Do you read several books a week, one a year and so on?
- Do you like to read but find you never have the time for it? Why?
- When and where do you read? Do you read in bed, in the bath, when eating breakfast, when commuting and so on?
- Do you discuss what you read with other people?
- Do you belong to a library from which you borrow books?
- Do you have a library of your own? Does it contain many books? What kinds of books does it contain?

2. Reading skills

- Assess your reading strengths and weaknesses. Which skills do you need to develop or refine?

- Consider the type of study you are undertaking and write down the reading skills that are appropriate for you. Explain which reading skills are not appropriate.

3. Purposes for reading

Consider the reading you have done over the past few weeks. Identify and write about tasks where you have used each level of reading.

14. Keeping a reading log

Introduction

Every student, academic and professional person needs to record references and information sources. Methods to do this vary widely, and it is important that each person develop a system that suits his or her own objectives. It is useful for students to develop a system in the first year of university study.

This exercise focuses on keeping a reading log for one unit. It is expected that you will use the activities beyond this exercise and that you will extend the skills developed to all of your units. When beginning a unit, you should consider whether or not you will keep a reading log. If you are intending to keep a learning log (described in Exercise 1), it is possible to combine that with your reading log to form one log. To do this you will need to set up clear categories that separate your personal reflections on learning from your summary and critique of reading in the unit. It is more efficient to develop a system for keeping a reading log before you begin any reading in the unit. Subsequent exercises in this chapter suggest the form and content of log entries.

This exercise encourages you

- to keep a reading log in all units of study;

- to develop a system for recording information and ideas stemming from reading;

- to develop a system for keeping a reading log that will satisfy your objectives;

- to consider objectives for keeping a reading log to maximise its usefulness;

- to read critically, analyse the material and contribute a personal comment on it.

Approximate time

45–60 minutes

Learning activities

Activity 1   The extent of required reading

Look through your unit materials and consider the amount and depth of reading required. Distinguish between the minimum requirements and additional reading, if any. What are the advantages of reading widely on the topics in the unit? If the unit requires a reading log, what instructions are you given and do you have to submit copies of reading log entries to your tutor?

Activity 2   Objectives for keeping a reading log

Consider your objectives for keeping a reading log. These objectives should not be limited to those units that require a reading log, as it can be useful to keep a reading log in all units that you study.

Two main objectives for keeping a reading log are:

- to help you retrieve information at a later time;
- to help you crystallise your ideas about the readings.

What other objectives might you have for keeping a reading log?

What to include in a reading log

Make a list of what should be included in a reading log to fulfil the objectives identified above.

For retrieving information at a later time, a reading log should include:

- the complete citation details, including author(s) and/or editor(s), year, article and/or book title, edition, publisher and place of publication and page numbers;

- a short description of the argument or main points (content), key terms, relevant or important ideas;

- a way to easily access or retrieve information (a system of ordering entries and records).

You may also like to include details such as the date when you read it and the library and catalogue number where you found the book.

To help crystallise your ideas, a reading log should include some personal reflection or comment on the material and a critical analysis of the information and ideas presented in the reading written in your own words.

Activity 3 Different systems for keeping a reading log

Your system for keeping a reading log can include one or a combination of the following:

- notebooks;
- loose-leaf sheets in folders;
- loose-leaf sheets in ring binders;
- cards;
- computer data base.

Your information can be organised according to:

- title;
- subject headings;
- author or source.

Advantages and disadvantages of different systems

Consider any systems you have used previously to record and store information. Consider their advantages and disadvantages. For example:

- **Notebooks** are portable and cheap, but it can be difficult to organise large lists of references relating to different subjects.

- **Loose-leaf sheets** are moveable and can be easily reorganised, but they can get very dog-eared.

- **Cards** are reasonably cheap, increasingly flexible and transportable and can be easily alphabetised. It is easy to carry a few cards with you in case you find a reference you want to record, and they can be kept in alphabetical order for easy location. However, cross-referencing cards is difficult, and rely heavily on you being able to remember an author's name.

- **Computers** facilitate retrieval as information can be sorted and located using key words, title or author, and references can be transferred to an essay without rewriting. However, unless you have a lap top computer, information cannot be added in different study locations.

Activity 4   Make reading log entries

Aim to make reading log entries for the books, articles or chapters that you preview and read in the following exercises in this chapter.

Enjoy reading and making your log entries!

15. Previewing a book

Introduction

This exercise is useful if you are required to read a book written by one or more authors (as opposed to an edited book of readings which is covered in the following exercise). Previewing is also useful when browsing the library for information on a specific topic when you are required to read only a chapter or two of a book or when you need to grasp the argument or theme in a book.

If a book is the main text in a unit, it is important to preview it before you begin reading. If you have started to read the book without previously previewing it, stop and preview it. In just a short time you will learn a great deal about the book as a whole and it will be much easier to relate the parts that you are reading to the overall argument presented.

This exercise encourages you

- to develop a system for previewing or overviewing that can be applied to all of your reading material prior to reading it;

- to read for a purpose;

- to ask questions about the material as you preview it;

- to 'get to know' a book quickly by developing and utilising specific skills.

Materials

A book that is a main or set text in a unit you are studying or one you must read for an essay or assignment. If such books are not required in your unit, choose a book that you have not read and that is well structured (that is, includes an introduction, conclusion, table of contents, chapter titles and headings within each chapter). Don't use a book of readings or a novel. If you cannot find a suitable book, preview this book or *A guide to learning independently* (Marshall and Rowland, 2006).

 15.1   Thorough preview of a book

Approximate time

45 – 60 minutes

Reading

Marshall & Rowland, 2006, Chapter 9, pp. 137–141 and 149–152.

Learning activities

Activity 1   Finding out what books are about

Choose a book to preview, preferably a unit text or one that may be useful for an assessment. Ensure that you have not read it before. Don't select an edited collection of readings or a novel. You may need to borrow a book from a friend or the local or university library.

'Get to know' the book quickly

Imagine that you have arranged to discuss this book with another student who is arriving in five minutes. However, you have been busy and haven't had time to even open the book. Find out what the book is about. Stop after five minutes.

In your learning log, take ten minutes to write a paragraph explaining what the book is about. Don't look at the book and don't copy sentences or paragraphs from the book. Just free write, don't worry about style or format. (Make sure you give complete citation details, including author(s), date, title and publication details.)

Analyse your method

In your learning log, describe how you went about finding out what the book is about. Answer the following questions.

- How did you 'get to know' the book?
- Which parts of the book did you use?
- Which parts of the book did you look at first, second and so on?
- Where in the book did you find the most information?
- What was missing from the book that could have helped?

If the book had an index, did you use it?

Few students use the index when previewing. Indexes are usually used when locating a specific key term or topic. However, an index, like a table of contents, can be helpful when previewing. Checking the number of references or pages related to specific terms or topics in the index can indicate the emphasis, importance or weight or lack thereof given to particular topics in the book.

Activity 2　Previewing a book

When to preview

When do you use previewing?

Previewing can be used:

- to accept or reject a book or article (for example, when browsing in a library or bookshop);
- to obtain an understanding of the content, orientation and organisation of the material before you read the text in depth;
- to help decide which parts of the material you do or don't need to read (that is, which parts are relevant to your needs);
- to find out where to start reading/using the material;
- to determine how fast or how slow (reading rate or speed) to read different sections of the material.

It is important to vary your reading rate according to your purpose and the complexity of material. (See Marshall and Rowland, 2006, pp.149–152.)

Levels of previewing

There are various levels of previewing that can be applied in different situations. For example:

- when browsing library shelves for books on a subject
  - quick five-minute preview;
- when reading a book in detail
  - preview whole book thoroughly, and then
  - preview each chapter before reading;
- when warming-up for a study session
  - quick five-minute preview;
- when intending to read an article or chapter in depth
  - preview the article or chapter in depth.

Activity 3   Previewing systematically

Preview the book

Take time to thoroughly preview the book you have chosen. (See
Table 9.1 in Marshall and Rowland, 2006, pp. 140–141.)

 15.1   As you preview answer the questions on the attached worksheet,
'Thorough preview of a boo'.

Think and write about the book

Discuss how the book relates to the whole unit and/or how the book
related to your purposes for reading it.

    In your learning log, summarise the argument or main point presented
in the book. Note any criticisms that you may have of the book.
Assess how the book fits into the unit and how useful it is to your
purposes. List any questions you have about this book.

Activity 4   Reflection on the process

    In your learning log, discuss any changes you need to make to
preview books more effectively.

Previewing a book

1. Finding out what books are about

Take ten minutes to write a paragraph explaining what the book is about.

Give complete citation details, including author(s), date, title and publication details.

Describe how you went about finding out what the book is about. Answer the following questions.

- How did you 'get to know' the book?
- Which parts of the book did you use?
- Which parts of the book did you look at first, second and so on?
- Where in the book did you find the most information?
- What was missing from the book that could have helped?

If the book has an index, did you use it?

2. Previewing systematically

Summarise the argument or main point presented in the book. Note any criticisms you may have of the book. Assess how the book fits into the unit and how useful it is to your purposes. List any questions you have about this book.

3. Reflection on the process

Discuss any changes you need to make to preview books more effectively.

Thorough preview of a book

15.1

Activity 4

Author(s) ....

Title ....

Subtitle ....

Questions that the title and subtitle suggest

....

....

....

....

....

Publication date .... Is this information significant? Why? ....

....

....

List important ideas that the author presents in the **preface, foreword or introduction**

....

....

....

....

....

....

....

Read the **table of contents** and change the chapter headings into questions. List five of these questions.

1. ....

2. ....

3. ....

4. ....

5. ....

If there are **appendices** in the book, list each one and explain how it might be useful.

....

....

....

Skim through the book and look at the graphs, pictures, maps, or charts; read the captions under them. List three that seem most interesting/useful, and state the reasons for your choices.

1. .... on page ....

Reason ....

....

....

2. .... on page ....

Reason ....

....

....

3. .... on page ....

Reason ....

....

....

Skim through several chapters to discover which study aids have been included. Indicate those that you find on the list below.

Chapter outline _____   Italics _____   Questions for study or review _____

Headings _____   Footnotes _____   Other study aids _____

Chapter summaries _____   References _____   _____

Glossary _____   Bibliography _____   _____

Use the **index** to survey what you know or don't know about the contents of the book. Read each column to see how many terms, names and places are familiar to you. From the entire index, select ten items that are familiar to you and ten items that you know little about. If you cannot find ten items that are unfamiliar, you probably have a basic knowledge of the subject.

Known	**Unknown**

1. _____	6. _____	1. _____	6. _____
2. _____	7. _____	2. _____	7. _____
3. _____	8. _____	3. _____	8. _____
4. _____	9. _____	4. _____	9. _____
5. _____	10. _____	5. _____	10. _____

List some authors and titles of books from the **bibliography** or **references** that you would like to read or that might challenge you to expand your knowledge of the subject.

....

....

16. Previewing edited books

Introduction

This exercise is useful if you are required to read a book that consists of a collection of writings by different authors. These books usually contain an introduction written by the editor and a series of chapters written by different authors in different styles. Although, some commercially available edited books can have a reasonably consistent style. Books that consist of a collection of readings from various sources will have a wide range of content, writing styles and formats. Such books are a common source of reading in many units of study, and will have been especially compiled to suit the purposes and content of a unit. This usually occurs when a commercial text covering the content is not available. This exercise should be applied at the beginning of a unit that has an edited book as the unit text. At this stage, it will be important to find out what the unit and the set texts are about. It will also be important to preview the unit as a whole, such as any study guides, the lectures, assignments, other set texts and any other materials.

This exercise encourages you

- to develop a system for previewing or overviewing edited books, which should be applied before you read them;

- to 'get to know' a book quickly by developing and using specific reading skills;

- to read for a purpose;

- to ask questions about the reading material as you preview it;

- to use a book of readings for various purposes.

Materials

An edited book of readings

Approximate time

45 – 60 minutes

Reading

Marshall & Rowland, 2006, Chapter 9, pp. 137–141.

Learning activities

Activity 1 Previewing the edited book

Reading is an active thinking process, and one way to ensure this is to ask questions about the material during your preview. For example, authors and/or editors carefully chose titles and subtitles to encapsulate key themes and ideas. Aim to think actively about the possible meanings and implications of these before and during reading. Otherwise, it can be easy to get lost in the details of difficult material and 'not be able to see the wood for the trees'.

Take time to systematically preview the edited book by answering the following questions.

The title of the edited book: What meaning(s) does the title convey? Does the title lead you to ask any questions?

The editor: Do you know anything about the editor(s)? Who is s/he? What else has s/he written?

The date: When was the book compiled? Is this significant? Why?

Table of contents: Is there a table of contents? Does this indicate the structure or organisation of the material, for instance, any sections or parts? Does the table of contents indicate the key themes or ideas covered? Do you recognise any of the authors of the chapters/readings? If so, what do you know about them? Is there a range of publication dates of the chapters/readings?

Preface, foreword or introduction: Is there an introductory section that indicates the purpose of the collection and the content that it covers? What important points are presented?

Section or parts: Is there an introduction and conclusion to each section or part? Do these lead you to ask any questions? If the material is not grouped, can you see any logic to the way it is presented?

Conclusion: Is there a concluding section to the reader?

Index: Does the reader contain an index? If so, are there any entries that are familiar to you. Is there greater emphasis given to certain topics? What are these?

The readings: Skim through the book. What are your initial thoughts about:

- the readings that have been included? Have the readings been especially written for this collection? Are the readings articles from journals, chapters from other books, lectures or other?
- the difficulty of the material. For instance, will it be difficult or easy to read? Why?

Read Marshall and Rowland, 2006, Chapter 9, pp. 137–141.

Activity 2   An interesting reading

Look through the edited book and find a reading that interests you the most. Why does this reading interest you? Make notes in your learning log.

Activity 3   A familiar reading

Look through the edited book and find a reading that is somewhat familiar. Why do you know something about the content of this reading? Make notes in your learning log.

Activity 4   A difficult reading

Look through the edited book and find a reading that will be difficult to read. Is the content unfamiliar or is the writing style complex? Is there some other reason why you think it will be difficult? Make notes in your learning log

Activity 5   Reflection on the process

In your learning log, discuss the process of previewing edited books and the usefulness of previewing in your study.

Previewing an edited book of readings

1. An interesting reading

Provide the complete citation details (author, year, title, page numbers, publisher and place of publication) of a reading that interests you.

Explain why this reading interests you.

2. A familiar reading

Provide the complete citation details (author, year, title, page numbers, publisher and place of publication) of a reading that is somewhat familiar.

Explain why you know about the content of this reading.

3. A difficult reading

Provide the complete citation details (author, year, title, page numbers, publisher and place of publication) of a reading that will be difficult.

Explain why you think this reading will be difficult.

4. Reflection

Discuss the process of previewing edited books and the usefulness of previewing in your study.

17. Note making from reading

Introduction

This exercise is designed to be used in conjunction with Exercise 18, 'Reading in depth'. It considers the system that can be used to 'mark up' texts and/or make notes from reading. Exercise 18 also provides examples of a text that has been 'marked up' and notes made from it.

The system for making notes from your readings outlined in this exercise is similar to the system used in Exercise 10, 'Learning from lectures'.

This exercise encourages you

- to develop an effective system of 'marking up' and making notes;

- to distinguish the thesis (or conclusion) from the supporting premises (or reasons) or the main point from the supporting details when making notes;

- to develop skills in making linear and non linear (patterned) notes.

Materials

From Exercise 18, 'Reading in depth'

18b.3 Linear notes: an example using numbers
18b.4 Linear notes: an example using columns and bolding
18b.5 Patterned notes: example 1
18b.6 Patterned notes: example 2

Approximate time

45 minutes

Reading

Marshall & Rowland, 2006, Chapter 9, pp. 152-155 & Chapter 10, pp. 165-168.

Learning activities

Activity 1 Objectives for 'marking up' and making notes

'Marking up' a reading and making notes from it can be completed more efficiently if you have clear objectives.

An objective for 'marking up' or making notes may include one or more of the following:

— to note a statement that you wish to quote in an assignment;

— to outline the argument in the reading for future discussion in an assignment, exam or tutorial;

— to indicate the structure of the text;

— to help you concentrate as you read;

— to help you remember what you read.

Your 'marking up' and note making will differ depending on your objectives. It is important to identify and articulate your objectives before you begin 'marking up' texts or making notes.

Activity 2 'Marking up' texts

Your system

Do you have a system that you use to 'mark up' a text? If so, your system may include some or all of the following:

— underlining, highlighting or vertical lines in the margin for main points;

— numbers in the margins for a series of points;

— marks or asterisks on the side of a page for points of interest;

— circles around transitional words, phrases and paragraphs;

— abbreviations to indicate content or structure;

— question marks for words, phrases or entire sections that you did not understand and will look up or ask about later;

— question marks to turn headings into questions;

— notes in the text (recording questions, answers, main points, reactions and so on).

Each device can help you understand and remember what you read.

How to 'mark up' texts

It is important to use a system that clearly separates the thesis and supporting points from your personal interests, reflections and ideas. Aim to underline judiciously and sparingly, highlighting only key terms and ideas. Highlighting or underlining slabs of text does not help you quickly retrieve key information.

 18b.1

Refer to Exercise 18 and note the system used to 'mark up' the introduction and conclusion, and the first section of the reading, 'The tragedy of the commons'.

Note that you should only 'mark up' texts that you own. Don't 'mark up' a text that does not belong to you. Reading a library book that someone else has marked for their own purposes can take longer to read as the marks can be distracting and are rarely of any help. Defacing books that you do not own is vandalism. If a book doesn't belong to you and you would like to keep your notes and the material together, photocopy the relevant sections and 'mark up' the photocopy.

Activity 3   Making notes from reading

Your system

Do you have a system that you use when making notes from a text?

Consider the methods that you use to make notes and answer the following questions.

- Have you recorded the author, year and title of the reading, its source and the page numbers?
- How have you separated the thesis from the supporting premises or reasons? Or how have you separated the main point from the supporting details?
- Have you used headings and subheadings to provide a framework for your information?
- Have you written in full sentences, phrases or point form?
- What abbreviations have you used?

- Have you used different coloured pens to distinguish information?
- Have you left extra space and wide margins in your notes?
- Have you written on only one side of the page (or card)?
- Have you used shorthand?
- Have you copied down extracts or quotations accurately?
- Have you handwritten your notes or typed them directly onto a computer?

Refer to Exercise 10 'Learning from lectures' for further clarification of note making methods.

Read Marshall and Rowland, 2006, pp. 152-155 and note what to make notes of as you read.

Linear and non linear techniques

- Do you use a linear or non linear (patterned) form of note making?
- Do you summarise what you read in a linear or non linear (patterned) form?

See Marshall and Rowland, 2006, pp. 165-168.

Exercise 18 encourages you to experiment with linear and patterned note making and to evaluate the effectiveness of both techniques. Begin Exercise 18 when you complete this one.

18b.4; 18b.5
18b.6
18b.7

Refer to Exercise 18 for examples of linear and non linear notes.

Activity 4   Organising your notes

It is important to organise your notes so that they are readily accessible to you. Your system of organising will depend largely on your objectives, that is, how you will use your notes.

Refer to Exercise 25, 'Researching information', for techniques on organising information.

Activity 5   Reflection on the process

In your learning log, discuss the process and method of 'marking up' and note making outlined in this exercise. Explain the usefulness of 'marking up' and note making in your study.

Note making from reading

Reflection

Discuss the process and method of 'marking up' and note making outlined in this exercise. Explain the usefulness of 'marking up' and note making in your study.

18. Reading in depth

Introduction

This exercise closely examines the way that authors write and structure their work. The activities in this exercise can be applied to a range of texts (chapter or short section of a book or an article) to gather information on and identify:

- the author's argument (the thesis and the supporting premises or reasons) or the main point (or theme) and supporting details (evidence, examples or illustrations) as an important preliminary to a critical evaluation of these;

- the author's style:

    - the use of reading aids (navigational guides), such as title, headings, subheadings and italics;

    - the paragraph structure, such as the use of topic sentences, main points and generalisations (as opposed to secondary points, elaboration and specific examples);

    - the sequencing of ideas and information, and the use of cohesive devices, such as transitional (linking or connective) words, phrases, sentences and paragraphs;

- the complexity of the material, which often depends on the sentence and paragraph structure.

This exercise emphasises the importance of:

    - previewing all study material before reading it;

    - reading with a purpose;

    - reading as an active thinking process, that is, asking and answering questions before and during reading;

    - adjusting your reading rate/speed depending on your reading purpose and the complexity of the material

    - understanding an argument fully prior to critically evaluating it.

This exercise provides an opportunity for you to apply the activities to study material (an article, chapter or section of a text) of your choosing and to see the activities applied to an example article (see the boxed text, 'The tragedy of the commons'). The provision of this example is primarily intended to aid your in depth reading of other academic texts.

It can take additional time to complete this exercise as it is packed with information.

Note that Exercise 17 'Note making from reading', is referred to several times in this exercise.

This exercise encourages you

- to dissect a piece of academic text (a chapter or section from a book or an article) using distinct reading objectives:

    - to preview or skim using the title, headings, introduction, conclusion, cohesive devices (transitional markers or connectives) and topic sentences;
    - to gain a detailed understanding using the structure of the material (revealed through previewing);
    - to identify the argument (the thesis and supporting premises or reasons) or the main point (theme) and supporting details (evidence, examples, illustrations);

- to read for a purpose;

- to preview all study material before reading it;

- to read the entire text in depth if your purpose is to fully understand the material;

- to apply the strategies for reading in depth when critically evaluating material.

Materials

A text (article or chapter) that is required reading for a unit you are studying, and which interests you. It does not matter if you have read this text previously.

Alternatively you can apply the activities in the exercise to the example article, 'The tragedy of the commons'[3], in the boxed text below.

You may choose to read the example article and apply the activities to it before you apply them to a unit text of your own choice.

---

[3] Garrett Hardin, 1968, 'The tragedy of the commons', *Science*, Vol. 164, pp. 1243–1248

Materials that can be applied to academic text

18a.1   Questions to ask when previewing material

18a.2   Patterned notes

18a.3   Summary of the text

From Chapter 6, 'Writing essays'

21.1   Essay structure: different pictorial representations

21.3   Essay structure: functional stages

27.2   Transitional words and phrases

'The tragedy of the commons'

'The tragedy of the commons'

In this article, particular attention is given to:

- the introduction
- the conclusion, 'Recognition of necessity'
- parts of the sections, 'What shall we maximize?' and 'Tragedy of freedom in a commons'
- the sections and parts used when previewing.

It doesn't matter if you have read this article previously.

18b.1   'The tragedy of the commons'

18b.2   The parts of the article used when previewing 'The tragedy of the commons'

18b.3   Functional stages of the introduction

18b.4   Linear notes: an example using numbers

18b.5   Linear notes: an example using columns

18b.6   Patterned notes: example 1

18b.7   Patterned notes: example 2

18b.8   Summary of the article

These materials have been fully prepared by several people. However, their 'reading' of the article may differ from your reading and you may find information that is not included here. These examples are not definitive answers, they are primarily intended to aid your learning and reading.

Approximate time

60 – 90 minutes

Reading

Marshall & Rowland, 2006, Chapter 9, pp. 133–159 & Chapter 10, pp. 165–168.

Clanchy & Ballard, 1991, pp. 19–38.

Learning Activities

Activity 1   Purposes for reading

Identify and articulate reading purposes

This exercise has very clearly defined purposes: to read an academic text for an in depth understanding and to use this approach to reading when critically evaluating material[4]. This exercise will show you how material is structured to aid your understanding of the content. A critical evaluation depends on understanding the argument (the thesis and the supporting premises or reasons). During this exercise you will be asked to make notes showing that you can identify the thesis and supporting premises presented in the text.

Articulating your purpose for reading before you begin reading any academic reading text can help you read more effectively.

Activity 2   Previewing

Your purposes for previewing

Reading is an **active thinking process** and one way to ensure that you read actively is to ask questions about the text during your preview.

There are various purposes for previewing material before reading it in depth. Previewing can be used:

–   to determine which sections or parts are most relevant to your needs;

–   to judge the complexity of the material;

–   to provide a navigational map or overview showing how the material is organised;

–   to develop an understanding of the author's writing style.

A preview should always note:

---

[4]   See Exercise 13, 'Understanding your reading habits and skills', Activity 3 for more information on purposes for reading.

- the title and subtitle;

- the abstract or summary (when provided);

- the main headings and subheadings;

- the introduction;

- the conclusion.

Preview the text

 18a.1 Preview the text by answering the questions in your learning log or on the attached worksheet, 'Questions to ask when previewing'.

The title of the material: What meanings does the title convey to you? Why do you think the author/publisher has chosen this particular wording? What does the title indicate about the material? What do you think the text is about?

'The tragedy of the commons'

- What is meant by 'commons'? (Perhaps consult a dictionary or encyclopaedia.)
- What meaning(s) does the word 'tragedy' convey?
- What does the abstract indicate about the content of the article?

Hardin begins with the 'commons' of medieval history, but extends his meaning to include government land, National Parks, the oceans and the atmosphere.

Hardin quotes Whitehead to describe tragedy as 'the remorseless working of things'.

The author: Do you know anything about this author(s)? Who is s/he? What else has s/he written?

The date: When was the text written? Is this significant? Why?

'The tragedy of the commons'

The article was written in 1968, which makes it quite an old academic paper. Is the material in the article still relevant today? Why or why not?

Headings within the text: Are there headings at different levels? What is the purpose of this? Do they reflect the structure or organisation of the material? Do they indicate the main points covered? Can you turn some of the headings into questions, and can you provide answer(s) to these questions? (Ask why, what, when, where or how about each heading.)

'The tragedy of the commons'

- Do the headings reflect the thesis of the article?
- Why has Hardin made some of his headings questions?
- Can you provide answers to these questions?

Introduction: Can you find a paragraph or sentence(s) that state the argument or thesi,s or the main point or theme of the text?

'The tragedy of the commons'

Look for leading phrases ('My thesis is that', 'I try to show here', 'I would like to focus your attention').

Look for words and phrases that are repeated.

Conclusion: Can you find a conclusion or a summary of the argument? Is there a statement (or restatement) of the thesis or the main point?

'The tragedy of the commons'

Look for leading phrases ('summary of this').

References: Is there evidence that the material has been well researched?

Body of the text: Skim through the text.

- What are your thoughts about the difficulty of the material? Will it be difficult or easy to read? Why?

- What is your impression of the writer's style (the use of language, sentence and paragraph structure and so on.)?

- Does the text contain any special features, for example, reading aids? Are any features missing?

'The tragedy of the commons'

This material was first presented as a lecture. This has affected the writing style, as it contains some features of spoken language, indicated below.

- Use of first person:
  'I would like to focus your attention.'
  'In our day ...'
  'I try to show here that ...'
  (In many disciplines, writing is impersonal and is in the third person.)

- Use of imperatives (commands or instructions to the audience:
  'Recall the game of tick, tack, toe ...'
  'Consider the problem ...'
  'Picture a pasture open to all ...'

- Use of interrogatives (asking questions and answering them):
  'How can I win the game of tick, tack, toe? It is well known that I cannot'
  'What shall we maximise? A fair defence ...'
  'What shall be the situation of mankind? Specifically, can Bentham's goal of "the greatest good for the greatest number" be realized?'
  'No – for two reasons'.

  (In many disciplines, writing is in the declarative mood, that is, normal statement form.)

- Use of explicit modality or opinions, such as 'I think' rather than 'it seems', 'probably', 'in all probability' and so on.

- Deliberate use of short sentences, such as 'Space is not escape', for rhetorical effect.

Note the use of non-gender inclusive language which may reflect when the article was written (1968), such as 'The rational man finds that his share ...'

This overview provides a basis for an in depth reading of the material.

18b.2

> **'The tragedy of the commons'**
>
> See the attached material, 'The parts of the article used when previewing 'The tragedy of the commons'.
>
> This prepared example clarifies the previewing process and shows which parts of the material to read during a preview.

Activity 3 The introduction

Examine the introduction

Take the first paragraphs in the introductory section and read one at a time. When you have completed this, answer the following questions.

- Does the introduction indicate how the material is structured? Which sentences do this?

- Does the introduction indicate what the text will argue, that is, the thesis and supporting premises or reasons?

- Is there a thesis statement in the introduction?

- What are the functional stages in the introduction?

18b.3

> **'The tragedy of the commons'**
>
> See the attached material, 'Functional stages of the introduction' to the 'Tragedy of the commons'. Note that this analysis shows: beginning to end development, paragraph structure, links between the second and the third sections.

21.3

(See also the material in Exercise 21, 'Essay structure: functional stages', for another analysis of functional stages.)

Identify any parts in the introduction that aim to interest or intrigue the reader or set the scene. This may be information that is not central to the thesis or main point of the text.

> **'The tragedy of the commons'**
>
> Take each paragraph in the introductory section and determine the role the introductory paragraphs play in the article, as outlined below.
>
> - Paragraph 1 raises interest.
> - Paragraph 2 provides a definition of a technical solution.
> - Paragraphs 3 and 4 show that not all problems have technical solutions, using a simple illustration to make the point.
> - Paragraph 5 states the thesis, that 'the population problem cannot be solved in a technical way.'
>
> The author argues like a mathematician with precise logic. It may seem obvious that not all problems have a technical solution. This thesis may have greater acceptance today than in 1968. However, many people still believe that all problems can be reduced to elements for which technical solutions can be found.
>
> Note the way information has been 'marked up' and the functional stages labelled in the introduction.

'Mark up' the introduction

When you have finished reading the introduction, 'mark up' important information, such as the argument, (thesis and supporting premises or reasons), the main point or the context of the text.

See Exercise 17, Note making from lectures', for strategies on 'marking up' texts.

> 18b.1 **'The tragedy of the commons'**
>
> Note how the introduction and first section have been 'marked up' and how the functional features have been labelled.

Activity 4   The conclusion

Examine the conclusion

Take the concluding section and examine how the argument (thesis and supporting premises or reasons) or the main point and supporting details in the text are tied together. Answer the following questions.

- Does the conclusion tie the material together?

- Does the conclusion repeat the argument (the thesis and the supporting premises or reasons)?

- Is there any other information included in the conclusion?

'The tragedy of the commons'

Consider the role of each paragraph in the conclusion 'Recognition of necessity'.

- How does Hardin group the different types of 'commons'?
- Does the conclusion refer to the idea of technical fix, which had such an important place in the introduction? Why not?
- Where does Hardin state the main conclusion? What is it?

'Mark up' the conclusion

When you have finished reading the conclusion, 'mark up' important information to show what parts have been incorporated.

The tragedy of the commons'

18b.1 Note how the conclusion has been 'marked to show its connection with the body of the article .

Activity 5   Paragraph structure

Read a section

When reading a text it is important to continually evaluate what you are reading to determine which ideas and information relate to your reading purpose and to the overall argument (thesis and supporting premises or reasons) or the main point and supporting details in the text. It is important to distinguish between the thesis or main point and the supporting premises or details.

Read a section of the text, particularly one that relates to the thesis or main point. Answer the following questions.

- What is the main point or idea in this section?

- How does it relate to the overall argument or thesis of the article or chapter?

Examine each paragraph

Now read each paragraph separately. Answer the following questions

- What is the main point or idea in this paragraph?

- What is the topic sentence of the paragraph? When you decide on the topic sentence, underline it.

- Which sentence(s) relate to the main point, explicitly or implicitly?

- How does this topic sentence or main idea in the paragraph relate to the whole section or to the overall argument or thesis of the article or chapter?

Answer the following questions.

- What evidence, examples or illustrations are presented to support this main point or idea?

- Are there any references to other authors or written work? Are they necessary to understand the context? Should you note and look up any references later?

- Has the author made any assumptions or generalisations about the topic?

Identify the overall paragraph structure

When you have completed this, answer the following questions.

- Is there an overall pattern to the way the author has presented main points or ideas?
- Is there a pattern to the use of topic sentences?
- Is the main point of each paragraph explicit or implied?
- Is there a particular way the author links paragraphs?

Different authors have different writing styles, and the main points or ideas can be organised and structured in different ways, and can sometimes be implied.

'The tragedy of the commons'

Apply this activity to the second section, 'What shall we maximise?'

How would you find out if the following statement were true: 'there is no prosperous population in the world today that has, and has had for some time, a growth rate of zero'?

Note the structure of the paragraphs.

Activity 6   Transitions and links

 21.1

Examine the graphic in Exercise 21, 'Essay structure: different pictorial representations'. Note that it is important to make links between the introduction and each section of the body, and between each section of the body and the conclusion. Note that it is also important to introduce and conclude each section or paragraph and then lead in to the next.

 27.2

Examine the table in Exercise 27, 'Transitional words and phrases' See also Marshall and Rowland, 2006, p. 217. (Note that this table is also used in the chapter on 'Writing essays' in the exercises on 'Editing the final draft'.)

Identify transitions and links

Skim through the introduction and the first section of the text. Circle any connective or transitional words, phrases or sentences.

Is there a pattern in the way that the author has used transitional markers or connectives?

18b.1

> **'The tragedy of the commons'**
>
> Note the use of transitional markers or links in the introduction. (These have been circled.)

Read the remaining text, and as you read:

- mark up the argument (or thesis) or the main point;
- circle transitional words or connectives;
- note the links or connections between sections;
- show the relationship between sections and the thesis or main point.

> **'The tragedy of the commons'**
>
> Consider the final paragraph of the second section 'What shall we maximise?' and the introductory paragraph of the third section, 'Tragedy of Freedom in a Commons'.
>
> ▪ How does one section link to the next?
> ▪ How do the ideas in the third section relate to the overall thesis of the article?

Activity 7 Making notes

See Exercise 17, 'Note making from lectures', for strategies on making notes from a reading.

Make linear notes

Develop linear notes of the text that clearly separate the thesis from the supporting premises or the main point from the supporting details.

Divide your page into two columns and place the thesis or main point in the left hand columns, and the supporting premises or details in the right hand columns. Use your own words and don't copy the text.

18b.4
18b.5

'The tragedy of the commons'

See the attached examples of linear note making related to this article, 'Linear notes: an example using numbers' and 'Linear notes: an example using columns'

Make patterned notes

18a.2 Develop patterned notes for the material using the worksheet provided. Place the thesis or main point in the ellipse in the middle of the page and place the supporting premises or details around the ellipse. Draw lines to show the connections between the thesis or main point and the supporting premises or details. You may need to turn the page sideways for this exercise.

Refer to Exercise 17, 'Note making from reading', for strategies on summarising material into patterned notes.

18b.6
18b.7

'The tragedy of the commons'

See the attached examples of patterned notes related to this article, 'Patterned notes: example 1' and 'Patterned notes: example 2'.

Activity 8   Reviewing and summarising the text

18a.3 Review your notes on the text so that you can remember and use what you have read. In your learning log or on the attached worksheet, answer the following questions.

- What is the thesis or main point presented in the text?
- What premises or details does the author present to support the thesis or the main point?
- What is the underlying theoretical perspective (world view or paradigm)?

Evaluate your summary

Read your summary and check that it:

- contains the argument (thesis and supporting premises) or the main point and supporting details;
- doesn't include any unnecessary examples, illustrations or direct quotations;
- doesn't include unnecessary details, such as names.

18b.8

> **'The tragedy of the commons'**
>
> See the attached summary of the article, 'Summary of the article'.

Activity 9 Share your notes and summary

It can be useful to share and compare your linear and patterned notes with those compiled by another student(s) or by your tutor. Ask your tutor for examples of linear and patterned notes.

Activity 10 Reflection on this approach to reading

Note that you won't need to apply each activity in this exercise to all of your readings to gain a detailed understanding.

In your learning log, discuss the approach to reading in depth outlined in this exercise. Answer the following questions.

- When do you think this method will be of most use?
- Will you continue to use this method? Why or why not?
- Which parts of this exercise will you utilise when reading in depth?
- Do you think there are advantages to adopting this approach to reading, even if it takes longer to read?
- Have you learned any new writing techniques from analysing the way academic authors write?
- What is the overall benefit for you in completing this exercise?

In your learning log, write a paragraph or two outlining the changes you need to make or strategies you need to adopt in order to make your reading more effective.

162

Activity 11 Apply the techniques in this exercise to another reading

Apply any relevant strategies or techniques to another reading, keeping in mind your purpose for reading. Note that you do not need to apply every activity in this exercise to each reading to gain an in depth understanding. Note also that it can take time to develop new skills and break old habits in becoming a more effective reader.

Reading in depth

1. Reflection on this approach to reading

Discuss the approach to reading in depth outlined in this exercise. Answer the following questions.

When do you think this method will be of most use?

Will you continue to use this method? Why or why not?

Which parts of this exercise will you utilise when reading in depth?

Do you think there are advantages to adopting this approach to reading, even if it takes longer to read?

Have you learned any new writing techniques from analysing the way academic authors write?

What is the overall benefit for you in completing this exercise?

2. Changes to be a more effective reader

Write a paragraph or two outlining the changes you need to make or strategies you need to adopt in order to make your reading more effective.

Questions to ask when previewing material

18a.1

Activity 2

Provide the complete citation details: author, year, title, publisher and place of publication.

Title

What meaning(s) does the title convey to you?

Author

Who is the author?

Date

When was the material written? Is this significant?

Headings

How do the headings reflect the structure or organization of the material?

What main points or topics will be covered?

Introduction

What is the thesis (conclusion) or the main point (or theme) of the material?

Conclusion

Does the material contain concluding sentences or paragraphs? If so, how do they summarise or conclude the material?

References

Is there evidence that the material has been well researched?

Body of the material

Comment on

- the difficulty of the material (Will it be difficult or easy to read? Why?)

- the writer's style (the use of language, sentence and paragraph structure, etc.)

Patterned notes

Activity 8

Write the thesis or main point of the reading in the ellipse in the middle of the page and then show the supporting premises or reasons for this thesis. You may need to turn the page sideways.

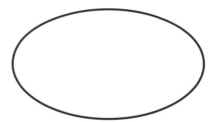

Summary of the text

Thesis or main point

Premises that support the thesis or details that support the main point

----

Underlying theoretical perspective (world view or paradigm)

18b.1

**Activities
2-10**

The Tragedy of the Commons

✳ The population problem has no technical solution; it requires a fundamental extension in morality.

Garrett Hardin

At the end of a thoughtful article on the future of nuclear war, Wiesner and York (1) concluded that: "Both sides in the arms race are . . . confronted by the dilemma of steadily increasing military power and steadily decreasing national security. *It is our considered professional judgment that this dilemma has no technical solution. If the great powers continue to look for solutions in the area of science and technology only, the result will be to worsen the situation.*"

I would like to focus your attention not on the subject of the article (national security in a nuclear world) but on the kind of conclusion they reached, namely that there is no technical solution to the problem. An implicit and almost universal assumption of discussions published in professional and semipopular scientific journals is that the problem under discussion has a technical solution. A technical solution may be defined as one that requires a change only in the techniques of the natural sciences, demanding little or nothing in the way of change in human values or ideas of morality.

In our day (though not in earlier times) technical solutions are always welcome. Because of previous failures in prophecy, it takes courage to assert that a desired technical solution is not possible. Wiesner and York exhibited this courage; publishing in a science journal, they insisted that the solution to the problem was not to be found in the natural sciences. They cautiously qualified their statement with the phrase, "It is our considered profes-

sional judgment. . . ." Whether they were right or not is not the concern of the present article. Rather, the concern here is with the important concept of a class of human problems which can be called "no technical solution problems," and, more specifically, with the identification and discussion of one of these.

It is easy to show that the class is not a null class. Recall the game of tick-tack-toe. Consider the problem, "How can I win the game of tick-tack-toe?" It is well known that I cannot, if I assume (in keeping with the conventions of game theory) that my opponent understands the game perfectly. Put another way, there is no "technical solution" to the problem. I can win only by giving a radical meaning to the word "win." I can hit my opponent over the head; or I can drug him; or I can falsify the records. Every way in which I "win" involves, in some sense, an abandonment of the game, as we intuitively understand it. (I can also, of course, openly abandon the game—refuse to play it. This is what most adults do.)

The class of "No technical solution problems" has members. My thesis is that the "population problem," as conventionally conceived, is a member of this class. How it is conventionally conceived needs some comment. It is fair to say that most people who anguish over the population problem are trying to find a way to avoid the evils of overpopulation without relinquishing any of the privileges they now enjoy. They think that farming the seas or developing new strains of wheat will solve the problem—technologically. I try to show here that the solution they seek cannot be found. The population problem cannot be solved in a technical way, any more than can the problem of winning the game of tick-tack-toe.

The author is professor of biology, University of California, Santa Barbara. This article is based on a presidential address presented before the meeting of the Pacific Division of the American Association for the Advancement of Science at Utah State University, Logan, 25 June 1968.

What Shall We Maximize?

Population, as Malthus said, naturally tends to grow "geometrically," or, as we would now say, exponentially. In a finite world this means that the per capita share of the world's goods must steadily decrease. Is ours a finite world?

A fair defense can be put forward for the view that the world is infinite; or that we do not know that it is not. But, in terms of the practical problems that we must face in the next few generations with the foreseeable technology, it is clear that we will greatly increase human misery if we do not, during the immediate future, assume that the world available to the terrestrial human population is finite. "Space" is no escape (2).

A finite world can support only a finite population; therefore, population growth must eventually equal zero. (The case of perpetual wide fluctuations above and below zero is a trivial variant that need not be discussed.) When this condition is met, what will be the situation of mankind? Specifically, can Bentham's goal of "the greatest good for the greatest number" be realized?

No—for two reasons, each sufficient by itself. The first is a theoretical one. 1. It is not mathematically possible to maximize for two (or more) variables at the same time. This was clearly stated by von Neumann and Morgenstern (3), but the principle is implicit in the theory of partial differential equations, dating back at least to D'Alembert (1717–1783).

The second reason springs directly 2. from biological facts. To live, any organism must have a source of energy (for example, food). This energy is utilized for two purposes: mere maintenance and work. For man, maintenance of life requires about 1600 kilocalories a day ("maintenance calories"). Anything that he does over and above merely staying alive will be defined as work, and is supported by "work calories" which he takes in. Work calories are used not only for what we call work in common speech; they are also required for all forms of enjoyment, from swimming and automobile racing to playing music and writing poetry. If our goal is to maximize population it is obvious what we must do: We must make the work calories per person approach as close to zero as possible. No gourmet meals, no vacations, no sports, no music, no literature, no art. . . . I think that everyone will grant, without argument or proof, that maximizing population does not maximize goods. Bentham's goal is impossible.

In reaching this conclusion I have made the usual assumption that it is the acquisition of energy that is the problem. The appearance of atomic energy has led some to question this assumption. However, given an infinite source of energy, population growth still produces an inescapable problem. The problem of the acquisition of energy is replaced by the problem of its dissipation, as J. H. Fremlin has so wittily shown (4). The arithmetic signs in the analysis are, as it were, reversed; but Bentham's goal is still unobtainable.

The optimum population is, then, less than the maximum. The difficulty of defining the optimum is enormous; so far as I know, no one has seriously tackled this problem. Reaching an acceptable and stable solution will surely require more than one generation of hard analytical work—and much persuasion.

We want the maximum good per person; but what is good? To one person it is wilderness, to another it is ski lodges for thousands. To one it is estuaries to nourish ducks for hunters to shoot; to another it is factory land. Comparing one good with another is, we usually say, impossible because goods are incommensurable. Incommensurables cannot be compared.

Theoretically this may be true; but in real life incommensurables *are* commensurable. Only a criterion of judgment and a system of weighting are needed. In nature the criterion is survival. Is it better for a species to be small and hideable, or large and powerful? Natural selection commensurates the incommensurables. The compromise achieved depends on a natural weighting of the values of the variables.

Man must imitate this process. There is no doubt that in fact he already does, but unconsciously. It is when the hidden decisions are made explicit that the arguments begin. The problem for the years ahead is to work out an acceptable theory of weighting. Synergistic effects, nonlinear variation, and difficulties in discounting the future make the intellectual problem difficult, but not (in principle) insoluble.

Has any cultural group solved this practical problem at the present time, even on an intuitive level? One simple fact proves that none has: there is no prosperous population in the world today that has, and has had for some

time, a growth rate of zero. Any people that has intuitively identified its optimum point will soon reach it, after which its growth rate becomes and remains zero.

Of course, a positive growth rate might be taken as evidence that a population is below its optimum. However, by any reasonable standards, the most rapidly growing populations on earth today are (in general) the most miserable. This association (which need not be invariable) casts doubt on the optimistic assumption that the positive growth rate of a population is evidence that it has yet to reach its optimum.

We can make little progress in working toward optimum population size until we explicitly exorcize the spirit of Adam Smith in the field of practical demography. In economic affairs, *The Wealth of Nations* (1776) popularized the "invisible hand," the idea that an individual who "intends only his own gain," is, as it were, "led by an invisible hand to promote . . . the public interest" (5). Adam Smith did not assert that this was invariably true, and perhaps neither did any of his followers. But he contributed to a dominant tendency of thought that has ever since interfered with positive action based on rational analysis, namely, the tendency to assume that decisions reached individually will, in fact, be the best decisions for an entire society. If this assumption is correct it justifies the continuance of our present policy of laissez-faire in reproduction. If it is correct we can assume that men will control their individual fecundity so as to produce the optimum population. If the assumption is not correct, we need to reexamine our individual freedoms to see which ones are defensible.

Tragedy of Freedom in a Commons

The rebuttal to the invisible hand in population control is to be found in a scenario first sketched in a little-known pamphlet (6) in 1833 by a mathematical amateur named William Forster Lloyd (1794–1852). We may well call it "the tragedy of the commons," using the word "tragedy" as the philosopher Whitehead used it (7): "The essence of dramatic tragedy is not unhappiness. It resides in the solemnity of the remorseless working of things." He then goes on to say, "This inevitableness of destiny can only be illustrated in terms of human life by incidents which in fact in-

volve unhappiness. For it is only by them that the futility of escape can be made evident in the drama."

The tragedy of the commons develops in this way. Picture a pasture open to all. It is to be expected that each herdsman will try to keep as many cattle as possible on the commons. Such an arrangement may work reasonably satisfactorily for centuries because tribal wars, poaching, and disease keep the numbers of both man and beast well below the carrying capacity of the land. Finally, however, comes the day of reckoning, that is, the day when the long-desired goal of social stability becomes a reality. At this point, the inherent logic of the commons remorselessly generates tragedy.

As a rational being, each herdsman seeks to maximize his gain. Explicitly or implicitly, more or less consciously, he asks, "What is the utility *to me* of adding one more animal to my herd?" This utility has one negative and one positive component.

1) The positive component is a function of the increment of one animal. Since the herdsman receives all the proceeds from the sale of the additional animal, the positive utility is nearly +1.

2) The negative component is a function of the additional overgrazing created by one more animal. Since, however, the effects of overgrazing are shared by all the herdsmen, the negative utility for any particular decision-making herdsman is only a fraction of −1.

Adding together the component partial utilities, the rational herdsman concludes that the only sensible course for him to pursue is to add another animal to his herd. And another; and another. . . . But this is the conclusion reached by each and every rational herdsman sharing a commons. Therein is the tragedy. Each man is locked into a system that compels him to increase his herd without limit—in a world that is limited. Ruin is the destination toward which all men rush, each pursuing his own best interest in a society that believes in the freedom of the commons. Freedom in a commons brings ruin to all.

Some would say that this is a platitude. Would that it were! In a sense, it was learned thousands of years ago, but natural selection favors the forces of psychological denial (8). The individual benefits as an individual from his ability to deny the truth even though society as a whole, of which he is a part, suffers.

1244

Education can counteract the natural tendency to do the wrong thing, but the inexorable succession of generations requires that the basis for this knowledge be constantly refreshed.

A simple incident that occurred a few years ago in Leominster. Massachusetts, shows how perishable the knowledge is. During the Christmas shopping season the parking meters downtown were covered with plastic bags that bore tags reading: "Do not open until after Christmas. Free parking courtesy of the mayor and city council." In other words, facing the prospect of an increased demand for already scarce space, the city fathers reinstituted the system of the commons. (Cynically, we suspect that they gained more votes than they lost by this retrogressive act.)

In an approximate way, the logic of the commons has been understood for a long time, perhaps since the discovery of agriculture or the invention of private property in real estate. But it is understood mostly only in special cases which are not sufficiently generalized. Even at this late date, cattlemen leasing national land on the western ranges demonstrate no more than an ambivalent understanding, in constantly pressuring federal authorities to increase the head count to the point where overgrazing produces erosion and weed-dominance. Likewise, the oceans of the world continue to suffer from the survival of the philosophy of the commons. Maritime nations still respond automatically to the shibboleth of the "freedom of the seas." Professing to believe in the "inexhaustible resources of the oceans," they bring species after species of fish and whales closer to extinction (9).

The National Parks present another instance of the working out of the tragedy of the commons. At present, they are open to all, without limit. The parks themselves are limited in extent—there is only one Yosemite Valley—whereas population seems to grow without limit. The values that visitors seek in the parks are steadily eroded. Plainly, we must soon cease to treat the parks as commons or they will be of no value to anyone.

What shall we do? We have several options. We might sell them off as private property. We might keep them as public property, but allocate the right to enter them. The allocation might be on the basis of wealth, by the use of an auction system. It might be on the basis of merit, as defined by some agreed-upon standards. It might be by lottery. Or it might be on a first-come, first-served basis, administered to long queues. These, I think, are all the reasonable possibilities. They are all objectionable. But we must choose—or acquiesce in the destruction of the commons that we call our National Parks.

Pollution

In a reverse way, the tragedy of the commons reappears in problems of pollution. Here it is not a question of taking something out of the commons, but of putting something in—sewage, or chemical, radioactive, and heat wastes into water; noxious and dangerous fumes into the air; and distracting and unpleasant advertising signs into the line of sight. The calculations of utility are much the same as before. The rational man finds that his share of the cost of the wastes he discharges into the commons is less than the cost of purifying his wastes before releasing them. Since this is true for everyone, we are locked into a system of "fouling our own nest," so long as we behave only as independent, rational, free-enterprisers.

The tragedy of the commons as a food basket is averted by private property, or something formally like it. But the air and waters surrounding us cannot readily be fenced, and so the tragedy of the commons as a cesspool must be prevented by different means, by coercive laws or taxing devices that make it cheaper for the polluter to treat his pollutants than to discharge them untreated. We have not progressed as far with the solution of this problem as we have with the first. Indeed, our particular concept of private property, which deters us from exhausting the positive resources of the earth, favors pollution. The owner of a factory on the bank of a stream—whose property extends to the middle of the stream—often has difficulty seeing why it is not his natural right to muddy the waters flowing past his door. The law, always behind the times, requires elaborate stitching and fitting to adapt it to this newly perceived aspect of the commons.

The pollution problem is a consequence of population. It did not much matter how a lonely American frontiersman disposed of his waste. "Flowing water purifies itself every 10 miles," my grandfather used to say, and the myth was near enough to the truth when he was a boy, for there were not too many people. But as population became denser, the natural chemical and biological recycling processes became overloaded, calling for a redefinition of property rights.

How To Legislate Temperance?

Analysis of the pollution problem as a function of population density uncovers a not generally recognized principle of morality, namely: *the morality of an act is a function of the state of the system at the time it is performed* (10). Using the commons as a cesspool does not harm the general public under frontier conditions. because there is no public; the same behavior in a metropolis is unbearable. A hundred and fifty years ago a plainsman could kill an American bison, cut out only the tongue for his dinner, and discard the rest of the animal. He was not in any important sense being wasteful. Today, with only a few thousand bison left, we would be appalled at such behavior.

In passing, it is worth noting that the morality of an act cannot be determined from a photograph. One does not know whether a man killing an elephant or setting fire to the grassland is harming others until one knows the total system in which his act appears. "One picture is worth a thousand words," said an ancient Chinese; but it may take 10,000 words to validate it. It is as tempting to ecologists as it is to reformers in general to try to persuade others by way of the photographic shortcut. But the essence of an argument cannot be photographed: it must be presented rationally —in words.

That morality is system-sensitive escaped the attention of most codifiers of ethics in the past. "Thou shalt not . . ." is the form of traditional ethical directives which make no allowance for particular circumstances. The laws of our society follow the pattern of ancient ethics, and therefore are poorly suited to governing a complex, crowded, changeable world. Our epicyclic solution is to augment statutory law with administrative law. Since it is practically impossible to spell out all the conditions under which it is safe to burn trash in the back yard or to run an automobile without smog-control, by law we delegate the details to bureaus. The result is administrative law, which is rightly feared for an ancient reason—*Quis custodiet ipsos custodes?*—"Who shall watch the watchers themselves?" John Adams said that we must have "a government of laws and not men." Bureau administrators, trying to evaluate the morality of acts in the total system, are singularly liable to corruption, producing a government by men, not laws.

Prohibition is easy to legislate (though not necessarily to enforce); but how do we legislate temperance? Experience indicates that it can be accomplished best through the mediation of administrative law. We limit possibilities unnecessarily if we suppose that the sentiment of *Quis custodiet* denies us the use of administrative law. We should rather retain the phrase as a perpetual reminder of fearful dangers we cannot avoid. The great challenge facing us now is to invent the corrective feedbacks that are needed to keep custodians honest. We must find ways to legitimate the needed authority of both the custodians and the corrective feedbacks.

Freedom To Breed Is Intolerable

The tragedy of the commons is involved in population problems in another way. In a world governed solely by the principle of "dog eat dog"—if indeed there ever was such a world—how many children a family had would not be a matter of public concern. Parents who bred too exuberantly would leave fewer descendants, not more, because they would be unable to care adequately for their children. David Lack and others have found that such a negative feedback demonstrably controls the fecundity of birds (*11*). But men are not birds, and have not acted like them for millenniums, at least.

If each human family were dependent only on its own resources; *if* the children of improvident parents starved to death; *if*, thus, overbreeding brought its own "punishment" to the germ line— *then* there would be no public interest in controlling the breeding of families. But our society is deeply committed to the welfare state (*12*), and hence is confronted with another aspect of the tragedy of the commons.

In a welfare state, how shall we deal with the family, the religion, the race, or the class (or indeed any distinguishable and cohesive group) that adopts overbreeding as a policy to secure its own aggrandizement (*13*)? To couple the concept of freedom to breed with the belief that everyone born has an

equal right to the commons is to lock the world into a tragic course of action.

Unfortunately this is just the course of action that is being pursued by the United Nations. In late 1967, some 30 nations agreed to the following (*14*):

The Universal Declaration of Human Rights describes the family as the natural and fundamental unit of society. It follows that any choice and decision with regard to the size of the family must irrevocably rest with the family itself, and cannot be made by anyone else.

It is painful to have to deny categorically the validity of this right; denying it, one feels as uncomfortable as a resident of Salem, Massachusetts, who denied the reality of witches in the 17th century. At the present time, in liberal quarters, something like a taboo acts to inhibit criticism of the United Nations. There is a feeling that the United Nations is "our last and best hope," that we shouldn't find fault with it; we shouldn't play into the hands of the archconservatives. However, let us not forget what Robert Louis Stevenson said: "The truth that is suppressed by friends is the readiest weapon of the enemy." If we love the truth we must openly deny the validity of the Universal Declaration of Human Rights, even though it is promoted by the United Nations. We should also join with Kingsley Davis (*15*) in attempting to get Planned Parenthood-World Population to see the error of its ways in embracing the same tragic ideal.

Conscience Is Self-Eliminating

It is a mistake to think that we can control the breeding of mankind in the long run by an appeal to conscience. Charles Galton Darwin made this point when he spoke on the centennial of the publication of his grandfather's great book. The argument is straightforward and Darwinian.

People vary. Confronted with appeals to limit breeding, some people will undoubtedly respond to the plea more than others. Those who have more children will produce a larger fraction of the next generation than those with more susceptible consciences. The difference will be accentuated, generation by generation.

In C. G. Darwin's words: "It may well be that it would take hundreds of generations for the progenitive instinct to develop in this way, but if it should do so, nature would have taken her revenge, and the variety *Homo contra-*

cipiens would become extinct and would be replaced by the variety *Homo progenitivus*" (*16*).

The argument assumes that conscience or the desire for children (no matter which) is hereditary—but hereditary only in the most general formal sense. The result will be the same whether the attitude is transmitted through germ cells, or exosomatically, to use A. J. Lotka's term. (If one denies the latter possibility as well as the former, then what's the point of education?) The argument has here been stated in the context of the population problem, but it applies equally well to any instance in which society appeals to an individual exploiting a commons to restrain himself for the general good—by means of his conscience. To make such an appeal is to set up a selective system that works toward the elimination of conscience from the race.

Pathogenic Effects of Conscience

The long-term disadvantage of an appeal to conscience should be enough to condemn it; but has serious short-term disadvantages as well. If we ask a man who is exploiting a commons to desist "in the name of conscience," what are we saying to him? What does he hear?—not only at the moment but also in the wee small hours of the night when, half asleep, he remembers not merely the words we used but also the nonverbal communication cues we gave him unawares? Sooner or later, consciously or subconsciously, he senses that he has received two communications, and that they are contradictory: (i) (intended communication) "If you don't do as we ask, we will openly condemn you for not acting like a responsible citizen"; (ii) (the unintended communication) "If you *do* behave as we ask, we will secretly condemn you for a simpleton who can be shamed into standing aside while the rest of us exploit the commons."

Everyman then is caught in what Bateson has called a "double bind." Bateson and his co-workers have made a plausible case for viewing the double bind as an important causative factor in the genesis of schizophrenia (*17*). The double bind may not always be so damaging, but it always endangers the mental health of anyone to whom it is applied. "A bad conscience," said Nietzsche, "is a kind of illness."

To conjure up a conscience in others

is tempting to anyone who wishes to extend his control beyond the legal limits. Leaders at the highest level succumb to this temptation. Has any President during the past generation failed to call on labor unions to moderate voluntarily their demands for higher wages. or to steel companies to honor voluntary guidelines on prices? I can recall none. The rhetoric used on such occasions is designed to produce feelings of guilt in noncooperators.

For centuries it was assumed without proof that guilt was a valuable, perhaps even an indispensable. ingredient of the civilized life. Now, in this post-Freudian world, we doubt it.

Paul Goodman speaks from the modern point of view when he says: "No good has ever come from feeling guilty, neither intelligence, policy, nor compassion. The guilty do not pay attention to the object but only to themselves. and not even to their own interests, which might make sense, but to their anxieties" (*18*).

One does not have to be a professional psychiatrist to see the consequences of anxiety. We in the Western world are just emerging from a dreadful two-centuries-long Dark Ages of Eros that was sustained partly by prohibition laws, but perhaps more effectively by the anxiety-generating mechanisms of education. Alex Comfort has told the story well in *The Anxiety Makers* (*19*); it is not a pretty one.

Since proof is difficult, we may even concede that the results of anxiety may sometimes, from certain points of view, be desirable. The larger question we should ask is whether, as a matter of policy, we should ever encourage the use of a technique the tendency (if not the intention) of which is psychologically pathogenic. We hear much talk these days of responsible parenthood; the coupled words are incorporated into the titles of some organizations devoted to birth control. Some people have proposed massive propaganda campaigns to instill responsibility into the nation's (or the world's) breeders. But what is the meaning of the word responsibility in this context? Is it not merely a synonym for the word conscience? When we use the word responsibility in the absence of substantial sanctions are we not trying to browbeat a free man in a commons into acting against his own interest? Responsibility is a verbal counterfeit for a substantial *quid pro quo*. It is an attempt to get something for nothing.

If the word responsibility is to be used at all, I suggest that it be in the sense Charles Frankel uses it (*20*). "Responsibility," says this philosopher, "is the product of definite social arrangements." Notice that Frankel calls for social arrangements—not propaganda.

Mutual Coercion
Mutually Agreed upon

The social arrangements that produce responsibility are arrangements that create coercion, of some sort. Consider bank-robbing. The man who takes money from a bank acts as if the bank were a commons. How do we prevent such action? Certainly not by trying to control his behavior solely by a verbal appeal to his sense of responsibility. Rather than rely on propaganda we follow Frankel's lead and insist that a bank is not a commons; we seek the definite social arrangements that will keep it from becoming a commons. That we thereby infringe on the freedom of would-be robbers we neither deny nor regret.

The morality of bank-robbing is particularly easy to understand because we accept complete prohibition of this activity. We are willing to say "Thou shalt not rob banks," without providing for exceptions. But temperance also can be created by coercion. Taxing is a good coercive device. To keep downtown shoppers temperate in their use of parking space we introduce parking meters for short periods, and traffic fines for longer ones. We need not actually forbid a citizen to park as long as he wants to; we need merely make it increasingly expensive for him to do so. Not prohibition. but carefully biased options are what we offer him. A Madison Avenue man might call this persuasion; I prefer the greater candor of the word coercion.

Coercion is a dirty word to most liberals now, but it need not forever be so. As with the four-letter words, its dirtiness can be cleansed away by exposure to the light, by saying it over and over without apology or embarrassment. To many, the word coercion implies arbitrary decisions of distant and irresponsible bureaucrats; but this is not a necessary part of its meaning. The only kind of coercion I recommend is mutual coercion. mutually agreed upon by the majority of the people affected.

To say that we mutually agree to

coercion is not to say that we are required to enjoy it, or even to pretend we enjoy it. Who enjoys taxes? We all grumble about them. But we accept compulsory taxes because we recognize that voluntary taxes would favor the conscienceless. We institute and (grumblingly) support taxes and other coercive devices to escape the horror of the commons.

An alternative to the commons need not be perfectly just to be preferable. With real estate and other material goods. the alternative we have chosen is the institution of private property coupled with legal inheritance. Is this system perfectly just? As a genetically trained biologist I deny that it is. It seems to me that. if there are to be differences in individual inheritance, legal possession should be perfectly correlated with biological inheritance—that those who are biologically more fit to be the custodians of property and power should legally inherit more. But genetic recombination continually makes a mockery of the doctrine of "like father, like son" implicit in our laws of legal inheritance. An idiot can inherit millions. and a trust fund can keep his estate intact. We must admit that our legal system of private property plus inheritance is unjust—but we put up with it because we are not convinced, at the moment. that anyone has invented a better system. The alternative of the commons is too horrifying to contemplate. Injustice is preferable to total ruin.

It is one of the peculiarities of the warfare between reform and the status quo that it is thoughtlessly governed by a double standard. Whenever a reform measure is proposed it is often defeated when its opponents triumphantly discover a flaw in it. As Kingsley Davis has pointed out (*21*), worshippers of the status quo sometimes imply that no reform is possible without unanimous agreement, an implication contrary to historical fact. As nearly as I can make out, automatic rejection of proposed reforms is based on one of two unconscious assumptions: (i) that the status quo is perfect; or (ii) that the choice we face is between reform and no action; if the proposed reform is imperfect, we presumably should take no action at all, while we wait for a perfect proposal.

But we can never do nothing. That which we have done for thousands of years is also action. It also produces evils. Once we are aware that the status quo is action, we can then compare its discoverable advantages and disadvantages with the predicted advantages and disadvantages of the proposed reform, discounting as best we can for our lack of experience. On the basis of such a comparison, we can make a rational decision which will not involve the unworkable assumption that only perfect systems are tolerable.

Recognition of Necessity

Perhaps the simplest summary of this analysis of man's population problems is this: the commons, if justifiable at all, is justifiable only under conditions of low-population density. As the human population has increased, the commons has had to be abandoned in one aspect after another.

First we abandoned the commons in food gathering, enclosing farm land and restricting pastures and hunting and fishing areas. These restrictions are still not complete throughout the world.

Somewhat later we saw that the commons as a place for waste disposal would also have to be abandoned. Restrictions on the disposal of domestic sewage are widely accepted in the Western world; we are still struggling to close the commons to pollution by automobiles, factories, insecticide sprayers, fertilizing operations, and atomic energy installations.

In a still more embryonic state is our recognition of the evils of the commons in matters of pleasure. There is almost no restriction on the propagation of sound waves in the public medium. The shopping public is assaulted with mindless music, without its consent. Our government is paying out billions of dollars to create supersonic transport which will disturb 50,000 people for every one person who is whisked from coast to coast 3 hours faster. Advertisers muddy the airwaves of radio and television and pollute the view of travelers. We are a long way from outlawing the commons in matters of pleasure. Is this because our Puritan inheritance makes us view pleasure as something of a sin, and pain (that is, the pollution of advertising) as the sign of virtue?

Every new enclosure of the commons involves the infringement of somebody's personal liberty. Infringements made in the distant past are accepted because no contemporary complains of a loss. It is the newly proposed infringements that we vigorously oppose; cries of "rights" and "freedom" fill the air. But what does "freedom" mean? When men mutually agreed to pass laws against robbing, mankind became more free, not less so. Individuals locked into the logic of the commons are free only to bring on universal ruin; once they see the necessity of mutual coercion, they become free to pursue other goals. I believe it was Hegel who said, "Freedom is the recognition of necessity."

The most important aspect of necessity that we must now recognize, is the necessity of abandoning the commons in breeding. No technical solution can rescue us from the misery of overpopulation. Freedom to breed will bring ruin to all. At the moment, to avoid hard decisions many of us are tempted to propagandize for conscience and responsible parenthood. The temptation must be resisted, because an appeal to independently acting consciences selects for the disappearance of all conscience in the long run, and an increase in anxiety in the short.

The only way we can preserve and nurture other and more precious freedoms is by relinquishing the freedom to breed, and that very soon. "Freedom is the recognition of necessity"—and it is the role of education to reveal to all the necessity of abandoning the freedom to breed. Only so, can we put an end to this aspect of the tragedy of the commons.

References

1. J. B. Wiesner and H. F. York, *Sci. Amer.* 211 (No. 4), 27 (1964).
2. G. Hardin, *J. Hered.* 50, 68 (1959); S. von Hoernor, *Science* 137, 18 (1962).
3. J. von Neumann and O. Morgenstern, *Theory of Games and Economic Behavior* (Princeton Univ. Press, Princeton, N.J., 1947), p. 11.
4. J. H. Fremlin, *New Sci.*, No. 415 (1964), p. 285.
5. A. Smith, *The Wealth of Nations* (Modern Library, New York, 1937), p. 423.
6. W. F. Lloyd, *Two Lectures on the Checks to Population* (Oxford Univ. Press, Oxford, England, 1833), reprinted (in part) in *Population, Evolution, and Birth Control*, G. Hardin, Ed. (Freeman, San Francisco, 1964), p. 37.
7. A. N. Whitehead, *Science and the Modern World* (Mentor, New York, 1948), p. 17.
8. G. Hardin, Ed. *Population, Evolution, and Birth Control* (Freeman, San Francisco, 1964), p. 56.
9. S. McVay, *Sci. Amer.* 216 (No. 8), 13 (1966).
10. J. Fletcher, *Situation Ethics* (Westminster, Philadelphia, 1966).
11. D. Lack, *The Natural Regulation of Animal Numbers* (Clarendon Press, Oxford, 1954).
12. H. Girvetz, *From Wealth to Welfare* (Stanford Univ. Press, Stanford, Calif., 1950).
13. G. Hardin, *Perspec. Biol. Med.* 6, 366 (1963).
14. U. Thant, *Int. Planned Parenthood News*, No. 168 (February 1968), p. 3.
15. K. Davis, *Science* 158, 730 (1967).
16. S. Tax, Ed., *Evolution after Darwin* (Univ. of Chicago Press, Chicago, 1960), vol. 2, p. 469.
17. G. Bateson, D. D. Jackson, J. Haley, J. Weakland, *Behav. Sci.* 1, 251 (1956).
18. P. Goodman, *New York Rev. Books* 10(8), 22 (23 May 1968).
19. A. Comfort, *The Anxiety Makers* (Nelson, London, 1967).
20. C. Frankel, *The Case for Modern Man* (Harper, New York, 1955), p. 203.
21. J. D. Roslansky, *Genetics and the Future of Man* (Appleton-Century-Crofts, New York, 1966), p. 177.

The parts of the article used when previewing 'The tragedy of the commons'

18b.2

Activity 2

Title: The tragedy of the commons

Abstract: *The population problem has no technical solution; it requires a fundamental extension in morality.*

Author: Garrett Hardin

Headings: What shall we maximize?
Tragedy of freedom in a commons
Pollution
How to legislate temperance?
Freedom to breed is intolerable
Conscience is self-eliminating
Pathogenic effects of conscience
Mutual coercion mutually agreed upon
Recognition of necessity

Introduction: The class of "no technical solution problems" has members. My thesis is that the "population problem", as conventionally conceived, is a member of this class. How it is conventionally conceived needs some comment. It is fair to say that most people who anguish over the population problem are trying to find a way to avoid the evils of overpopulation without relinquishing any of the privileges they now enjoy. They think that farming the seas or developing new strains of wheat will solve the problem – technologically. I try to show here that the solution they seek cannot be found. The population problem cannot be solved in a technical way, any more than can the problem of winning the game of tick-tack-toe.

Conclusion: **Recognition of Necessity**

Perhaps the simplest summary of this analysis of man's population problems is this: the commons, if justifiable at all, is justifiable only under conditions of low-population density. As the human population has increased, the commons has had to be abandoned in one aspect after another.

5 paragraphs

The only way we can preserve and nurture other and more precious freedoms is by relinquishing the freedom to breed, and that very soon. "Freedom is the recognition of necessity" – and it is the role of education to reveal to all the necessity of abandoning the freedom to breed. Only so, can we put an end to this aspect of the tragedy of the commons.

References: (21 references used for this material)

Functional stages of the introduction 'The tragedy of the commons'

18b.3

Para	Functional stage	Content	Macro-topic
1	**Orientate to topic** **context** (give general background to the topic)	At the end of a thoughtful article on the future of nuclear war, Wiesner and York *(1)* concluded that: "Both sides in the arms race are... confronted by the dilemma of steadily increasing military power and steadily decreasing national security. *It is our considered professional judgment that this dilemma has no technical solution.* If the great powers continue to look for solutions in the area of science and technology only, the result will be to worsen the situation."	**Introduction**
2	**Orientate to topic** **Define terms**	I would like to focus your attention not on the subject of the article (national security in a nuclear world) but on the kind of conclusion they reached, namely that there is no technical solution to the problem. An implicit and almost universal assumption of discussions published in professional and semi-popular scientific journals is that the problem under discussion has a technical solution. <u>A technical solution may be defined as one that requires a change only in the techniques of the natural sciences, demanding little or nothing in the way of change in human values or ideas of morality.</u>	
3	**Orientate to topic**	In our day (though not in earlier times) technical solutions are always welcome. Because of previous failures in prophecy, it takes courage to assert that a desired technical solution is not possible. Wiesner & York exhibited this courage; publishing in a science journal, they insisted that the solution to the problem was not to be found in the natural sciences. They cautiously qualified their statement with the phrase, "It is our considered professional judgment..."	

	State purpose (to state the purpose of the essay)	Whether they were right or not is not the concern of the present article. Rather, the concern here is with the important concept of a class of human problems which can be called "no technical solution problems", and, more specifically, with the identification and discussion of one of these.	
4	**Orientate to topic** (by giving an example)	It is easy to show that the class is not a null class. Recall the game of tick-tack-toe. Consider the problem, "How can I win the game of tick-tack-toe?" It is well known that I cannot, if I assume (in keeping with the conventions of game theory) that my opponent understands the game perfectly. Put another way, there is no "technical solution" to the problem. I can win only by given a radical meaning to the word "win". I can hit my opponent over the head; or I can drug him; or I can falsify the records. Every way in which I "win" involves, in some sense, an abandonment of the game, as we intuitively understand it. (I can also, of course, openly abandon the game—refuse to play it. This is what most adults do.)	
5	**State thesis**	The class of "No technical solution problems" has members. <u>My thesis is that the "population problem," as conventionally conceived, is a member of this class.</u> How it is conventionally conceived needs some comment. It is fair to say that most people who anguish over the population problem are trying to find a way to avoid the evils of over-population without relinquishing any of the privileges they now enjoy. They think that farming the seas or developing new strains of wheat will solve the problem—technologically. <u>I try to show here that the solution they seek cannot be found. The population problem cannot be solved in a technical way, any more than can the problem of winning the game of tick-tack-toe.</u>	

Linear notes: an example using numbers 'The tragedy of the commons'

18b.4

Activity 8

Summary

1. Freedom of land has been abandoned by:

   i) enclosure, privatisation;

   ii) regulation of hunting, fishing, grazing.

2. Freedom of air and water now being abandoned by:

   i) restricting sewage disposal;

   ii) restricting pollution.

3. Freedom from noise and visual pollution now under threat by:

   i) noise restriction;

   ii) limiting advertising hoardings, etc.

4. The necessity to abandon the freedom to breed has not yet been recognised.

Linear notes: an example using columns 'The tragedy of the commons'

18b.5

Activity 8

Main points	Supporting points	Comments
Introduction There is no technical solution to the problem of overpopulation.	Not <u>all</u> problems can be solved technically eg. tick-tack-toe (trivial but easy to prove)	*This article was written before 1968. The common belief in technical fix has waned since then.*
There needs to be a change in human values or ideas of morality.	nuclear conflict	
What shall we maximise? Maximum population is not the same as maximum good per person. Optimum population is less than maximum population.	The world is finite. It is mathematically impossible to maximise for 2 variables (max. good and max. number) at the same time Minimum subsistence living maximises number but is not considered 'optimum'	*This mathematical logic is elegant for those that understand it, but is not necessary for the argument.*
'Maximum good per person' has different meanings for different people. We need criteria and a system of weighting to determine optimum population.	Natural selection is nature's solution. In human populations the most rapidly growing are often the most miserable, so positive growth rate does not indicate sub-optimum population.	*The claim that no prosperous population in the world today has had for some time a growth rate of zero could be dated.* *Some European countries now have a zero or negative growth*
The idea that population will be self regulating needs to be critically examined. If it is found to be incorrect then we need to see which 'freedoms' are unjustified.	The free market principle (Adam Smith) justifies the policy of *laissez faire* ie. decisions reached individually for individual good will be best for the whole society	*This section points to how the argument will proceed.*

Patterned notes: example 1
'The tragedy of the commons'

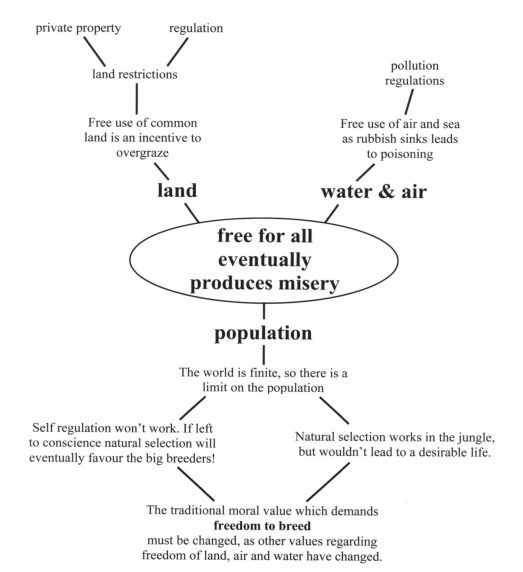

private property   regulation

land restrictions

Free use of common
land is an incentive to
overgraze

pollution
regulations

Free use of air and sea
as rubbish sinks leads
to poisoning

land   **water & air**

**free for all
eventually
produces misery**

population

The world is finite, so there is a
limit on the population

Self regulation won't work. If left
to conscience natural selection will
eventually favour the big breeders!

Natural selection works in the jungle,
but wouldn't lead to a desirable life.

The traditional moral value which demands
freedom to breed
must be changed, as other values regarding
freedom of land, air and water have changed.

Patterned notes: example 2
'The tragedy of the commons'

Activity 8

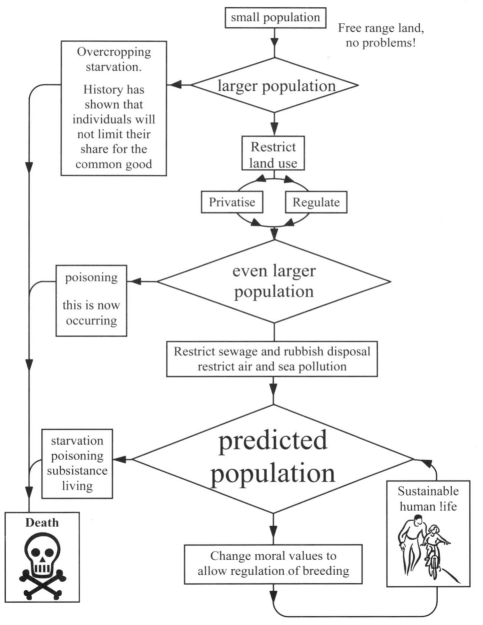

small population

Free range land,
no problems!

larger population

Overcropping
starvation.

History has
shown that
individuals will
not limit their
share for the
common good

Restrict
land use

Privatise   Regulate

even larger
population

poisoning

this is now
occurring

Restrict sewage and rubbish disposal
restrict air and sea pollution

predicted
population

starvation
poisoning
subsistance
living

Sustainable
human !life

Death

Change moral values to
allow regulation of breeding

Summary of the article
'The tragedy of the commons'

Argument

There must be some coercion (rules) to prevent human overpopulation as this is the only way to avert tragedy.

Premises used to support this argument

1. Not all problems have a technical fix. Some problems need a change in values rather than clever inventions for their solution. Overpopulation is one of these problems.
2. Eventually (and 'soon' is inferred), we must reach zero population growth.
3. An optimum population is less than a maximum population.
4. Individuals working for self gain will not promote public interest without coercion. Devices for coercion include:
   - private property   Unfair to the poor!
   - regulatory laws   Who makes the regulations?
   - taxing devices   Who controls the taxes?
5. The welfare state works against natural selection methods to reduce overpopulation.
6. Conscience is, in the long term, self eliminating.
7. Methods of coercion need not be perfect, just better.
8. The existing morality, as defined by the UN needs to be changed. Freedom to breed needs to be relinquished just as other freedoms have been given up over history.

Assumptions

1. The world available to the human population is finite. Space is not an escape.
2. We should work for the greater good of the greatest number.
3. Guilt is not a valuable, even indispensable ingredient of civilised life.
4. Humans should assume control over their own destiny.

CHAPTER 5

Using numeracy

Within and outside educational settings most people encounter printed, oral and/or electronic quantitative material. In university, many disciplines use mathematical or symbolic representations to communicate a message. Thus, it is important to take note of them and work at understanding what they are saying.

In this book numeracy is defined as '…competence in the mathematical skills needed to cope with everyday life and the understanding of information presented in mathematical terms like graphs, charts, or tables'[1]. Many of these mathematical[2] demands are quantitative, and in this chapter the terms 'numeracy' and 'quantitative' are used in

---

[1] Encarta® World English Dictionary © 1999 Microsoft Corporation, Bloomsbury Publishing Plc.

[2] Encarta defines mathematics as 1 the study of the relationships among numbers, shapes and quantities. It uses signs, symbols, and proofs and includes arithmetic, algebra, calculus, geometry and trigonometry; and 2 the calculations involved in a process, estimate, or plan.

relation to the mathematical demands evident in study. Many of the uses of mathematics don't involve numbers, and many require approximations rather than precise calculations.

This chapter is not aimed at students studying mathematics or those who are competent with mathematics. It is designed for students in disciplines where quantitative material is presented in readings or lectures or where quantitative representations are required in assignments. This chapter is intended for students who don't have a strong mathematical background and/or are anxious about their mathematical ability.

This chapter contains two exercises[3]. Exercise 19 focuses on situations in everyday life that involve numeracy and examines strategies for reading quantitative information presented in university study. Exercise 20 focuses on reading and interpreting study material presented in tables, graphs and other forms. The activities in this exercise can be applied to the article provided or to an academic article containing quantitative information that you are required to read in a unit you are studying.

---

[3] The material in this chapter has been rewritten with input from Marian Kemp and Exercise 20 includes the Five Step Framework she developed. Originally the material in this chapter was adapted by Marian Kemp, Lorraine Marshall and Mary Dale from material prepared by Sue Willis, Barry Kissane and Anne Chapman in the School of Education, Murdoch University.

19. Numeracy in everyday life and in study
- Everyday uses of mathematics
  - your everyday uses of mathematics
  - different uses of numeracy
  - the role of educated guesses
- Types of quantitative representation
  - quantitative representations in everyday life
  - quantitative representations in study
- Attitude to mathematics
  - your attitude to mathematics
- Reading quantitative information
- The role of numeracy in study

Using Numeracy

20. Reading quantitative information
- Deciding on material
- Previewing material systematically
  - identifying types of mathematical and symbolic representations
  - identifying the argument or main point
- Academic texts containing quantitative information
- A framework for interpreting quantitative material
- Interpreting tables
  - types of tables
  - the characteristics of tables
  - applying the Five Step Framework to a table
- Interpreting graphs
  - types of graphs
  - reading graphs
  - techniques for drawing graphs
  - applying the Five Step Framework to a graph
- Analysing maps, plans and diagrams
- Interpreting flow diagrams
- Reviewing the whole article
- Difficulties with reading quantitative representations
- Reflections

19. Numeracy in everyday life and in study

Introduction

This exercise explores how you use different levels of numeracy in everyday life. For university students 'everyday life' may include activities such as shopping, sport, travel, paid employment, leisure and study. The exercise also examines your attitude towards mathematics and you approach when reading quantitative information.

This exercise encourages you

- to identify the numeracy demands placed on you in everyday life and in your study and to examine how you approach these demands;

- to recognise those situations where you are required to read, interpret and evaluate quantitative information;

- to understand the importance of making an educated guess in certain situations involving mathematical calculations;

- to examine your attitudes towards mathematics.

Materials

19.1   Everyday uses of numeracy
19.2   It's the good guess that counts
19.3   Different types of mathematical and symbolic representations
19.4   Reading quantitative information.

Approximate time

60 minutes

Reading

Marshall & Rowland, 2006, Chapter 13, pp. 234-237.

Learning activities

Activity 1   Everyday uses of mathematics

Your everyday uses of mathematics

In your learning log, record your uses of mathematics over the past week in your everyday life. Include any uses of mathematics in your study that are unrelated to university mathematics units.

Different uses of numeracy

Read the extract, 'Everyday uses of numeracy'.

In your learning log, consider and explain a situation where you used mathematics to solve a problem or make a decision about something that was not obviously mathematical. Discuss the mathematics that you used and list the steps that you took to solve the problem or make the decision.

The role of educated guesses

Read the extract, 'It's the good guess that counts', by John Maddox.

In your learning log, reflect on and describe occasions where it has been more appropriate to make educated guesses rather than provide exact calculations.

Activity 2   Types of quantitative representation

Quantitative representations in everyday life

Examine some newspapers, magazines and other publications, and list the different types of representations that comprise quantitative information.

Look closely for examples that may have been designed to mislead the reader, such as graphs without scales or with distorted scales.

19.3   Examine the attached diagram, 'Different types of mathematical and symbolic representations', and compare the various representations that you found with this diagram.

Quantitative representations in study

Preview your study materials, such as your unit guide, unit reader, required texts or reference books, and identify any different types of quantitative representations. Relate these examples to the diagram.

In your learning log, list the different types of quantitative representations evident in both everyday situations and in study material.

Activity 3   Attitude to mathematics

Your attitude to mathematics

Some people are confident in their ability to tackle the mathematical demands of everyday life and others are not. If you lack confidence, the previous activities will have highlighted how much you use mathematics in everyday life and hopefully will have been productive for you.

In your learning log, describe one positive experience and one negative experience that you have had with mathematics.

Explore your attitudes towards mathematics and the basis of this by answering the following questions.

- Do you enjoy reading and interpreting quantitative information? Why or why not?

- What factors or situations in your life have influenced your attitude towards mathematics?

- How do you deal with the everyday mathematical demands that you encounter?

- With which types of mathematical demands do you cope effectively?

- Do you readily learn new concepts that are presented in a symbolic form? Why or why not?

- Do you readily question and analyse written material but avoid graphs and tables? If so, why?

Activity 4   Reading quantitative material

In your learning log, answer the following questions.

- How do you read numbers, tables, graphs and symbols and other numerical or quantitative representations? Do you skim over them quickly? Why?

- When do you read mathematical representations in depth?

Activity 5   The role of numeracy in study

19.4

Read the attached material, 'Reading quantitative information', and consider the role of numeracy in your study. Answer the following questions.

- What definition of numeracy is used?

- Why is it important to read quantitative information critically?

This reading intends to help prepare you for the following exercises.

Numeracy

1. Everyday uses of mathematics

Record your uses of mathematics over the past week in your everyday. Include any uses of mathematics in your study that are unrelated to university mathematics units.

Consider and explain a situation where you used mathematics to solve a problem or make a decision about something that was not obviously mathematical. Discuss the mathematics that you used and list the steps that you took to solve the problem or make the decision.

Describe occasions where it has been more appropriate to make educated guesses rather than provide exact calculations.

2. Types of quantitative representation

List the different types of quantitative representations evident in both everyday situations and in study material.

3. Attitude to mathematics

Describe one positive experience and one negative experience that you have had with mathematics

Explore your attitudes towards mathematics and the basis of this by answering the following questions.

- Do you enjoy reading and interpreting quantitative information? Why or why not?

- What factors or situations in your life have influenced your attitude towards mathematics?

- How do you deal with the everyday mathematical demands that you encounter?

- With which types of mathematical demands do you cope effectively?

- Do you readily learn new concepts that are presented in a symbolic form? Why or why not?

- Do you readily question and analyse written material but avoid graphs and tables? If so, why?

4. Reading quantitative material

- How do you read numbers, tables, graphs and symbols and other numerical or quantitative representations? Do you skim over them quickly? Why?

- When do you read mathematical representations in depth?

Everyday uses of numeracy[4]

19.1

Activity 1

Supermarket shopping: My task is to buy some coffee for the staff morning tea fund. I want to get the best value for money so I need to know which size jar represents the best value, that is, the lowest cost per 100 grams of coffee. This is too much trouble to work out exactly while shopping, so I use a 'rough 'n ready' calculation. I can buy 375g of coffee for $9.50, or the special at $4.25 for 250g. Doubling the special is $8.50 for 500g, so I buy the special. Here accuracy is unnecessary but efficiency and approximation are important.

Petrol consumption: I am driving from Perth to Albany. The fuel is running low near Mt Barker, and fuel is more expensive in Mt Barker than Albany. Have I got enough fuel to get to Albany? I not sure about my car's fuel consumption over long trips. I realise that I have used seven-eighths of a tank and have one eighth left. I ask myself: Is the distance between Mt Barker and Albany more than one-eighth of my journey? I need to improvise and use maths to solve the problem. In this case, I need to do a simple mental calculation and a precise calculation is unnecessary. In fact, a 'precise' calculation would be no better than the imprecise data fed into it.

Trip to the airport: What is the best route? What do I mean by best? Shortest? Fastest? Most scenic? Least traffic? Perhaps the most reliable? For example, on one route I can rely on reaching the airport in exactly 45 minutes. The other route is often faster (only 30–35 minutes when I get a good run), but heavy traffic occasionally means that the trip can take 55–60 minutes. What is the best route?

Informal measurements: I make informal measurements when I jump a puddle (or decide not to risk it and walk around); when I project my voice to be heard at the back of a lecture room but drop it to speak to a small group; when I hit a tennis ball; when I pace my running to where I think a ball will descend etc.

Using the library: The library catalogue system is essentially mathematical as it involves the elaborate classification of published material (placing it into sets) and the arrangement and ordering of the material according to an overall plan. As publications belong to more than one set, they are cross classified and locatable under these various classifications. Thus, when I use the library I make use of mathematics. At the very least, I need to be able to order decimals if I am to find books.

Studying: I use mathematical process and ideas when I organise and structure the content of a unit, when I allocate time and when I judge the pace of a presentation. Also, almost every article in my unit reader requires a reasonable level of numeracy.

---

[4]   Anne Chapman, 1988, 'Using numeracy: Some everyday examples used by a student', written for this book.

It's the good guess that counts[5]

The more we extol the virtues of numeracy, the more obvious it becomes that often we do not know what we are talking about. For some, the acid test is that we should be able to divide 325.86 by 32.59 without making a mistake. For others, numeracy means knowing that $100 - 11 = 1$ is a calculation in the binary scale. Nobody sets much store by the calculation of the square root of 325.86 – as pocket calculators now do that.

If these three simple examples were alternative responses to a multiple-choice question asking which is the essential ingredient of numeracy, prudent respondents should be careful to tick the box marked 'None of these'. In doing so, they should worry a little about the vagueness of a concept that is well on the way to dominating part of the curriculum. So what does it mean?

The place to start is with the need of the ordinary school-leaver who leaves school at 16 with no immediate thought of taking a job involving maths. Some mathematical skills are nevertheless essential. It is reasonable to hope that everybody will be able to ensure that their pay slip has been properly calculated.

Do-it-yourself buffs need some old-fashioned measuration, as in 'How many rolls of wallpaper with a repeating pattern every 3 feet will be needed to cover the walls of a room?' Those who drive will need simple ratios to tell whether the few gallons of petrol in their tank will let them get to the next service station on the motorway. Those who have money left over with which to buy things need an eagle eye at the checkout counter and a flair for ratios if they are looking for the best buy in pineapple chunks. Gamblers need to know about odds, or probability, and everybody needs to know something about sampling errors in order to make sense of the public opinion polls.

By carrying on in this way, it should of course be possible to define the essence of numeracy, the mathematical equipment that all adults need. However, the definition would be deficient in at least two important respects. First, adults are much less in need of exact calculations than of being able to make numerical guesses that are accurate. Will five rolls of wallpaper do the job? Roughly how long will it take to drive to the Costa Brava? Is it better to finesse the Queen of Spades or to play for the drop? If the gross national product is roughly £1,000,000m, is the GNP per head more like £2,000 than £1,000?

The importance of these skills of estimation is widely and grossly underestimated, yet in everyday maths – everyday life – they are the skills that matter. There is a sense in

---

5   J. Maddox, n.d., 'It's the good guess that counts', Science Diary, Letts, UK.

which it is more valuable to know that £1,000 per annum is roughly £20 a week than that it is £19.230769 per week. £20 per week is a number that you can easily use on other calculations, in working out the weekly equivalent of a princely salary, for example. The other number I have given is useless by comparison. For most people, calculations like these are a mystery. They should not be, for these are the kinds of sums that people who use maths professionally engage in all the time, even on much more exalted planes than this simple arithmetic.

Unfortunately, the word has falsely got around that maths is above all a means of arriving at precision. For many purposes it is the opposite. To be able to guess confidently is more useful than to be able to calculate slavishly, to the umpteenth decimal place. So much should be firmly in the minds of all those who have bought themselves electronic calculators, and who discover that it is still something of a problem to be able to tell just by looking whether the answer that flickers up in green electronic numbers has the decimal point where it ought to be.

Guessing confidently needs a much more comprehensive battery of skills than the act of lavish calculation. So a flair for estimation is one forgotten part of numeracy. The ability to learn mathematical techniques that one has not previously encountered is another. Here I have in mind the problems of the school-leavers who take jobs that they suppose will not entail maths and who then discover that it is (as it is) quite inescapable.

There are the battalions of architects and designers who thought they would take up something artistic because they were not much good with numbers at school, and the armies of people who thought they would make a career in marketing (which is widely supposed to require just charm) and who have then discovered that real life is mostly about numbers after all.

Sooner or later, all those people have to knuckle down to learn manipulative tricks that they would not in any case have been taught at school. They do so, in the end, with much pain. For a school-leaver, the essential equipment for life ahead is an ability to learn techniques that have not already been taught.

My own suspicion [that is the author's] is that if the maths curriculum was designed in such a way that most school-leavers had this extra flair for guessing and for flexibility, most of the other needs of the under-16's would automatically be catered for. Some have to use maths in learning other subjects, and some have to use it as a basis for further specialised study in maths or physics. It will not, however, have escaped attention that the securing of these goals would be a great advance on what most people now understand of maths when they leave school.

Different types of mathematical and symbolic representations

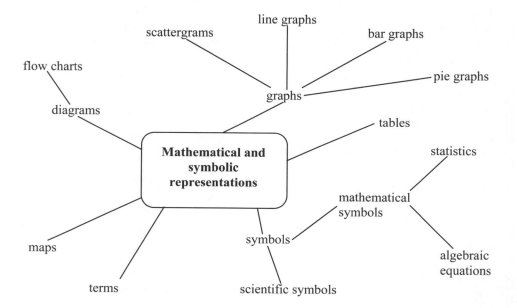

Reading quantitative information

19.4

Activity 4

In university the amount of numerical or quantitative information students are expected to read and how they are expected to work with it will vary between disciplines. This information, whether printed, oral or electronic, can comprise verbal, tabular, graphical and symbolic representations. Verbal representation are written or spoken text and may include mathematical terms such as birth rates, decreasing inflation, exponential growth, or inversely proportional. These representations can be embedded in prose so that the mathematical meaning is within the words. Tabular representation includes information in tables ranging from the straightforward, such as bus timetables, to the more complex, such as data found in statistical reports. They include numerical data related to different categories and are often longitudinal. Graphic representations include bar graphs, line graphs or pie graphs and are frequently found in newspapers. These can be misleading unless the reader pays attention to the legends, axes and scales. Symbolic representations are typically restricted to scientific and mathematical areas and are found in the form of formulae.

Authors (and your unit coordinators) expect you to interact in different ways with the numerical or quantitative material presented within their fields. Some authors expect you to interpret the data directly, while others will interpret it for you. Regardless of the expectation, however, you still need to critically evaluate the author's interpretation in the same way that you would evaluate an argument put forward by anyone.

Although it is common for students to skim over tables, graphs, numbers and symbols, it is only by paying attention to them that students can decide whether to accept the inferences and conclusions of the author that are based on the data. This does not necessarily mean that every number in a table, for example, needs to be considered in detail, but having an ability to make inferences, consider comparisons, see the 'big picture' and pick up inconsistencies are invaluable skills. In some cases it is helpful to transform types of representations, for example, from a table to a graph, from formulae to words, from words to a graph and so on. It has been suggested that the ability to generate these transformations can help to make the information more accessible and understandable.

Thus, in order to absorb and understand numerical information when reading a text, such as quantities and percentages, it is necessary to read more slowly than you would otherwise. Often texts can include terms that have a specific mathematical meaning and distinguishing between the mathematical usage and everyday usage can require careful thought. For example, 'mean', 'random', 'odd', 'even', 'normal' and 'generally' have different meanings in mathematical language and everyday language.

Students have varying ability and willingness to engage with the quantitative aspects of texts or readings. Some students are confident and efficiently tackle these aspects. Other students are more reluctant to deal explicitly with quantitative information, perhaps because they lack mathematical knowledge, fear mathematics or don't realise the importance of working with this type of material. Dealing directly with numerical or quantitative information does not require being good at mathematics, but it does require thinking carefully about what you read. Some people who are very good at mathematics don't realise the importance of thinking critically about the quantitative aspects of what they are reading.

In addition, it is important for you to reflect on your readings and to identify those that are or aren't easy to understand, especially those involving quantitative information. This can help you consider and decide on the most appropriate way to present your own research findings or quantitative information. For example, you may decide to include a table for detailed information, a graph to show trends or text to explain reasons for changes.

Once you have decided to examine numerical or quantitative information you need to decide what to do with it. A framework for this is included in the following exercise. This process involves using some mathematical skills, and interpreting and evaluating what you read.

20. Reading quantitative information

Introduction

This exercise includes a series of strategies for reading and interpreting quantitative information. These can be applied to the report provided, 'Financial disadvantage in Australia 1990 to 2000: the persistence of poverty in a decade of growth' (referred to in the text boxes in each activity), or to material containing quantitative information that you are required to read in a unit you are studying.

In this exercise you are asked to preview the material and analyse the quantitative information it contains using a Five Step Framework. This framework and the strategies will help you formulate questions that can enable you to understand the full meaning of quantitative material, such as that included in your study materials and information in the media.

If you are confident with your mathematics ability, you may decide to may decide to preview and analyse an article in your study. However, if you have difficulty with this or are anxious about your mathematical ability use the article and worksheets provided. When you have completed the exercise, transfer what you have learned to other study material.

Mathematics is best learned by doing, not just reading. It can help to have immediate feedback, so answers have been provided[6].

This exercise encourages you

▪ to develop skills in reading, interpreting and evaluating quantitative material presented in tables, graphs, flow charts and diagrams;

▪ to develop skills in presenting quantitative material in your written work.

Materials

This exercise can be completed using the report provided or material (an article, chapter or report) containing quantitative information from a unit you are studying. You don't need to read the material before beginning this exercise. The information in this exercise is applied to the quantitative material in the report provided, which is referred to in the text boxes in each activity.

---

[6] Answers to the questions in this exercise are provided in the Appendix, so that you are not tempted to read them before beginning the work yourself.

20.1 An extract from 'Financial disadvantage in Australia 1990 to 2000. The persistence of poverty in a decade of growth'. Executive Summary and Sections 1 and 2 of Part A. (The full report is available from the website listed below.[7])

20.2 Previewing: questions to ask and notes on parts of the report

20.3 Apply the Five Step Framework to Table 1 'Estimated poverty rates and other characteristics of Australians, 1990 to 2000'. Questions

20.4 Apply the Five Step Framework to Figure 3 'Trends in poor, middle average and top incomes, after adjustment for inflation, 1990 to 2000a'. Questions

See the Appendix for answers to the questions.

20.5 'Estimated poverty rates and other characteristics of Australians, 1990 to 2000'. Answers

20.6 'Trends in poor, middle average and top incomes, after adjustment for inflation, 1990 to 2000a'. Answers

Approximate time

60 minutes

Reading

Marshall & Rowland, 2006, Chapter 13, pp. 234-7.

---

[7] A. Harding, R. Lloyd & H. Greenwell, 2001, *Financial Disadvantage in Australia 1990 – 2000,* Section A. html document:
http://www.smithfamily.com.au/documents/Fin_Disadv_Report_Nov_2001_4D837.pdf

Learning activities

Activity 1   Deciding on material

Decide whether you will use the report provided or an article from a unit you are studying.

This exercise leads you through a series of strategies for reading and interpreting texts containing quantitative information.

Activity 2   Previewing material systematically

Read the information in Exercises 18, 'Reading in depth', that explains previewing.

Preview the material systematically and answer questions about the key parts: author (s), title and/or subtitle, subject headings, introduction, conclusion, quantitative and symbolic representations.

20.1
20.2

'Financial disadvantage in Australia 1990 to 2000. The persistence of poverty in a decade of growth'

Preview this extract.

See the attached information that lists the parts to examine when previewing.

Identifying types of mathematical and symbolic representations

19.3

Refer to the diagram from Exercise 19, 'Different types of mathematical and symbolic representations'. Identify and examine the types of representations in the material. Compare these with the diagram. You will be asked to analyse in detail some of these types of representations.

20.1
20.2

'Financial disadvantage in Australia 1990 to 2000. The persistence of poverty in a decade of growth'

In the report provided there is a pie graph, a table and two line graphs.

Identifying the argument or main point

Using your preview as a guide, read the body of the material in sufficient depth so that you can identify the argument or main point.

Depending on the material and your reading purpose, it may be preferable to examine the quantitative information before reading the material.

20.1
20.2

'Financial disadvantage in Australia 1990 to 2000. The persistence of poverty in a decade of growth'

Read the report. You should have an overview of the argument from your preview, so you may not find it necessary to read the report before examining the tables and graphs.

Activity 3   Academic texts containing quantitative information

Re-read your log entry from Exercise 19.

19.4

Re-read the extract from Exercise 19, 'Reading quantitative information'.

In your learning log, answer the following questions.

- How do you usually read academic texts that contain quantitative information?
- How do you usually read tables and graphs in study materials?

Remember that to understand quantitative information you need to read more slowly than you would otherwise.

Graphs and tables provide alternate ways to look at quantitative information. Tables give detailed information about particular instances whereas graphs give a view of overall trends. You can extract information from both tables and graphs about particular values and trends, and make comparisons and draw conclusions about the information presented.[8]

---

[8]   Adapted from R. C. Aukerman, 1972, *Reading in the secondary school classroom*, McGraw Hill, USA, p. 203.

Activity 4 A framework for interpreting quantitative material

Below is a Five Step Framework[9] for interpreting data in graphs and tables. These steps are used by experienced people when interpreting quantitative information.

Examine these steps carefully. You will be asked to apply these steps in the following activities.

Step 1: Getting started

Examine the title, headings, footnotes and source to understand the context and evaluate the credibility of the data. For example, read the title and headings to find out exactly what information is being presented, read the labels and numbers on the table or graph.

Step 2: WHAT do the numbers mean?

Make sure you know the meanings of all the numbers (totals, subtotals, averages and so on) and symbols (%, '000, $m and so on) in the table. Look for the largest and smallest values in one or more rows or columns to get an idea of the range of the data.

Step 3: HOW do they change or differ?

Examine the data in a single set of numbers, such as an entire row or column. Consider the variation over the whole set to see how the numbers change or differ. Repeat this for other sets of numbers.

Step 4: WHERE are the differences?

What are the relationships in the table that connect the variables? Use your observations from Step 3 to help you make comparisons between columns or rows and to look for similarities and differences, such as changes over time, or comparisons between categories (for example, gender, food groups, countries).

Step 5: WHY do they change?

Suggest plausible reasons for the relationships in the data by considering relevant factors, such as social, environmental or

---

[9] Marian Kemp, 2006,

economic. For example, look for connections between sudden or unexpected variations in the data with changes in state, national and international policies or with major events.

Activity 5 Interpreting tables

Types of tables

There are two main types of tables that you may encounter in everyday life and in study.

- Firstly, tables that provide specific information, such as those on food packets or medicines or bus and train timetables.
- Secondly, tables containing data that has been collected, collated and possibly include a range of data such as traffic statistics, global climate changes, recycling practices, environmental concerns or poverty statistics. These tables can be simple or complex, but provide data at a level of accuracy not possible in graphic form. Due to the detail in such tables it is important to develop strategies for reading them.

The characteristics of tables

The following summary describes the characteristics of a well-presented table.[10]

It is useful to consider a table as being made up of a series of lists or vertical columns, each with its own heading, which are then aligned side by side so that the data correlate horizontally. It should be clear whether a heading applies to information alongside it or below it. In general (there are always exceptions) a heading should apply to the information beneath it not beside it.

A table should be compact and have a minimum number of blank spaces or repetitions. However, if this can only be achieved by an elaborate system of footnotes, colour codings, compressions or words turned sideways, a table may not be appropriate. The table may show that you have understood how the data fits together, but may be difficult for readers to understand.

In your learning log, answer the following question.

---

[10] Sue Habeshaw & Di Steeds, 1993, *53 interesting communication exercises for science students*, 2nd edn, Technical Education Services Ltd, Bristol, UK, p. 189.

- What types of information are particularly suitable for tables?
- What kind of information needs to be included in a table?
- What are the advantages of using a table?

If you are collecting data for a project, aim to record measurements in tabular form when possible. This is compact, easy to follow, makes it easy to identify mistakes and enables you to record the data systematically and note any omissions.

Applying the Five Step Framework to a table

Select a table from the material and apply the Five Step Framework to the table.

20.1
20.2

'Financial disadvantage in Australia 1990 to 2000. The persistence of poverty in a decade of growth'

Apply the Five Step Framework to the table, 'Estimated poverty rates and other characteristics of Australians, 1990 to 2000'. Interpret the table using the Five Step Framework.

20.3

Refer to the attached worksheet for information on the systematic application of the framework to the table. Answer the questions on the worksheet or in your learning log.[11]

Activity 6   Interpreting Graphs

Types of graphs

There are various types of graphs.

- Pie graphs (or pie charts) are commonly used to show portions of a whole.
- Line graphs are primarily used to show trends and to help make comparisons, often over time.
- Bar or column graphs are usually used for discrete data (separate quantities, such as numbers of fish or categories, such as kinds of fast food) and histograms are usually used for continuous data, such as heights, weights or time taken.

---

[11] If you unable to complete a problem, it can be useful to work backwards from the answer. Using answers sensibly is a useful study skill and is not cheating. Ask your tutor or another person if you continue to have difficulty.

'Financial disadvantage in Australia 1990 to 2000. The persistence of poverty in a decade of growth'

This article contains a pie chart (or pie graph), and two line graphs. All three graphs include data provided in the table 'Estimated Poverty rates and other characteristics of Australians, 1990 to 2000', that was examined in the previous Activity. The graphs use selected data from the table and present the data visually, which helps in forming comparisons.

The pie chart in Figure 1, 'Estimated number of Australians in poverty in 2000 = 2,432,000 or 13%' uses information from the table to show the relative number of adults and children who together make up the number in poverty in 2000. The reader must refer to the table in order to understand the derivation of the 12.3% and the 14.9%, which are percentages of the total numbers of adults and children (as defined in the footnotes) in 2000. Usually, the percentages of a pie chart to add up to 100%; however, in this case it is the two numbers that add up to the total number of people in poverty.

Reading graphs

Graphs often appear easy to interpret, but still must be read carefully in order to make sense of the information and not jump to erroneous conclusions.

When reading a graph it is important to look carefully at the scales and keys (legends) so you can interpret it correctly. In many cases the scales are not labelled or are labelled incorrectly, which can be confusing. In these situations there is insufficient information to be able to draw valid conclusions.

Techniques for drawing graphs

Consider how you go about drawing a graph. The following strategies should be considered:

- collect the data (preferably in table form);
- choose the style of graph (line, pie, bar, or scatter graph);
- choose the scales;
- draw the axes, label them and use suitable scales;
- graph the data;

- carefully examine the graph carefully to ensure there are no unexpected anomalies because of a drawing mistake;
- give the graph a title;
- provide any necessary explanation in text.

Note that you were asked to draw a bar graph in Exercise 5, Organising and planning study' and a line graph in Exercise 6, 'Concentrating'. You may find it useful to refer to these now.

Read Marshall and Rowland, 2006, pp. 234-7.

Applying the Five Step Framework to a graph

Select a graph from the material and apply the Five Step Framework to the graph. As you apply Step 1, check that the graph includes all of the correct information, such as correctly labelled scales.

20.1
20.2

'Financial disadvantage in Australia 1990 to 2000. The persistence of poverty in a decade of growth'

Apply the Five Step Framework to the line graph in Figure 3, 'Trends in poor, middle average and top incomes, after adjustment for inflation, 1990 to 2000a'. This graph shows particular data extracted from the table examined previously (see Activity 5) and allows you to make comparisons, but it is not possible to see the same detail evident in the table.

20.4

Refer to the attached worksheet for information on the systematic application of the framework to the graph. The worksheet enables you to develop strategies for interpreting a graph.

Activity 7   Analysing maps, plans and diagrams

Diagrams and plans are particularly useful when describing experimental methods. A diagram need not be photographically true or artistic. It is often most useful when it is schematic and simplistic, indicating only the features relevant to the experiment.[12]

Flow diagrams are a specific type of diagram and are explained in the following activity.

---

[12] Adapted from G. L. Squires, 1985, *Practical Physics*, Cambridge University Press, Cambridge.

In your learning log, answer the following questions.

- What are the advantages of using maps, plans or diagrams?
- What types of information are particularly suitable for maps, plans or diagrams?
- Could the same information be conveyed in words?
- What kind of information needs to be included in the map, plan or diagram?
- Is it always necessary to include a scale?
- Is it useful to have both a caption and a title?
- What happens when too much detail is included?

Activity 8 Interpreting flow diagrams

A flow diagram is a specific type of diagram that shows a series of actions or processes undertaken in a complex activity, such as in decision making, production lines or computer programs.

Translate the information provided in a flow diagram into words by answering the following questions.

- What is the diagram showing?
- Is the information conveyed qualitative or quantitative?
- Does the diagram show the main ideas and/or detailed information?
- Is it useful to have both a caption and a title?
- Is it important to include both numbers and arrows?

When you have completed this, answer the following questions:

- What are the advantages of using flow diagrams?
- What types of information are particularly particularly suitable for flow diagrams?
- What kind of information needs to be included in the diagram?

Note that flow diagrams often include the following mistakes:

- no title or insufficient explanation;
- no beginning and end, or no inputs and outputs;
- poorly or incorrectly labelled arrows and boxes;

- inclusion of too much detail;
- failure of the box scale or arrow to reflect the true magnitude of the phenomenon.

Consider how you could use flow diagrams in your study. Use them where appropriate in your report writing.

Reflect on the old Chinese proverb, 'A picture is worth a thousand words', but use a picture only when it conveys information in a useful way.

Activity 9 Reviewing the whole article

Review the whole article to fully recall what you have read. In your learning log, evaluate the quantitative representations in the material.

Note that although many academic journals successfully use figures, diagrams or information in boxes that are not referred to in the main text, this is not recommended when presenting information in your reports.

Activity 10 Difficulties with reading quantitative representations

Refer to the activities completed and consider which quantitative representations (tables, graphs, maps, plans or diagrams) were most difficult to understand.

Select an article containing quantitative information from a unit you are studying and repeat this exercise applying the Five Step Framework. Choose a range of quantitative informatiaon and apply some of the procedures you have learned.

Remember that for a full understanding different kinds of text must be read at different rates. Your reading rate depends on your reading purpose and the difficulty of the material. In particular, mathematical material often contains denser information than an equivalent length of prose and must be read at a different rate. Skim reading will not be sufficient for this material. It must be read carefully, slowly and actively if meaning is to be acquired.

Your individual preference will help you decide what is most useful, but some valuable techniques when reading mathematical information include:

– writing brief notes;
– drawing a diagram;
– writing an equation;
– transforming a table to a graph or vice versa;
– drawing a rough sketch graph.

An important skill in reading quantitative information is learning to ask the right questions. Most of the questions you have been asking about the information are related to acquiring meaning from the data.

Activity 11 Reflecting on the exercise

It is important for you to take time to reflect on the exercise you have just completed.

In your learning log, evaluate what you have gained from this exercise. Has it helped your reading? Has it changed how you will approach quantitative material in the future?

List any questions or problems. Contact your tutor or another person who can assist you with these.

Reading quantitative information

1. Academic texts containing quantitative material

Answer the following questions.

- How do you usually read academic texts that contain quantitative information?
- How do you usually read tables and graphs in your study materials?

2. Interpreting tables

Answer the following questions.

- What types of information are particularly suitable for tables?
- What kind of information needs to be included in a table?
- What are the advantages of using a table?

3. Analysing maps, plans and diagrams

Answer the following questions.

- What are the advantages of using maps, plans or diagrams?
- What types of information are particularly suitable for maps, plans or diagrams?
- Could the same information be conveyed in words?
- What kind of information needs to be included in the map, plan or diagram?
- Is it always necessary to include a scale?
- Is it useful to have both a caption and a title?
- What happens when too much detail is included?

4. Reviewing the whole article

Review the whole article to fully recall what you have read. Evaluate the quantitative representations in the article.

5. Reflecting on the exercise

Evaluate what you have gained from this exercise. Has it helped your reading? Has it changed how you will approach quantitative material in the future?

List any questions or problems.

An extract from 'Financial disadvantage in Australia 1990 to 2000'.
Executive Summary and Sections 1 and 2 of Part A[13]

20.1

Activity 1-6

Executive Summary

This report provides estimates of trends in poverty in Australia over the past decade. There is no consensus among researchers as to the best measure of poverty. In this report we have used a common measure of relative poverty, setting the poverty line at half the average family income of all Australians. In 2000, this poverty line for a single income couple with two children was $416 a week. This is after the payment of income tax and before the payment of housing costs.

In 2000, about one in every eight Australians lived in income poverty – 13 per cent of all Australians. The risk of being in poverty was higher for children than adults, with 14.9 per cent of children and 12.3 per cent of adults being in poverty. While progress was made in the first half of the 1990s in the fight against child poverty, these gains were fully eroded during the second half of the 1990s. Poverty among adults increased steadily during the decade. These changes led to a gradual increase in poverty among all Australians during the 1990s.

Sole parents remain the group at most risk of being in poverty, although there has been a pronounced fall in their risk of being in poverty since the beginning of the decade. Single people, particularly young singles, have fared worst in the past decade – with almost one in every five single people now being in poverty. There has been a slight increase in the poverty rate among couples with children, and it is this increase that underlies the minor rise in child poverty during the 1990s.

Government cash benefits are now the main family income source for almost six out of ten people in poverty. The poverty rate among those relying on government benefits has increased sharply, from 24 per cent at the start of the decade to 31 per cent by the end of the decade. More than half of all Australians who are unemployed live in a family that is poor.

While the growth of part-time, low paid and casual work has prompted concerns about the possible rise of working poverty, there has been little change in the poverty risk faced by families whose main income source is wages and salaries during the past decade. About 15 per cent of all Australians in poverty in 2000 lived in families whose main income source is wages and salaries, much the same as in 1990. While full-time employment generally protects a family from being in poverty, part-time employment is less likely to do so. With the growth of part-time employment, part-time workers make up a growing share of the poor.

Perhaps defying conventional wisdom, the poverty rate among women is now lower than for men. While the poverty risk for both men and women aged 15 years and over was exactly the same at the beginning of the 1990s, by 2000 men faced a slightly higher risk of being in poverty. This appears to be due to the sharp falls in poverty rates among female sole parents and the rising poverty rates among single males. Single males have fared much worse than single females as changes to industry structure and labour market conditions have impacted more harshly upon them during the past decade.

Poverty rates generally decrease with age, although for a large part of the decade poverty among those in the 50 to 64 year age bracket was higher than for people aged 25 to 49 or over 65. The key change during the past decade has been the steady increase in poverty rates among the aged. While the risk of being in poverty used to be much lower for the aged than for those of workforce age, now the risk is relatively similar.

A rather different picture is gained, however, if poverty is assessed after housing costs have been met. Because owner-occupiers have relatively low housing costs, their poverty rates fall as the focus shifts from a before to an after-housing picture. Conversely, the poverty rates of home purchasers and renters increase. The aged have high rates of outright home ownership and their risk of being in poverty has not changed during the 1990s if poverty is assessed after housing costs have been paid. On the other hand, poverty among adults aged 25 to 44 years has become more serious, with almost one-fifth of adults aged 25 to 44 years being in poverty on an after-housing basis.

Financial Disadvantage in Australia 1990 to 2000: The persistence of poverty in a decade of growth

vii

---

[13] Reprinted with permission from the Smith Family Australia www.smithfamily.com.au

The results by State fluctuate, and it is not clear whether the year-to-year changes reflect real variation or sampling error for the smaller states. NSW had the highest poverty rate in 2000, with 13.9 per cent of its residents being in poverty. Poverty has also increased in the other States, with only Queensland and Tasmania remaining relatively unchanged.

The depth of poverty does not appear to have changed greatly during the 1990s, with the average gap between a poor family's income and the poverty line increasing from $112 in 1990 to $118 in 2000 (after taking out the impact of inflation). However, it appears that the severity of poverty increased in the second half of the 1990s.

There is no agreement about where to set the poverty line and what equivalence scale to use. In Part C we present results for 12 possible poverty lines. In 11 of these 12 cases poverty rates increased during the 1990s, while in the remaining case poverty was stable. It thus appears that Australia did not manage to make any progress in the fight against poverty, despite falls in unemployment during the period.

1. Introduction

This is the second edition of an annual comprehensive report on financial disadvantage among Australians. The key goal of this annual report is to provide authoritative and up-to-date estimates of financial disadvantage (or 'poverty') in Australia. While last year's report (Harding and Szukalska 2000a) primarily focussed on poverty during a single year, this year's report provides estimates of trends in poverty over the past decade.

The concept of 'poverty' is vague and consequently the measurement of poverty is far from straightforward. There has been much discussion, over many years, about how best to define or characterise poverty (see Saunders 1994, pp. 221-30 and Osberg 2000, pp. 3-7 for recent reviews of the debate). Typically, poverty is regarded as a state of deprivation, a situation where one's standard of living has fallen below some acceptable minimum level. Absolute poverty occurs when families do not have sufficient income to pay for such basic necessities as food and housing. However, most poverty studies in developed countries have focussed on relative poverty, where a family's income is low relative to that of other families (for Australian examples, see the Commission of Inquiry into Poverty 1975; Johnson 1987; King 1997; ABS 1998).

Income poverty lines are levels of income. If a family's income (adjusted to take account of the family's size and structure) falls below the poverty line then the family is considered to be in poverty. In the main part of this study, we have used a common measure of relative poverty, setting the poverty line at half the average family income of all people in Australia. (This measure does not adjust income to take account of housing costs.) As a measure of relative poverty, the half average poverty line has the advantage of being relatively transparent, as it is explicitly linked to the income distribution (Osberg 2000, p. 4). It can also be updated in a natural and consistent manner by calculating the average for each point in time.

Some researchers prefer to set the poverty line at half the median (or middle) income of all people in Australia (ABS 1998). This implies a judgement that the living standards of the poor should be compared to those of people in the middle of the income distribution. The median also has the advantage of being less affected by extreme values than the average. For example, large increases in the highest incomes will cause the average to increase but alone will not have an effect on the median.

However, in this report we have used the 'half average income' poverty line, as it better captures relative deprivation in times of rising income inequality (see Harding and Greenwell 2001). As the top income earners become better off, then the poor are relatively worse off. That is, they are poorer in relative terms. Using the 'half average income' line thus denotes acceptance of the proposition that the living standards of the poor should be measured against the living standards of all of the population, including the very affluent.

The issues surrounding the way in which poverty is measured are discussed further in Part B. Measurement of poverty is also dependent upon the quality of data used. In this case, our data sources are the Income Survey confidentialised unit record files, released by the Australian Bureau of Statistics. Results are derived from surveys conducted in 1990, 1994-95, 1995-96, 1997-98, and 1999-00 but throughout the report the years are referred to as 1990, 1995, 1996, 1998 and 2000 for simplicity. There are some concerns about the comparability of the surveys conducted after the mid 1990s with that conducted in 1990. Again, these issues are explored in more detail in Part B.

Because there is no consensus about the most appropriate poverty line to use, Part C provides estimates of poverty trends using a range of poverty lines, both before and after taking account of housing costs.

In Part A, Section 2 examines trends in aggregate poverty between 1990 and 2000, while Section 3 undertakes further analysis by family type. Section 4 looks at whether there have been changes in the major income sources of families in poverty, while Section 5 explores the labour force and educational characteristics of families in poverty. Section 6 disaggregates the poverty picture by age and gender, while Section 7 explores the impact of housing tenure and state of residence. Section 8 considers whether the depth of poverty in Australia has changed – how far below the poverty line those families in poverty actually are. Finally, Section 9 summarises the findings of this report.

In this report, we define dependent children to mean all children aged less than 15 and all 15 to 24 year olds engaged in full-time study and still living at home with their parents, in accordance with the ABS definition (ABS 1999, p. 68). Adults is defined as the residual. That is, the number of adults equals the total number of people in the Australian population minus the number of dependent children. The head of the family is the ABS 'reference person'. For readability we use the term family to mean the ABS income unit.

What is Poverty?

It is hard to gain agreement about how poverty should be defined and measured in our society. For some people poverty means that a family cannot afford to buy food or adequate shelter. But in industrial economies like Australia a relative poverty definition is more commonly used. In this study we have set the main poverty line at half the average family income of all Australians. Family income has been adjusted to take different family size and composition into account, using the Henderson equivalence scales.

Using this method, we estimate that in 2000 the poverty line for a single income couple with two children was $416 a week. This means that the 'cash in the hand' of such a family has to be more than $416 a week for this family not to be in poverty. Cash income is measured as all income received from such sources as wages and investments, plus cash benefits from government such as the age pension, minus any income tax paid. This is called disposable income.

The poverty line varies for different types of families, because larger families need more income to survive than smaller families. For example, for a single employed person the poverty line is $225 a week.

2. Who is in poverty today?

The latest ABS data suggest that almost one in every eight Australians live in income poverty today, when the poverty line is set at half the average family income of all Australians (Figure 1). This represents 2.4 million people, or 13 per cent of the population. Last year's report showed that the risk of being in poverty is higher for children than adults, and the same result was evident in 2000 – with 14.9 per cent of all dependent children in poverty compared with 12.3 per cent of adults.

Has this picture changed over the past decade? Comparison with 1990 suggests that poverty has increased slightly over the 1990s (Table 1). For children, there is a decline in poverty rates between the beginning and the middle of the decade and then an apparent increase in the second half of the decade. For adults, the picture is quite different and appears to be one of consistent but slow increase in the risk of poverty. Because adults so greatly outnumber children, the pattern for adults prevails and results in the slow but steady increase in poverty rates among all Australians over the 1990s (Figure 2).

Figure 1   Estimated number of Australians in poverty in 2000ª
2,432,000 or 13 per cent

Adults
1,688,000
(poverty rate 12.3%)

Dependent Childrenᵇ
743,000
(poverty rate 14.9%)

Notes:

a) Using the before-housing half average income poverty line (Henderson equivalence scale). See p.29 for further explanation.

b) Dependent children means all children aged less than 15 and all 15 to 24 year olds engaged in full-time study and still living at home.

Figure 2   Estimated poverty rates, 1990 to 2000ª

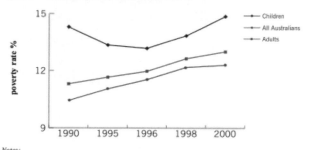

Notes:
a) Using the before-housing half average income poverty line (Henderson equivalence scale).

Table 1   Estimated poverty rates[a] and other characteristics of Australians, 1990 to 2000[b]

	1990	1995	1996	1998	2000
Half average income poverty line					
Poverty rates					
Children	14.3	13.3	13.1	13.8	14.9
Adults	10.4	11.0	11.5	12.2	12.3
All Australians	11.3	11.7	12.0	12.6	13.0
Number in poverty[c] '000					
Children	511	633	627	684	743
Adults	1261	1427	1510	1633	1688
All Australians	1772	2060	2137	2317	2432
Real (inflation adjusted) equivalent disposable incomes of the:[d]					
Poor	$224	$229	$233	$250	$262
Middle (median)	$686	$669	$650	$693	$723
Average (mean)	$766	$759	$747	$798	$832
95th percentile	$1482	$1514	$1490	$1611	$1654
Ratio between incomes of the:					
Middle/poor	3.06	2.92	2.79	2.77	2.76
Average/poor	3.42	3.31	3.20	3.20	3.18
Half median income poverty line					
Poverty rates					
Children	9.0	8.4	8.7	8.5	9.6
Adults	8.0	8.2	8.5	8.4	8.4
All Australians	8.2	8.2	8.6	8.4	8.7

Notes:

a) Using the before-housing half average income poverty line (Henderson equivalence scale).

b) Results are derived from surveys conducted in 1990, 1994-95, 1995-96, 1997-98, 1999-00 but throughout the report the years are referred to as 1990, 1995, 1996, 1998 and 2000 for simplicity.

c) The increasing number of people in poverty is due to two factors – the increasing proportion of people in poverty and the increasing population.

d) These are 'equivalent' incomes for all families (weighted by the number of people). 'Equivalent' incomes are adjusted for the needs of the family, and vary with the number and labour force status of the adults and the number and age of children. All dollars in this report are 2000 dollars, with values for earlier years inflated by the Consumer Price Index. The 'poor' here means those defined as poor using the half average income poverty line, and the figures given are the average incomes for all poor people. The 'middle' means the median family income and the 'average' indicates the mean family income.

These results suggest a discernable increase in poverty over the 1990s, when using the 'half average income' poverty line. But has this been due to a decline in the incomes of the poor? Or to strong economic growth lifting average incomes for those in work and thus the poverty line? Or is movement at the top of the income distribution affecting the average income and thus the poverty line? Figure 3 indicates that the average incomes of poor families, after taking out the impact of inflation, have increased by $38 a week during the 1990s.

How does this growth compare with the incomes of non-poor families? Figure 3 also shows the change in median (middle) family incomes over this period, and suggests that there has also been a slight increase in median family incomes, of $37 a week between 1990 and 2000. Finally, Figure 3 traces the change in average Australian incomes over the past two decades. It shows that average

215

incomes have increased by $66 a week – almost twice as much as for middle and poor families. As a result of these differential growth rates, the gap between middle and average incomes has been growing, up from $80 in 1990 to $109 in 2000.

While average incomes have increased strongly, this growth appears to have been primarily driven by increases at the top end of the income distribution, as shown by the rising average real incomes of those at the 95th percentile of the income distribution indicated in Table 1. The incomes of those at the 95th percentile have increased by $172 a week during the 1990s.

The 1990s have thus seen a widening gap between the incomes of the poor and the incomes of the very affluent, rather than between the incomes of the poor and the incomes of middle Australian families. It is the rising incomes of the affluent that are generating much of the growth in the half average income poverty line, and thus the increase in poverty rates apparent in the 1990s.

This divergence between the increases in middle family incomes and incomes at the top end means that a somewhat different impression of poverty trends is gained if the poverty line is set at half of middle family income rather than half of average family income. If the poverty line is set at half median income rather than half average income, poverty has remained relatively stable over the 1990s. As the lower shaded rows in Table 1 indicate, using a half median income poverty line results in poverty remaining at 8.2 per cent in 1990 and 1995, and then rising to 8.7 per cent in 2000.

Irrespective of the poverty line used, both sets of results indicate that Australia has not been successful in reducing poverty in the 1990s, despite falling unemployment.

Figure 3   Trends in poor, middle, average and top incomes, after adjustment for inflation, 1990 to 2000[a]

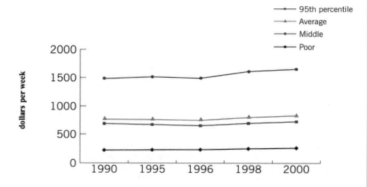

Notes:

a) All figures are for equivalent disposable family income, adjusted by the CPI to 2000 dollars. 'Poor' families are those in poverty using the Henderson half average income poverty line.

Previewing: questions to ask and notes on parts of the report

20.2

Activity 2

Part of report	Questions to ask and notes
Author	Who is the author? *Ann Harding is Director of NATSEM at the University of Canberra.* Who are the Smith Family and NATSEM? The Smith family researches different forms of disadvantage. NATSEM is the National Centre for Social and Economic Modeling.
Title and subtitle	Financial disadvantage in Australia 1990 to 2000: The persistence of poverty in a decade of growth This is an executive summary of the full report.
Headings	An executive summary of the report Who is in poverty today?
Introduction	This report provides estimates of trends in poverty in Australia over the past decade. There is no consensus among researchers as to the best measure of poverty.
Conclusion	Irrespective of the poverty line used, both sets of results indicate that Australia has not been successful in reducing poverty in the 1990s, despite falling unemployment.
Boxed information	The text in the highlighted box entitled 'What is Poverty?' describes how the term poverty is used in this article. **Questions to ask about 'WHAT IS POVERTY?'** How would statisticians have calculated 'half the average income for all Australians'? Where would statisticians have located the data for this calculation? How does the income for a single employed person in poverty compare with a family with two children? Why is the income for a single person more than half that for a family? What is the Henderson index? *The Henderson Index was developed by Professor R.F. Henderson in the 1970s, and 'calculates the amount of money people need to cover their basic living costs and maintain a minimum standard of living'[14].*
Mathematical representations	**Pie chart** Estimated number of Australians in poverty in 2000 = 2,432,000 or 13%)

[14] http://www.rpdc.tas.gov.au/soer/glossary/155/index.php

	Table Estimated poverty rates and other characteristics of Australians, 1900 to 2000 **Graphs**: Estimated poverty rates, 1900 to 2000 Trends in poor, middle, average and top incomes, after adjustment for inflation, 1900 to 2000

Apply the Five Step Framework to Table 1
20.3

'Estimated poverty rates and other characteristics of Australians, 1990 to 2000'.

Activity 5

Questions

Step 1: Getting started

Q1.1: What is the general topic being examined?

Q1.2: As well as poverty rates, what kinds of characteristics are used to make comparisons in the table?

Q1.3: Where does the table come from? What evidence is there that the information is reliable?

Terms and footnotes

Q1.4: How is an average (mean) income calculated from a set of incomes?

Q1.5: What is meant by 'half average income poverty line'?

Q1.6: How is the median income worked out from a set of incomes? What does it represent?

Q1.7: What is meant by 'half median income poverty line'?

Q1.8: How are 'children' defined?

Q1.9: To make valid comparisons the incomes for the years 1990 to 1998 have been adjusted to be reported as 2000 dollars (see footnote d below the table). What does this mean?

Step 2: WHAT do the numbers mean?

There are two main sections to this table that give data for different aspects of poverty. The first is based on ''half average income poverty line' and the second 'half median income poverty line'.

A. 'Half average income poverty line'

Q2.1: In the first column of the table for poverty rates, what is the meaning of the number 14.3?

Q2.2: In the last column of the table for 'Number in poverty', what is the meaning of the number 743?

Q2.3: In the last column of the table for real (inflation adjusted) equivalent disposable incomes, what are the meanings of the numbers 723 and 832?

Q2.4: In the last column of the table for real (inflation adjusted) equivalent disposable incomes, what are the meanings of the numbers 2.76 and 3.18?

B. 'Half median income poverty line'

Q2.5   What is the meaning of the number 9.0 in the first column of the table for poverty rates?

Q2.6: What is the meaning of the number 8.7 in the last column of the table for poverty rates?

Step 3: HOW do the numbers change?

A. 'Half average income poverty line'

Q3.1: For which year was the poverty rate for children (as measured by the 'half average income poverty line')
the least? .... the most? ....

How did the poverty rate for children change between 1990 and 2000?

Increased   Decreased   Stayed about the same   Fluctuated
Other: --

Q3.2: For which year was the poverty rate for adults (as measured by the 'half average income poverty line')
the least? .... the most? ....

How did the poverty rate for adults change between 1990 and 2000?

Increased   Decreased   Stayed about the same   Fluctuated
Other: --

B. 'Half median income poverty line'

Q3.3: For which year was the poverty rate (as measured by 'half median poverty line') for children
the least? .... the most? ....

How did the poverty rate for children change between 1990 and 2000?

Increased   Decreased   Stayed about the same   Fluctuated
Other: ....

Q3.4: For which year was the poverty rate for adults as measured by the 'half median income poverty line'
the least? .... the most? ....

How did the poverty rate for adults change between 1990 and 2000?

Increased   Decreased   Stayed about the same   Fluctuated
Other: ....

C. Numbers in poverty

Q3.5: For which year was the number of children in poverty (as measured by the 'half average income poverty line')
the least? .... the most? ....

How did the number of children in poverty change between 1990 and 2000?

Increased   Decreased   Stayed about the same   Fluctuated
Other: ....

Q3.6: For which year was the number of adults in poverty
the least? .... the most? ....

How did the number of adults in poverty change between 1990 and 2000?

Increased   Decreased   Stayed about the same   Fluctuated
Other: ....

Step 4: WHERE are the differences?

In Step 3 you will have noticed some changes for particular categories over time. In Step 4 some of these changes are compared. They might both increase, or both decrease, change in the same way, change in opposite directions or fluctuate in some other ways. ·

Q4.1:   For the half average income poverty line

Compare the changes over time for children, adults and all Australians to see the similarities and differences in the ways they change. What do you notice?

Q4.2:   For the half median income poverty line

Compare the changes over time for children, adults and all Australians to see the similarities and differences in the ways they change. What do you notice?

Q4.3:   What are the main differences and similarities for the half average income poverty line and half median income poverty line that you observed in questions 4.1.and 4.2?

Step 5: WHY do the numbers change?

Use the text and any other available sources to help you give responses to these questions:

Q5.1:   What kinds of environmental, social and economic factors might have influenced the changes in poverty that you have seen in this table?

Apply Five Step Framework to the graph in Figure 3 'Trends in poor, middle average and top incomes, after adjustment for inflation, 1990 to 2000a'. Questions

20.4

Activity 6

Line Graph: Trends in poor, middle average and top incomes, after adjustment for inflation, 1990 to 2000a

This graph shows visually some data extracted from the table. You can see that the graph allows us to make comparisons but we cannot see the detail that is available in a table. The framework exercise below helps you to develop strategies for interpreting a graph.

Step 1: Getting started

Q1.1: What is the general topic being examined?

Q1.2: To what does the 'a' refer in the title of the graph?

Q1.3: What are the four categories used to make comparisons?

Q1.4: What evidence is there that the information is reliable? Where does the table come from?

Terms and footnotes

Q1.5: From the text how is 'poor' defined in this context?

Q1.6: In this context what is meant by middle (also called the median and 50th percentile)?

Q1.7: In this context what is meant by average?

Q1.8: For a set of data the 95th percentile is the number below which 95% of the data lie. What precisely does it mean in this context?

Q1.9: In this context what is meant by adjusted for inflation?

Q1.10: In what measure is the vertical axis calibrated?

Q1.11: How is the horizontal axis calibrated?

Step 2: WHAT do the numbers mean?

Firstly look at the legend to distinguish between the different lines.

Q2.1: From the graph, approximately how many dollars per week were the poor people earning in 1990?

Q2.2: Approximately how many dollars per week were the middle people earning in 1995?

Q2.3: Approximately how many dollars per week were the average people earning in 1996?

Q2.4: Approximately how many dollars per week were the 95th percentile (top 5%) people earning in 2000?

Step 3: HOW do they change?

From the graph answer the following questions as accurately as you can

Q3.1: For which year was the income for the 95th percentile (top 5%)
the least? .... the most? ....

How did the income for the top 5% change between 1990 and 2000?

Increased   Decreased   Stayed about the same   Fluctuated

Other: --

Q3.2: For which year was the income for the average people
the least? .... the most? ....

How did the income for the average people change between 1990 and 2000?

Increased   Decreased   Stayed about the same   Fluctuated

Other: _____

Q3.3: For which year was the income for the middle people
the least? .... the most? ....

How did the income for the middle people change between 1990 and 2000?

Increased   Decreased   Stayed about the same   Fluctuated

Other: _____

Q3.4: For which year was the income for the poor people
the least? .... the most? ....

How did the income for the poor people change between 1990 and 2000?

Increased   Decreased   Stayed about the same   Fluctuated

Other: _____

Step 4: WHERE are the differences?

In Step 3 you will have noticed some changes for particular categories over time. In Step 4 some of these changes will be compared. They might both increase, or both decrease, change in the same way, change in opposite directions or fluctuate in some other ways.

Q4.1: What is the relationship between the 95th percentile and the average income levels illustrated in the graph?

Q4.2: What is the relationship between the graphs of the average and poor people's income?

Step 5: WHY do they change?

Use the text and any other available sources to help you respond to these questions:

Q5.1: What kinds of environmental, social and economic factors might have influenced the changes in income that you have seen in this graph?

CHAPTER 6

Writing essays

Essays are an important component of the required work in most disciplines at university. As essays require an extended period of planning and production, it is advisable to begin the first exercises in this chapter well in advance of the due date for your essay. The exercises in this chapter are not intended to represent clearly delineated stages in the essay writing process. In reality, from your first thoughts about the topic your essay starts evolving, and as you read and write your understanding of the topic will become more complex. As this occurs your manner of developing and presenting the essay will also become more sophisticated.

The exercises in this chapter urge you:

- to choose and analyse your essay question carefully and to refer back frequently to this analysis so that relevance is maintained;

–   to read and assess other essays so that you understand clearly what is expected of you in essay writing;

–   to write, write and keep writing your own ideas in your own words, before and during your research and use these notes to stimulate and clarify your thinking on the essay.

> An essay is constructed like a freight train. The argument is the engine, supplying power and direction and pulling the rest behind it. The cars are the paragraphs, each carrying a topic sentence and a load of specific sentences; the couplings are transitions holding the cars together, and the caboose is the conclusion, letting the reader know that the essay has come to an end. It is important to realise that the train exists to carry the freight: the essay is the vehicle for getting the meaningful specifics of your topic to the reader in an orderly condition, so they can unload and use them.[1]

---

[1]   Adapted from Frank Morgan, 1968, *Here and now: an approach to writing through perception*, Harcourt, Brace & World, p. 153.

21. Understanding the nature of university essays
- The structure of essays
- The sample essay
  - read the essay question
  - preview the essay
  - read the essay
- The organisation of the essay
- The introduction
- The conclusion
- The paragraphing
  - paragraphs 2 and 3
  - paragraphs 4 to 6
  - paragraph 7
  - paragraph 7 to 11
  - the conclusion
- Essay presentation
- Tutor's comments on the essay
- Compare this essay to your previous essays
- Refer back to this essay

22. Understanding tutor's expectations and your objectives
- Expectations of university essays
  - what you think is expected
  - information on the essay
  - information on what is expected
  - differences in expectations
- Your objectives for essay writing

23. Choosing an essay question
- Information on the essay
- Choosing the best essay question
  - the list of essay questions
  - allow time to choose
- Analyse the essay question

24. Analysing an essay question
- The essay writing process
  - your approach to essay questions
  - your approach to essay writing
  - the circular model of essay writing
- Selecting a question
- Analysing a question
- Initial analysis of the question
  - write out your analysis
- Revised analysis of the question

Writing essays

27. Editing the final draft
- The creative and editing aspects of essay writing
- University essays
  - expectations of your tutor
  - your audience
  - information on essays
- A process for editing essays
  - re-read the essay question
  - preview the essay
  - read essay for positive aspects
  - give first impressions
- The introduction
  - what an introduction should contain
  - examine and comment on the introduction
- The conclusion
  - what a conclusion should contain
  - examine the conclusion
- The organisation of the essay
  - examine the overall organisation of the essay
  - examine paragraph structure
  - examine transitions or links
- Referencing
  - what is expected
  - examine the referencing
- The mechanics of the essay
  - what is expected
  - examine the mechanics
- Evaluate the essay overall
- Evaluate essay writing skills

25. Researching information
- Previous research situations
- Primary and secondary sources
- Research skills and methods
- Problems with research
- Critical thinking in the research process

26. Writing the first draft
- The essay writing process
  - your essay writing process
  - different approaches to essay writing
  - the creative and editing aspects of essay writing
- Assessing progress on the essay
- The argument and structure of essays
  - your argument and structure
  - verbalising and structuring your argument
  - free writing your argument
  - sharing your written work
- The importance of writing to you
- Strategies to improve writing
- Using the free writing piece

21. Understanding the nature of university essays

Introduction

Are you just beginning university study and have to write your first essay? You may have previously written essays in secondary school or for a course you took, but you now want to know what is expected of you in university essays. Perhaps you want to see an example of a finished university essay before beginning your own.

This exercise is designed to help you understand the nature of university essays. A first year university essay has been included for you to read and comment on. However, this represents one type of university essay, and you should refer to the following exercise for information on the different types of essays that result from different types of questions. In this exercise you are asked to read the essay, and then you are guided step by step through it. Finally, you are provided with information on the shape, structure and functional stages of essays.

It is very important to read through the essay yourself before you read the notes on it. You will be referred back to this essay as you work through the other exercises in this chapter.

Note that when examining the sample essay in this exercise you are asked to work through steps that are similar to those in Exercise 18, 'Reading in depth'.

This exercise encourages you

- to develop an understanding of the nature of the university essay genre;

- to examine the structural and functional stages of a university essay.

Materials

21.1   Essay structure: different pictorial representations

21.2   Essay structure: introduction, body and conclusion

21.3   Essay structure: functional stages

21.4   Example of a student essay

21.5   Essay outline: functional stages

21.6   Connecting the conclusion to the body of the essay

21.7   Essay marking guide

Approximate time

45 minutes

Reading

Marshall & Rowland, 2006, pp. 87–92.

Learning activities

Activity 1   The structure of essays

21.1
21.2

Examine the attached graphics, 'Essay structure: different pictorial representations', 'Essay structure: introduction, body and conclusion', and note that university essays should include:

- an introduction, a body and a conclusion;
- an introduction that states the thesis and presents the supporting premises or reasons (or the main points) in the order that they will be covered in the body;
- a conclusion that restates the thesis and draws together the supporting premises or reasons;
- transitions indicating the links between paragraphs and sections.

21.3

Refer to the attached graphic, 'Essay structure: functional stages', and note that depending on the type of essay question, introductions in university level essays usually include the following stages:

- an introduction to the essay question or topic and background information (context);

- a summary of the content that will be covered in the essay;

- a statement of the argument (thesis and supporting premises), the viewpoint presented and the conclusions reached.

The above points apply to persuasive or argumentative essays. Other essays may require a statement of purpose, while other essays may require a statement of scope. Also the order of the stages in the introduction can also vary.

Activity 2   The sample essay

Read the essay question

21.4

Read the attached example essay question, 'Example of a student essay', and take a few minutes to consider how you might answer this question.

Preview the essay

Before you read the essay in depth, preview the example essay as outlined in Chapter 4, 'Reading'. Read the introduction and conclusion first.

Read the essay

21.4

Read the entire sample essay.

This essay was selected as it features many of the structural and functional stages of a 'good' university essay. This essay is constructed like a freight train. If you haven't already done so read the quotation at the beginning of this chapter.

Note that the paragraphs in the sample essay have been numbered to help you work through this exercise. Note that it is not the convention to number paragraphs in your essays.

Activity 3 — The organisation of the essay

Examine the entire essay and answer the following questions.

- Do the introduction and the conclusion explain the organisation or structure of the essay?

- How many parts are there to the essay, and where does each part begin and end? In other words, which paragraphs answer the first and second parts of the question?

- How many sections are there to the essay and where does each section begin and end? In other words, which paragraphs develop particular themes?

Part 1 (paragraphs 2 to 20) answers the question, 'What is a paradigm according to Kuhn?'.

Part 2 (paragraphs 7 to 11) gives an example of a paradigm (postmodernism) in cultural studies.

Section 1 comprises paragraphs 2 and 3, section 2 comprises paragraphs 4, 5 and 6, and section 3 comprises paragraphs 7 to 11.

Activity 4   The introduction

21.5

Read the attached information, 'Essay outline: Functional stages' and then read the introductory paragraph.

Note that the introduction to the essay:

–   indicates the purpose of the essay;

> I will briefly examine the concept of a scientific paradigm as conceived by Thomas Kuhn.

–   outlines the essay or explains the order in which the different aspects of the topic will be treated;

> For this purpose I will consider work by Kuhn himself, as well as work about him by Alan Chalmers, Phillip Cooke and Keith Roby. I will then apply the five components of a scientific paradigm to the concept of postmodernism ...

The writer has divided the body of the essay into two parts. The first part presents her understanding of the theories of Kuhn and three other thinkers on the concept of a paradigm. The second part applies the components of a paradigm to the concept of postmodernism.

–   states the thesis.

> This examination leads me to the thesis that postmodernism is a paradigm and its current influence is such that it is the dominant paradigm in cultural studies.

Activity 5   The conclusion

Read the concluding paragraph.

Note that the conclusion to the essay:

–   restates the thesis;

> I believe that the concept of a paradigm, as conceived by Thomas Kuhn, is applicable to postmodernism as a dominant paradigm within the Humanities.

    – summarises the supporting premises and draws the information together;

> This essay has shown that the components of a paradigm can all be transcribed onto the theory of postmodernism ... which focus it as a dominant force.

    – qualifies the thesis and suggests directions for future research.

> However, as a final point, it should be noted that through its very premises, postmodernism challenges the development and maintenance of paradigms, and could demand a reworking of this concept in the future.

Activity 6   The paragraphing

Paragraphs 2 and 3

Each paragraph contains one supporting premise or key point. Read paragraphs 2 and 3 of the essay.

Can you identify what the writer is doing in paragraph 2?

Paragraph 2 explains to the reader what a paradigm is. The second sentence defines a paradigm and the quote emphasises this definition.

Can you identify what the writer is doing in paragraph 3?

Paragraph 3 explains that paradigms are established and replaced in a cycle of stages, which include dominance, crisis and revolution.

Paragraphs 4 to 6

Read paragraphs 4 to 6 (the first section of the essay).

The first sentence in paragraph 4 explains what these paragraphs will discuss.

> In his book *What is this thing called science?* (1976), Chalmers outlines five general components of the Kuhn paradigm.

The first sentence in paragraph 5 links the paragraphs ('the fourth component') and sets out a key point.

> The fourth component of a Kuhn paradigm is that metaphysical beliefs guide the work within a paradigm, equally as much as scientific beliefs.

The key point is developed by the inclusion of a quote and a well-chosen example.

Paragraph 7

Read paragraph 7, the introductory paragraph to the second part of the essay. Paragraph 7 is a more complex paragraph than the previous paragraphs and is an excellent example of how a paragraph can be developed.

Paragraph 7 introduces the second part of the essay

Restate thesis	Postmodernism, can be seen to operate as a dominant paradigm within present academic structures, particularly in the Humanities. I shall
State outline	now consider the concept of post modernism, focusing on its relation to the components of a paradigm, as summarised by Chalmers, and outlined above. I do not attempt a complete
State scope	review of post modernism or of those cultural components grouped within the concept, but instead briefly observe its relation to the epistemology of the academic 'world'. As Jean-
Define term	Francois Lyotard (1992: 138) suggests: ...the word *postmodern*... is the condition of knowledge in the most highly developed societies.
Elaboration of definition	Postmodernism proposes a model for the present cultural state, which envelopes cultural activity, thought and diversity (at least within 'highly developed societies'), and is accepting of different forms of the 'subject' or 'individual', as indicative of its inherent plurality.

Paragraphs 7 to 11

Read paragraphs 7 to 11 and identify the supporting premises or key points in the paragraphs, the transitions or links between paragraphs, and any references back to the thesis.

The conclusion

21.6 Refer to the attached material, 'Connecting the conclusion to the body of the essay'. Note how the conclusion relates to the introduction and the body of the essay, and how each sentence in the conclusion relates to the parts of the essay and draws out the supporting premises and key points.

Activity 7   Essay presentation

Examine the presentation of the essay. Note that the essay has a cover sheet and is clearly set out. Although the student's name has been provided, the tutor's name has been deliberately omitted.

Activity 8   Tutor's comments on the essay

The tutor assessed and provided feedback on the essay using an essay marking guide. Read the tutor's comments on the essay, 'Essay marking guide'.

This marking guide outlines the assessment criteria. Note that it differs from the marking guide included in Exercise 22.

Would you have made the same comments on this essay? Remember, that each tutor will note different features of an essay. Can you find other aspects of this essay worth noting that the tutor has missed?

Activity 9   Compare this essay to your previous essays

Consider previous essays that you have written and assess your performance. Compare what was expected of you in previous essays with what was expected in this essay. In your learning log, discuss the skills that you need to develop or refine for upcoming essays you have to write.

Use this sample essay as a guide as you write your own essays.

Activity 10   Refer back to this essay

Refer to this exercise as you work through this chapter, particularly for Exercise 28, 'Editing the final draft'. Use this example essay and the attached materials to help you edit your essays.

Understanding the nature of university essays

Compare the sample essay with your previous essays

Consider previous essays that you have written and assess your performance. Compare what was expected of you in previous essays with what was expected in this essay. Discuss the skills that you need to develop or refine for upcoming essays you have to write.

Essay structure:
different pictorial representations

21.1

Activity 1

1. Amount of information

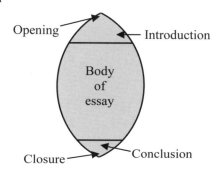

2. Links within the essay

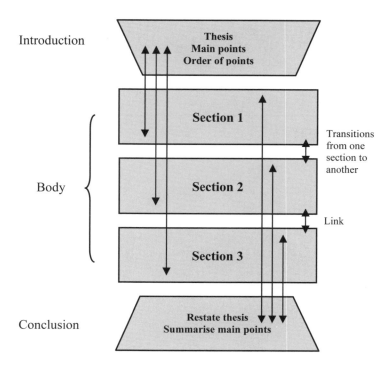

Essay structure:
introduction, body and conclusion

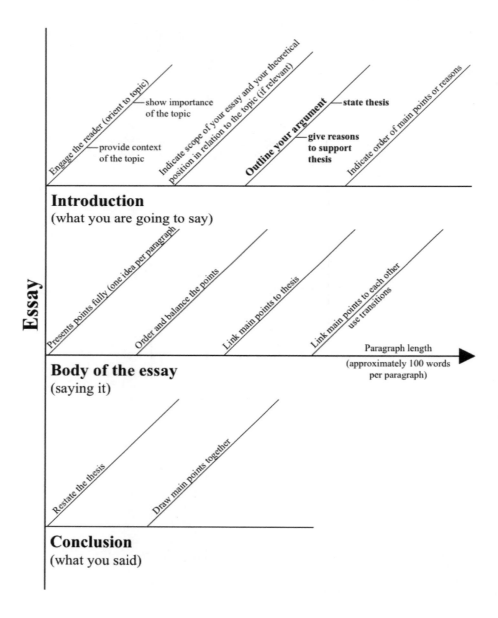

Essay

Introduction
(what you are going to say)

Engage the reader (orient to topic)

—show importance
of the topic

—provide context
of the topic

Indicate scope of your essay and your theoretical
position in relation to the topic (if relevant)

Outline your argument

—state thesis

—give reasons
to support
thesis

Indicate order of main points or reasons

Body of the essay
(saying it)

Presents points fully (one idea per paragraph)

Order and balance the points

Link main points to thesis

Link main points to each other
use transitions

Paragraph length
(approximately 100 words
per paragraph)

Conclusion
(what you said)

Restate the thesis

Draw main points together

Essay structure: functional stages[2]

21.3

Activity 1

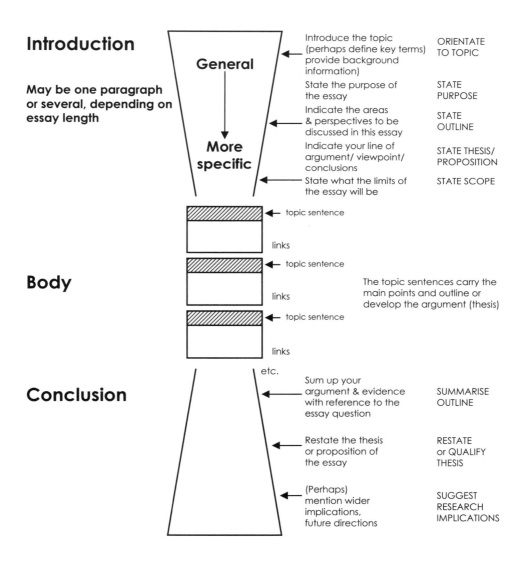

Introduction

May be one paragraph
or several, depending on
essay length

General

↓

More
specific

Introduce the topic
(perhaps define key terms)
provide background
information)

ORIENTATE
TO TOPIC

State the purpose of
the essay

STATE
PURPOSE

Indicate the areas
& perspectives to be
discussed in this essay

STATE
OUTLINE

Indicate your line of
argument/ viewpoint/
conclusions

STATE THESIS/
PROPOSITION

State what the limits of
the essay will be

STATE SCOPE

Body

topic sentence

links

topic sentence

links

topic sentence

links

etc.

The topic sentences carry the
main points and outline or
develop the argument (thesis)

Conclusion

Sum up your
argument & evidence
with reference to the
essay question

SUMMARISE
OUTLINE

Restate the thesis
or proposition of
the essay

RESTATE
or QUALIFY
THESIS

(Perhaps)
mention wider
implications,
future directions

SUGGEST
RESEARCH
IMPLICATIONS

---

[2]   Adapted from Essay Writing materials by Language & Learning Services, Monash University.

241

Example of student essay[3]

Murdoch University

Structure, Thought and Reality
A105

Christy Newman

Section A: question 2

What is a paradigm according to Kuhn? Give an example
of a paradigm from one of the disciplines you are studying.

---

[3] This essay was written by Dr Christy Newman in 1994 when she was a first year student
taking a first semester foundation course at Murdoch University. Note that there are some
inconsistencies in the student's spelling and occasional referencing errors. Dr Christy Newman
currently works for the University of NSW.

1. In this essay I will briefly examine the concept of a scientific paradigm as conceived by Thomas Kuhn. For this purpose I will consider work by Kuhn himself, as well as work about him by Alan Chalmers, Phillip Cooke and Keith Roby. I will then apply the five components of a scientific paradigm to the concept of post-modernism, which is as influential in my studies of the Humanities and Social sciences as certain scientific paradigms are for the Science student. This examination leads me to the thesis that postmodernism is a paradigm and its current influence is such that it is the dominant paradigm in cultural studies.

2. Thomas Kuhn, in his book *The Structure of Scientific Revolutions* (1970) outlined a revolutionary way of viewing the history of science, and indeed of viewing the development of other academic disciplines. He wrote that science was grouped, and had always been grouped, into 'paradigms' of research, and that these paradigms were the constructed presuppositions that a group of scientists carried with them when researching the 'world' around them. As Alan Chalmers (1976: 90) summarises,

> A paradigm is made up of the general theoretical assumptions and laws and techniques for their application that the members of a particular scientific community adopt.

Kuhn's main point in identifying specific paradigms and claiming that all science was inherently constructed through a paradigm, was to expose the processes involved in scientific research.

3. Kuhn believed that a cycle underlay this process of creating paradigms, which was identifiable in specific stages. The first stage occurs when a particular paradigm is accepted as the most accurate base of research which holds the 'key' to the answers sought. The second occurs when peculiarities or unexpected information are found, and become too disturbing to be ignored. This creates a state of crisis where the base paradigm is severely threatened as the accepted state of 'truth' or 'normality'. This crisis then becomes a 'revolution' where the entire state of belief is challenged by a new paradigm which seems to hold a better, more accessible key to the answers. This then gradually establishes the new paradigm as superior to the old, until it becomes the new base structure of research and susceptible to its own crisis and revolution.

4. In his book *What is this thing called science?* (1976), Chalmers outlines five general components of the Kuhn paradigm. The first is that it contains 'explicitly stated laws and theoretical assumptions' (1976: 90). These are the basis of the mode of research that a scientist or group of scientists work within. The second and third components, state that it will include:

standard ways of applying the fundamental laws to a variety of types of situations... instrumentation and instrumental techniques necessary for bringing the laws of the paradigm to bear on the real world will also be included in the paradigm.(1976: 90)

Kuhn points out that after a paradigm 'revolution', these last components of the paradigm are unlikely to change as much as the first component. That is, the actual ways and means of working within science change less than do the belief structures.

5. The fourth component of a Kuhn paradigm is that metaphysical beliefs guide the work within a paradigm, equally as much as scientific beliefs. Keith Roby in the book *Challenges for Einstein's Children* (1984:22) states

    As Kuhn suggests in his analysis of fundamental science the 'paradigm'...which the scientist tacitly acquired through his training, includes metaphysical commitments - that is to the search for knowledge as a prime value, to a certain image of nature, to beliefs in order and rationality.

For example, Albert Einstein, initiated a revolution of the scientific paradigm, by working on research which challenged and disproved it. His work on nuclear power was based on scientific and theoretical beliefs which were eventually proved true, and the metaphysical component of his research was the belief in human progress and nuclear power as a part of that progress.

6. The final component of a paradigm is that it will 'contain some very general methodological prescriptions such as making serious attempts to match the paradigm with nature' (Chalmers, 1976: 90), so that it will remain the accepted format. Phillip Cooke writes that Kuhn's paradigms explain why scientific breakthroughs are so often disputed and disregarded:

    Scientific discoveries were sometimes made by accident by a wild guess or even mystical belief. When such discoveries had been tested and found to be valid the scientist often had difficulty in convincing his peers of their validity, particularly where the new knowledge challenged the prevailing professional consensus.

The concept of the paradigm was developed by Kuhn to expose the structure of the scientific world and its 'ways' of developing knowledge. It is my belief that this concept need not only apply to science, but also to other disciplines.

7. Postmodernism, can be seen to operate as a dominant paradigm within present academic structures, particularly in the Humanities. I shall now consider the concept of post modernism, focusing on its relation to the components of a paradigm, as summarised by Chalmers, and outlined above. I do not attempt a complete review of post modernism or of those cultural components grouped within

244

the concept, but instead briefly observe its relation to the epistemology of the academic 'world'. As Jean-Francois Lyotard (1992: 138) suggests:

> ...the word *postmodern*... is the condition of knowledge in the most highly developed societies.

Postmodernism proposes a model for the present cultural state, which envelopes cultural activity, thought and diversity (at least within 'highly developed societies'), and is accepting of different forms of the 'subject' or 'individual', as indicative of its inherent plurality.

8.   As defined above post modernism fulfils the 'requirements' of a paradigm which were previously outlined, but in a more general sense than do scientific paradigms. The first component of a paradigm is its 'explicitly stated laws and assumptions' (Chalmers, 1976:91). Although the nature of post modernism is rigorously debated rather than explicitly stated, it does assume certain accepted characteristics. These are based upon its removal or progression away from Modernism. Silverman argues:

> The meaning and function of postmodernism is to operate at places of closure, at the limits of modernist productions and practices, at the margins of what proclaims itself to be new and a break with tradition, and at the multiple edges of these claims to self-consciousness and auto-reflection. Post modernism... examines the ends, goals, hope of modernist activity, situating it in its context of premodernist frameworks.

The paradigm of post modernism exudes such theoretical adjectives as 'fragmented', 'plural', 'dispersed', 'multiple', 'discontinuous' and 'decentred'. Post modernism claims all evidence supporting these plural tendencies as indicative of its existence, in the same way that a scientist collects information as supportive of the scientific paradigm.

9.   The second and third components of a paradigm concern its methods of instrumentation. Speaking very generally, the paradigm of post modernism relies upon an electronic technology and a global mass media. Postmodernism itself was identified and is debated and observed within highly theoretical academic institutions. It assumes a capitalist economy and multinational domination. It re-examines text, tradition and discourse. It deconstructs ideology and those aspects of culture which manifest themselves as constructed through ideology. These are just a few of the 'tools' of this paradigm. It is a paradigm which is so general and so encompassing that it leaves little unaffected. In Kuhn's words, 'Paradigms determine large areas of experience at the same time' (1970:129). In particular it is the theoretical debate over the concept of post modernism and subsequent academic teaching, that function as the equivalent of the instruments of scientific research.

10. The fourth component of a paradigm is the general metaphysical beliefs which focus the research. The paradigm of post modernism is characterised by a metaphysical nihilism. It does not accept such sentiments as 'truth', 'reason' or beauty'. Instead it is based on a total reconstruction of structure and thought. As Silverman (1990: 1) states:

> Postmodernist thinking involves rethinking - finding the places of difference within texts and institutions, examining the inscriptions of indecidibility, noting the dispersal of signification, identity, and centered unity across a plurivalent texture of epistemological and metaphysical knowledge production.

Postmodernism is relentless in its pursuit of a total and meticulous reworking of the concept of culture, allowing little constructive rejuvenation to balance the deconstruction. Phillip Cooke writes:

> If postmodern thinking has a purpose it is an ironic, subversive one, not necessarily a positive or reforming one.

Therefore, the metaphysics of postmodern thought work to define and perpetuate the total paradigm of postmodernism.

11. Chalmer's fifth component can be seen within the paradigm of postmodernism as a general 'philosophy' proposing the thorough application of the laws, theories and beliefs of postmodernism on the present culture. And just as –

> A failure to solve a puzzle is seen as a failure of the scientist rather than as an inadequacy of the paradigm. (Chalmers, 1976: 92)

– events, beliefs, religions, theories and so on, that do not agree with the 'laws' of postmodernism are considered irrelevant, or at least 'deconstructable'. So although postmodernism is accepting of many formations or manifestations of culture in its essentially plural form, it excludes those that are too far removed. For example, just as telepathic communication is not acknowledged as existent by the dominant scientific paradigms, so the phenomenon of prayer or of true "belief" is not accepted by the paradigm of postmodernism. Or, as a more general observation, those human 'subjects' who may believe in the priority of spirit over the rational, the sacred and mystic over the cultural myth, risk being labelled as naively modernist or pre-modernist, because of their non-accordance with the paradigm of postmodernism.

12. In conclusion, I will summarise the main points of this essay. I believe that the concept of a paradigm, as conceived by Thomas Kuhn, is applicable to postmodernism as a dominant paradigm within the Humanities. This essay has shown that the components of a paradigm can all be transcribed onto the theory of

postmodernism. It has certain characteristics that serve as its laws and assumptions. It has methods of development and observation which serve as its instrumentation. It has metaphysical principles and a general purpose which focus it as a dominant force. This essay has been an exercise in self-reflexivity, in its attempt to expose postmodernism as being equally as encompassing in structure, as those historical knowledges which it attempts to replace. However, as a final point, it should be noted that through its very premises, postmodernism challenges the development and maintenance of paradigms, and could demand a reworking of this concept in the future.

13. Reference list

Barns, I. (ed) (1984) *Challenges for Einstein's Children: Keith Roby's Vision of Science in Community Life*, Perth: Keith Roby Memorial Fund, Murdoch University.

Chalmers, A.F. (1976, 1982) *What is this thing called Science*, Brisbane: University of Queensland Press.

Cooke, P. (1990)*Back to the Future: Modernity, Postmodernity and Locality*, London: Unwin Hyman.

Kuhn, T. (1970)*The Structure of Scientific Revolutions*, Chicago: Chicago University Press.

Lyotard, J. (1992) 'Answering the Question: What is Postmodernism?', (ed) Charles Jencks, *The Post-Modern Reader*, London: Academy Editions.

Silverman, H.J. (1990) *Postmodernism – Philosophy and the Arts*, New York: Routledge.

Essay outline: functional stages[4]

Question:

What is a paradigm according to Kuhn? Give an example of a paradigm from one of the disciplines you are studying.

(No. of words = 1,780)[5]

Para	Functional stage	Content	Macro-topic
1	State purpose	– examine the concept of a scientific paradigm	Introduction
	State outline	– consider work by Kuhn and work about him by Chalmers, Cook, Roby – apply 5 components of a scientific paradigm to the concept of postmodernism	
	State thesis	– postmodernism is a paradigm and its current influence is such that it is the dominant paradigm in cultural studies	
2	Explain theory	– explain Kuhn's theory/ his revolutionary way of viewing the history of science and development of other academic disciplines	**Explanation of theory** **(Kuhn's theory)**

---

[4]　This analysis was developed by Sally Knowles based on the framework developed by Carolyn Webb, (ed.), 1991, *Writing an essay in the Humanities and Social Sciences*, Learning Assistance Centre, University of Sydney.

[5] This word count includes 1,456 of the student's own words and paraphrases, and 323 words that are directly quoted so that 18% of the essay comprises quotations. Hence, the tutor's caution against "over quoting".

Para	Functional stage	Content	Macro-topic
	Define terms	– define paradigms as constructions and as assumptions of specific scientific communities	
	Explain purpose of theory	– explain need to expose processes involved in scientific research	
3	**Explain theory**	– explain how paradigms are created – outline 5 stages of cycle: (1) paradigm accepted as most accurate (base structure of research) (2) non-conformity can no longer be ignored (3) crisis – base paradigm threatened (4) crisis – becomes a revolution challenged by a new, better paradigm (5) establishes new paradigm as superior until it becomes the new base structure of research – cycle (1–5) starts again	**Explanation of theory**
4	**Explain theory**	– outline Chalmers' 5 general components of the Kuhn paradigm (1) it contains 'explicitly stated laws and theoretical assumptions' as the basis of the mode of research that groups of scientists/ a scientist works within (2) it includes standard ways of applying fundamental laws	**Explanation of theory (Chalmers' interpretation of Kuhn's theory)**

Para	Functional stage	Content	Macro-topic
		(3) it includes instrumentation and instrumental techniques necessary for bringing the laws of the paradigm to bear on the real world	
5	**Explain theory**	(4) metaphysical beliefs guide the work within a paradigm, equally as much as scientific beliefs give examples (Roby)	**Explanation of theory (Chalmers' interpretation of Kuhn's theory)**
6		(5) it 'contain[s] some very general methodological prescriptions such as making serious attempts to match the paradigm with nature' so that it will remain the accepted format. give example (Cooke)	**Explanation of theory (Chalmers' interpretation of Kuhn's theory)**
	Explain purpose of theory	– explain reason for paradigm: to show structure of the scientific world and its 'ways' of developing knowledge	
	Establish conditions for thesis	– state that concept is applicable to other disciplines	
7	**Restate thesis**	– Introduce postmodernism (PM) as dominant paradigm within present academic structures (esp. Humanities)	**Application of theory (Postmodernism as a dominant paradigm)**
	State outline	– consider concept of PM focusing on its relation to the components of a paradigm	

Para	Functional stage	Content	Macro-topic
	State scope	– not a complete review: briefly observe relation to the epistemology of the academic 'world'	
	Define term	– define PM (Lyotard)	
	Elaboration of definition	– PM proposes a model for the present cultural state	
8	**Restate thesis**	– PM fulfils requirements of a paradigm in a more general sense than do scientific paradigms	**Application of theory (Postmodernism as a dominant paradigm)**
	Present evidence to confirm thesis	– show how PM is a paradigm how it matches Chalmers' 5 components:	
	Present evidence to confirm thesis	first component: • PM has accepted characteristics that serve as its laws give examples of how PM uses theoretical adjectives to support claims that it exists (Silverman)	
9		second and third component • PM has methods of development and observation that serve as its instrumentation give examples of 'tools'	
10		fourth component: • PM is characterised by a nihilist metaphysical principle (e.g. it rejects truth/reason/beauty)	

Para	Functional stage	Content	Macro-topic
		• based on total reconstruction of structure and thought (Silverman) give examples of how paradigm is defined and perpetuated through metaphysics (Cooke)	**Application of theory (Postmodernism as a dominant paradigm)** *cont..*
11	**Present evidence to confirm thesis**	fifth component: • PMP has a general purpose which focuses it as a dominant force (e.g. it excludes formations or manifestations of culture that are too far removed)	
12	**Summarise outline** **Restate thesis** **Summarise evidence/outline** **Establish conditions for qualification of thesis** **Qualify thesis/ suggest directions for future research**	– summarise main points – Kuhn's concept of a paradigm is applicable to postmodernism as a dominant paradigm within the Humanities – shown that the 5 components of a paradigm can all be transcribed onto the theory of postmodernism – restate characteristics of PM & how they match Kuhn & Chalmers' definition of a paradigm – exposed PM as equally as encompassing in structure as those historical knowledges it attempts to replace – suggest need to rework the concept of a paradigm	**Conclusion**

Connecting the conclusion to the body of the essay

21.6

Activity 6

Paragraphs of the essay:

Sentences of the conclusion:

Paragraph 1 **1. INTRODUCTION**

Explanation of theory

2. Explanation of Kuhn's theory of a paradigm & definition of terms

3. Explanation of 5 stages of how paradigms are created

4. Outline of Chalmers' 5 general components of the Kuhn paradigm

5.

6.

Application of theory

7. Postmodernism is the dominant paradigm within the present academic structure (esp. Humanities)

   Definition of postmodernism

8. Postmodernism is a paradigm. Show evidence that is matches Chalmers' interpretation of Kuhn's theory

9.

10.

11.

12. Conclusion

Paragraph 12 **1. CONCLUSION**

In conclusion, I will summarise the main points of the essay.

I believe that the concept of a paradigm, as conceived by Thomas Kuhn, is applicable to postmodernism as a dominant paradigm within the Humanities.

This essay has shown that the components of a paradigm can all be transcribed onto the theory of postmodernism.

It has certain characteristics that serve as its laws and assumptions.

It has methods of development and observation which serve as its instrumentation.

It has metaphysical principles and a general purpose which focus it as a dominant force.

This essay has been as exercise in self-reflexivity, in its attempt to expose postmodernism as being equally as encompassing in structure, as those historical knowledges which it attempts to replace.

However, as a final point, it should be noted that through its very premises, postmodernism challenges the development and maintenance of paradigms, and could demand a reworking of this concept in the future.

Essay marking guide

Student's name: *Christy Newman* .... Date:................

Tutor:...

Essay topic: *What is a paradigm according to Kuhn? Give an example of a paradigm* ......

from one of the disciplines you are studying ....

Rating scale
(Rate student performance for each)

A. Definition of topic

excellent   4   3   2   1   poor

1. Does the essay answer the question?   ☑ ☐ ☐ ☐

Comment:

You have answered both parts of the question and successfully dissected the question into its constituent parts and clearly related it to the issues involved.

B. Structure of the essay

2. Does the introduction:
   - engage the reader's interest?   ☐ ☑ ☐ ☐
   - indicate the scope and theoretical position?   ☑ ☐ ☐ ☐
   - outline the thesis and supporting points?   ☑ ☐ ☐ ☐
   - indicate the order of the main points?   ☐ ☑ ☐ ☐

3. Is there an effective **conclusion** which:
   - restates the thesis?   ☑ ☐ ☐ ☐
   - draws the main points together?   ☑ ☐ ☐ ☐
   - suggests any wider implications?   ☑ ☐ ☐ ☐

4. Does the body of the essay develop the argument in a clear and logical way by:
   - presenting the points fully (one idea per paragraph)?   ☑ ☐ ☐ ☐
   - ordering and balancing the points?   ☑ ☐ ☐ ☐
   - linking the main points to the thesis?   ☑ ☐ ☐ ☐
   - linking the points to each other?   ☑ ☐ ☐ ☐

Comment:

Your argument is clear and logically developed. You could have begun with a more general statement about the organisation of knowledge in a discipline at any particular time, or said something about the popularity of the word 'paradigm', in an effort to introduce the reader to your topic in a slightly less abrupt way.

C. Research/Content

5. Is there evidence of adequate reading and research?   ☑ ☐ ☐ ☐

6. Are main points supported by evidence, examples, sources & quotations?   ☑ ☐ ☐ ☐

7. Does the writer:
   - use terms and concepts accurately and with confidence?   ☑ ☐ ☐ ☐
   - relate his/her discussion to relevant themes and issues?   ☑ ☐ ☐ ☐

8. Does the essay show evidence of original thought?   ☑ ☐ ☐ ☐

Comment:

You show familiarity with the sources in both the history of science and cultural studies. Make sure you introduce your quotes and follow or precede them with a brief introduction in your own words (ie. suggest why they support your argument). Also, clearly indicate to which paragraphs the quotes belong. Be careful of over quoting. The analysis is more cohesive if you begin and end paragraphs in your own words.

D. Presentation

9. Fluency and style of writing   ☑ ☐ ☐ ☐

10. Spelling, grammar, paragraphing   ☑ ☐ ☐ ☐

11. Neatness and legibility   ☑ ☐ ☐ ☐

12. Is a standard referencing format used consistently and correctly to acknowledge sources of quotations and paraphrases?   ☑ ☐ ☐ ☐

Comment:

The standard of presentation is excellent.

E. General comment:

An excellent piece of work, superbly referenced and well structured which provides a lucid and critical approach to complex and difficult material. You gave a clear methodological explication of the concept of a paradigm within Kuhn's theory and your example of postmodernism was really interesting and quite daring.

Grade:
HD
High Distinction

22. Understanding tutor's expectations and your objectives

Introduction

Before you choose your essay topic and before you start working on the essay, it is important to consider the unit co-ordinator's objectives in setting the essay and your tutor's or marker's expectations. It is also important that you formulate your own goals and objectives for doing the essay. Naturally, one of your goals will be to pass the unit, but you need to think beyond this and consider the skills and content you hope to learn.

As you go through the process of writing your essay, it is important to keep in mind the criteria that the tutor or marker will use to judge your essay. When you write other assignments, consult the steps outlined in this exercise.

This exercise encourages you

- to develop an awareness of the expectations that your tutor or marker has of your essays;

- to consider, develop and articulate your objectives for writing essays.

Materials

An essay that you are required to write for a unit.

22.1   Expectations of university essays

22.2   Essay marking guide

22.3   Plagiarism and collusion: a caution to students

Approximate time

30 minutes

Reading

Marshall & Rowland, 2006, pp. 87–92.

Learning activities

Activity 1   Expectations of university essays

What you think is expected

Ask yourself:
What is expected from me in this essay?
In your learning log discuss what you think your tutor expects.

Information on the essay

Carefully read any instructions on the essay.

If necessary, use your dictionary or glossary to help you understand the meaning of any terms or words included.

Information on what is expected

Reflect on Exercise 21, 'Understanding the nature of university essays' in which you examined a sample essay.

22.1
22.2

Read the attached information, 'Expectations of university essays', and the example of criteria for marking, 'Essay marking guide'.

Read Marshall and Rowland, 2006, pp. 89–92.

22.3

As you research and write your essay, keep in mind the material on plagiarism and collusion, 'Plagiarism and collusion: a caution for students'.

Differences in expectations

In your learning log, compare any differences in what you previously thought was expected with what is actually expected in your essay.

Activity 2   Your objectives for essay writing

Read Marshall and Rowland, 2006, pp. 88–89 and answer the questions in your learning log.

In your learning log consider and explain your objectives for writing this essay. For example:

- to complete a piece of work required in a unit;
- to increase your knowledge in an area;
- to read more about an area that interests you;
- to practise and improve your writing skills.

Understanding tutor's expectations and your objectives

1. Expectations of university essays

What is expected from you in this essay? Discuss what you think your tutor expects.

Compare any differences in what you previously thought was expected with what is actually expected in your essay.

2. Your objectives for essay writing

Explain your objectives for writing this essay. For example: to complete a piece of work required in a unit, to increase your knowledge in an area, to read more about an area that interests you, to practise and improve your writing skills

Expectations of university essays[6]

22.1

Activity 1

1. Relevance to the set topic

You are expected to:

– recognise and take into account the assumptions and implications in the wording of the topic;

– deal with the topic and its key terms;

– focus consistently on key ideas and terms;

– cover all parts of the set topic.

2. Use of sources

You are expected to:

– read with an open and questioning mind;

– read to understand the *parts* of the argument, and their relationship to the *whole*;

– evaluate continuously what you are reading, in terms of the argument and the relevance of the material to the topic.

3. Reasoned argument

You are expected to:

– select only points relevant to the topic and your argument;

– structure material so as to present the main ideas logically and coherently;

– ensure each section of the argument is internally consistent, and that it supports or extends the central idea;

– take into account alternative points of view or interpretations.

4. Presentation

You are expected to:

– use the tone and style of academic writing, and of the discipline in which the essay is being written;

– use specialist terminology accurately (but only when necessary);

– use the correct format for quotations;

– use the referencing and bibliographical conventions of the discipline;

– present graphic and numerical data accurately;

– edit the essay for grammar, spelling and punctuation errors.

---

[6] Adapted from John Clanchy & Brigid Ballard, 1991, *Essay writing for students: a practical guide*, 2nd edn, Longman Cheshire, Melbourne, pp. 4–11.

Essay marking guide

Activity 1

Student's name:.. Date:.........................

Tutor:...

Essay topic:..

....

Rating scale
(Rate student performance for each)

A. Definition of topic

excellent 4   3   2   1 poor

1. Has the topic been clearly defined? Is the essay on the topic? ☐ ☐ ☐ ☐

Comment:

B. Structure of the essay

2. Does the introduction present a clear statement of the issues to be covered? ☐ ☐ ☐ ☐

3. Does the essay have a clear structure or organisation in which
    - the main points are developed logically? ☐ ☐ ☐ ☐
    - the relevance of the material to the theme or argument is clear ☐ ☐ ☐ ☐

4. Is there an effective **conclusion** which: draws the main points together? ☐ ☐ ☐ ☐

Comment:

C. Content

5. Is there evidence of adequate reading and research? ☐ ☐ ☐ ☐

6. Is the breadth of coverage adequate? ☐ ☐ ☐ ☐

7. Are the issues and ideas analysed in sufficient depth? ☐ ☐ ☐ ☐

8. Are arguments supported by evidence, examples, sources and quotations? ☐ ☐ ☐ ☐

Comment:

D. Analysis

9. Are the arguments logical and consistent? ☐ ☐ ☐ ☐

10. Are opinions based on fact and/or logic? ☐ ☐ ☐ ☐

11. Does the essay show evidence of original thought? ☐ ☐ ☐ ☐

Comment:

E. Presentation

12. Fluency and style of writing ☐ ☐ ☐ ☐

13. Spelling, grammar, paragraphing ☐ ☐ ☐ ☐

14. Presentation of data: effective uses of figures and tables; correct use of units and quantities ☐ ☐ ☐ ☐

15. Sources: Are sources acknowledged? Are references cited? Are references presented correctly? ☐ ☐ ☐ ☐

Comment:

F. General comment:

Grade:

Plagiarism and collusion: A caution to students[7]

Students coming to university from other educational institutions are sometimes surprised at the serious view that is taken of certain practices relating to the submission of work for assessment.

For example, having perhaps been encouraged at school or in some other institution to build up essays by stringing together quotations or paraphrases from sources such as reference books and encyclopaedias, they find that in at university not only is more emphasis placed on personal critical analysis, but failure to identify the source of every quotation or paraphrase used is regarded as a serious offence. Another mistake is to suppose that attempts to improve one's marks by submitting work done by another person will, if detected, be treated lightly, as though it were just the luck of the game to be found out.

The two examples given above are cases, respectively, of *plagiarism* and *collusion*. Australian universities take a serious view of both *plagiarism* and *collusion* and impose drastic penalties. The following comments will help you to understand why, and will indicate how you can steer clear of these offences.

What are plagiarism and collusion? Isn't it reasonable to get help from others?

The word *co-operation* refers to joint effort, between students, or between staff and students, and is to be encouraged as it can often be a valuable way to learn. It is sometimes acceptable to make joint submissions for assessment, if the tutor clearly specifies conditions which allow this such as for group projects. Clearly then, *co-operation* (when the situation permits it, and if it is practised openly and honestly) is not an offence but a positive aspect of your learning.

Collusion refers to any form of joint effort (between students, or between students and other persons) which is intended to deceive an assessor as to who was actually responsible for producing the material submitted for assessment.

Plagiarism refers to the act of using the work of another scholar without indicating this by a reference, and/or quotation marks when exact phrases are borrowed because the ideas expressed (and the wording of them) are not one's own. When you are paraphrasing someone else's work in your own words or using an idea from another author, you must indicate the source of those ideas by using a full reference. The only difference between directly quoting another's words and paraphrasing or summarising is

---

7   Adapted from materials developed in the School of Education, Murdoch University.

in the use of quotation marks or indented text (for shorter or longer quotes): **both** need to be fully referenced.

Plagiarism can sometimes occur unintentionally, but it may also be a deliberate attempt to deceive. Both collusion and plagiarism are considered offences because an individual *fails* to *acknowledge* the help obtained from another person. The attempt to claim credit for work that is not one's own is unethical and unacceptable in the university culture.

What's so wrong about collusion and plagiarism?

Students sometimes ask: why does the university treat these things so seriously? The answer has to do with what universities see as their functions. In particular, they set out to advance knowledge by sound scholarship. This requires, amongst other things, the correction of error and the exposure of falsehood. Academic staff who might otherwise be tempted to produce dishonest work are usually restrained by the knowledge that their work will be publicly reported in academic journals where both their methods and their results will come under careful scrutiny. Cases where academics have cheated make headlines, but the reason for this is precisely because they are fairly rare and universally frowned upon.

Universities have several functions, including training for various vocations. But at all times they are expected to teach in a way which helps and requires students to acquire the skills of intellectual inquiry. To this end, universities are expected to assess their students to see whether this expectation has been met. By the awarding of a degree the university is guaranteeing to the public, amongst other things, that the graduate has through their own efforts made the grade in this respect.

Where students attempt to deceive their assessors as to the level of achievement they have actually reached, this is not only immoral but puts the university's reputation at risk. It is therefore in the university's interest to treat such offences severely. Part of the immorality in such behaviour, incidentally, is that it is unfair to other students who have attempted to do honest work. University lecturers are expected to make clear to students the university's policies on plagiarism and to report instances of such deception to the university administration for further action.

It is acknowledged, however, that many students are ignorant of what really constitutes plagiarism or collusion. The following examples may help you to recognise these.

Examples of plagiarism

Consider the following examples involving three students writing essays on the subject of school discipline. Each uses a definition in the 1972 Dettman Report on school discipline, the original of which is as follows:

The discipline of a school is the state or condition of order or good behaviour among the students.

The following discussion explores the acceptability or otherwise of the use of this source:

Student A:

'Discipline' refers to the state of order or good behaviour in a school.

Student A fails to reference what is clearly a paraphrase of the Dettman definition.8 It amounts to plagiarism because it is not referenced: the inference is that these words and ideas are entirely the student's. It is an unacceptable paraphrase because, with the omission of two words and changes in the last three, the words are taken directly from the Report. An acceptable paraphrase involves rephrasing the same ideas in your own words which usually involves using synonyms and changing the grammatical structure (i.e. the sentence structure) of the original quotation. It is also poor academic work because the student gives no sign of realising that this is but one definition or way of regarding school discipline. But most of all, it is dishonest because it involves plagiarism.

Student B:

'The discipline of a school is the state or condition of order or good behaviour among the students.'

The quotation marks indicate correctly that this definition has been borrowed from another source, although the quotation is inexact because the word 'discipline' was underlined in the original, and the quotation has not been referenced (i.e. there is no in-text citation of the author, date and page number)9. Since quoting from other sources is not the only reason why writers may put quotation marks around words, the present example is therefore ambiguous, and open to the charge of plagiarism.

Student C:

One definition says that 'The discipline of a school is the state or condition of order or good behaviour among the students' (Dettman, 1972, 7). This

---

8   Note that definitions are better directly quoted because they are, by nature, carefully worded expressions of the concept or topic under discussion, and they must always be fully referenced.

9   This applies to the Harvard referencing system, but a numbered reference would be necessary if the Footnote or Endnote referencing system were being utilised.

definition emphasises the external signs of control, but makes no reference to the state of mind of the students...

Correct. This student has quoted accurately and acknowledged the source as required. She has also shown signs of independent thinking by indicating what she considers to be a shortcoming of the definition. She has not assumed it is right because it is printed in a book.

It is surprisingly easy for assessors who know their subject to detect instances of plagiarism, sometimes running to long quotes which the student takes from a work not in a reading list provided by the lecturer. Most assessors regard the offence as sufficiently serious to warrant their searching for the original in their own time to confirm their suspicions. It can and has led to an automatic fail in that subject or even exclusion from the university.

Examples of collusion

Whereas plagiarism is sometimes unintentional, collusion is always deliberate. It involves, as was said earlier, the submission for credit of work that is not your own. Sometimes students have attempted to have a friend sit an exam on their behalf, or they have copied essays written by friends and submitted them for assessment. Assessment by written assignments tests skills which formal exams miss, but if a lecturer discovers cases of collusion, then this puts pressure on that lecturer to revert to the more traditional, and often less effective, formal exam. This, again, is unfair to the honest students.

It is quite proper for people studying the same unit to investigate and discuss a topic together. This is co-operation, and is often a valuable learning experience. It is another thing, however, for students to submit separate essays which are almost identical or mostly the work of one of them. Alert assessors usually find this sort of thing easy to pick up, and they are then obliged to take disciplinary action. Whatever help you get from discussing your topic with other people, you must record your own thinking in writing in your own way.

Policies on plagiarism

Most universities have policies regarding plagiarism and collusion and you should check the policies used in the institution in which you are studying. Usually when a student is deemed by the assessor to have violated the accepted rules of scholarship by plagiarism or collusion, the assessor must first discuss the matter with the unit co-ordinator, in order to gauge how far the matter should be taken, bearing in mind the length of time the student has been involved in tertiary study. Most institutions have a graduated series of penalties which reflect the severity of the plagiarism. Penalties include giving warnings, failing the work, reduction in the overall grade of the unit, or other more severe disciplinary action.

23. Choosing an essay question

Introduction

Choosing an essay question or assignment task is not always easy. This exercise helps you consider the list of possible questions or tasks and encourages you to think about the various alternatives and choose carefully. It is preferable to make a well considered choice at the beginning than to find that halfway through your first draft, a week before the due date, that you have chosen the wrong question and can't write on the topic!

This exercise encourages you

- to develop strategies for thinking about your essay;

- to consider guidelines on choosing an essay question or assignment task.

Materials

From your unit study guide:

- the essay questions or assignment tasks;
- information on the essay or assignment.

 23.1 Choosing your essay question

 23.2 Choosing your essay question (blank form)

Approximate time

20 minutes

Reading

Marshall & Rowland, 2006, pp. 92–94.

Learning activities

Activity 1   Information on the essay

Make sure that you understand any administrative procedures, deadlines and limitations relating to your choice of topic for the essay.

You should realise that the tutor's expectations are usually evident in the question or topic itself. In other words, the questions or topics are worded and chosen to teach you certain skills and content. So if problem solving skills are required, this will be built into the wording of the question. If critical analysis is expected, the question will include words that indicate this.

Activity 2   Choosing the best essay question

23.1

Examine the attached diagram, 'Choosing your essay question'.

It is easier to write about a question that:

–   interests you;
–   you know something about;
–   has available sources of information.

Answer the questions in the three ellipses as you consider which essay question or topic interests you and which to choose.

The list of essay questions

Read the list of essay questions in your unit study materials. If the list is long, make a short list of possible questions (up to 5). Don't limit yourself to one question at this stage, unless the choice is obvious.

When you read the list of essay questions, don't be dismayed if you don't know anything about any of the questions. This is a common reaction. Don't panic. The following exercises will help you choose and write your essay.

Allow time to choose

It is very important to allow yourself a week or so to think about your choice of essay question. For each question in your short list, search the Net or preview and skim read texts or readings for a preliminary understanding of the ideas involved in each. Find out if the resources you need are available, but don't begin serious research until you have analysed the essay question (see Exercise 24).

Activity 3 Analyse the essay question

 23.2 Complete the attached worksheet, 'Choosing your essay question', before beginning Exercise 24, 'Analysing your essay question'.

Choosing your essay question

23.1

Activity 2

Choosing your essay question can be the most difficult part of an essay. This framework can help you consider and choose from the list of questions provided.

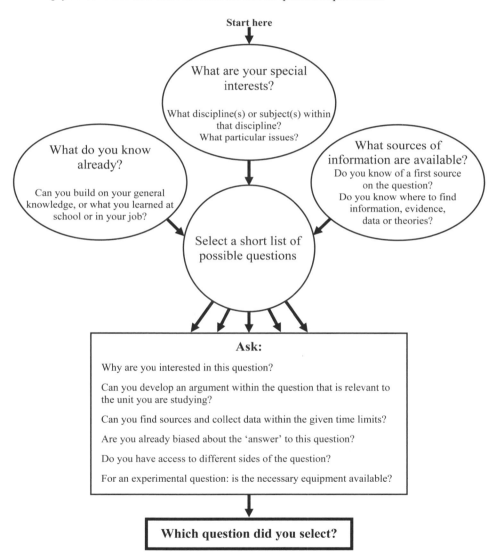

Start here

What are your special interests?

What discipline(s) or subject(s) within that discipline?
What particular issues?

What do you know already?

Can you build on your general knowledge, or what you learned at school or in your job?

What sources of information are available?
Do you know of a first source on the question?
Do you know where to find information, evidence, data or theories?

Select a short list of possible questions

Ask:

Why are you interested in this question?

Can you develop an argument within the question that is relevant to the unit you are studying?

Can you find sources and collect data within the given time limits?

Are you already biased about the 'answer' to this question?

Do you have access to different sides of the question?

For an experimental question: is the necessary equipment available?

Which question did you select?

Choosing your essay question

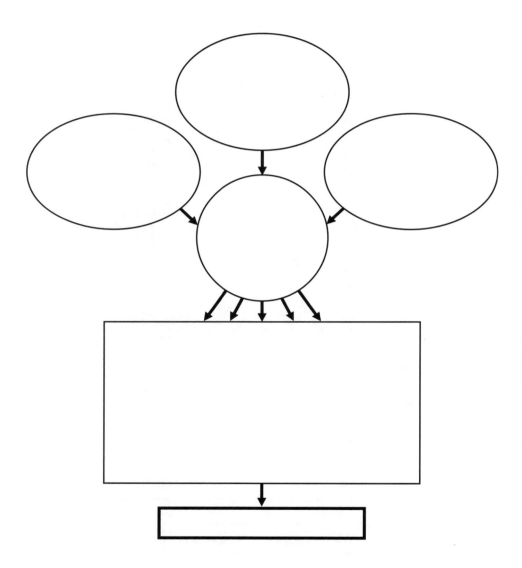

24. Analysing an essay question
Introduction

Many students jump straight into their research (usually reading) for an essay without carefully analysing (defining or interpreting) their chosen essay question. Analysing a question, and writing out an initial definition of the topic first, provides a guide for Net and library research, and helps develop an argument (thesis and supporting premises) on which to base the essay. This initial analysis of the question can form the basis of your essay but is subject to change as a result of research and reading.

Tutors often comment that a major problem with many essays is that students have not analysed the essay question thoroughly. If an essay question isn't carefully analysed, the whole essay can be inadequate. In fact it is possible to write a well-structured and well-written essay, but receive a poor grade because the essay doesn't answer the question fully, and thus misses the point. As mentioned in previous exercises, one of the essay marking criteria is a clear definition of the question. Thus, it is essential that the essay explicitly address the essay question and not deviate from it.

In this exercise you use set essay questions to develop strategies for analysing an essay question. You will be able to adapt and apply these strategies to other essays and assignments that you undertake. This exercise also asks you to write out your analysis (or interpretation) of your chosen essay question.

This exercise encourages you

- to develop strategies for analysing a chosen essay question before commencing research or reading;

- to write down your initial analysis (definition or interpretation) of the essay question.

Materials

The list of questions or topics set for an essay in your unit.

24.1   Essay writing process: circular model
24.2   Directive words

24.3   Analysing an essay question
24.4   Initial analysis of your essay question

From Exercise 23

23.2   Choosing your essay question

From Exercise 26

26.1   Revised analysis of your essay question

Approximate time

45–60 minutes

Reading

Marshall & Rowland, 2006, pp. 94–100.

Learning activities

Activity 1   The essay writing process

Your approach to essay questions

In your learning log, consider and answer the following questions.

- What do you do first when confronted with a question or topic on which you will write an essay?

- What questions do you ask about the essay question or topic?

- How do you usually go about analysing an essay question or topic?

Your approach to essay writing

In your learning log, reflect on and discuss the following questions.

When developing and writing an essay do you usually examine the question or topic, research it, draw up a plan, write a draft, write a final copy and then submit it as shown in the linear model below?

Topic
↓
Research
↓
Plan
↓
Rough Drafts
↓
Final Draft

Do you think this is the best way to write an essay?

The circular model of essay writing

24.1

To see an alternate model of essay writing, examine the attached graphic, 'Essay writing process: circular model'. This model emphasises defining and re-defining the question or topic as you research.

Note that:

- writing is central to the process;
- it is important to analyse the topic before commencing detailed research on it;
- your analysis of the topic may change as your research and read about the topic.

This graphic is referred to in following exercises.

Activity 2 Selecting a question

 23.2

Refer to the worksheet, 'Choosing your essay question' from Exercise 23. To complete this exercise, use the essay question that you have chosen and on which you hope to write your essay.

It is possible that when you have completed this exercise you will change your mind and choose another question from your short list of possible questions. Remember that it is better to change at this stage rather than when you are half way through writing your essay.

Activity 3 Analysing a question

Read Marshall and Rowland, 2006, pp. 94–100. The questions below ask you to think about the content, argument and structure of your essay.

1. What is the question about? ....Content

2. What do I already know about the question? ....Content

3. What might my thesis or theme be? ....Argument

4. How much breadth or depth can this essay have?.........Scope

5. What are the possible main points? ....Content

6. How will I structure my answer to the question? ....Structure

7. How role might my personal opinion
    play in this essay? ....Approach

When analysing your question or topic it is important to consider and tentatively decide on:

—   an argument (thesis [or conclusion] and supporting premises or [reasons]);

—   how you will approach (structure or organise) the essay.

Applying the questions on 'Analysing an essay question' to your chosen topic

24.3

When you have selected the question on which you intend to write, examine the attached worksheet, 'Analysing an essay questions, and apply each of the seven question to your chosen essay question or topic. Don't worry if you cannot answer all of these questions at this stage.

24.2

As you work through these questions, refer to the attached information, 'Directive words'.

Activity 4   Initial analysis of the question

Write out your analysis

24.4

Based on the above activities, complete the attached worksheet, 'Initial analysis of your essay question'. This worksheet should summarise your early thinking about the question or topic. You are asked to rephrase the question or topic using your own words and indicate:

—   the thesis of your essay;

—   the supporting premises or reasons;

—   how you might approach, structure or organise your essay.

You are also asked to list:

—   provisional reading in the citation format required for the essay;

—   any questions and problems.

At this stage, it is important that you know how to research and find information in the library and on the Net.

Activity 5　Revised analysis of the question

As you research and read about your essay question or topic, your thinking about it may change and you may need to revise your analysis.

26.1 If necessary complete the worksheet 'Revised analysis of your essay question' included in Exercise 26, 'Writing the first draft'.

Analysing an essay question

1.　The essay writing process

Your approach to essay questions

Consider and answer the following questions.

- What do you do first when confronted with a question or topic on which you will write an essay?

- What questions do you ask about the essay question or topic?

- How do you usually go about analysing an essay question or topic?

Your approach to essay writing

Reflect on and discuss the following question.

When developing and writing an essay do you usually examine the question or topic, research it, draw up a plan, write a draft, write a final copy and then submit it as shown in the linear model?

Essay writing process: Circular model

24.1

Activity 1

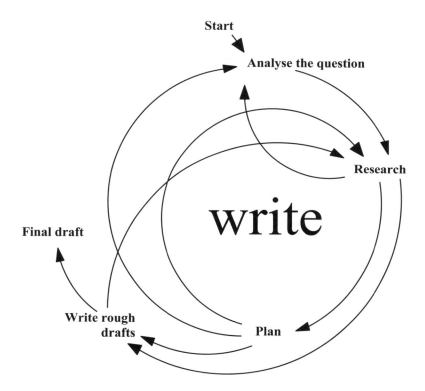

Creating an essay is a process of developing knowledge.

As you learn more about the question or topic, you go back and rethink your original propositions and thoughts and thus your analysis of the question. It is a feedback loop and as such is unlikely to be linear. It is a creative process.

Analysing an essay question

Topic ....

Content questions

1. **What is the question about?** List the key terms and ideas and their meaning.

   ....

   ....

   ....

   What assumptions seem to underlie the question?

   ....

   ....

   ....

2. **What do you already know about the question?**

   ....

   ....

   ....

   ....

3. **What are the possible main points of the question?**

   ....

   ....

   ....

   ....

   What key words will you use for library search?

   ....

   ....

Argument questions

4. **What might you thesis (or conclusion) be?**

   • What interests you most about the topic?

   ....

   ....

- What aspects of the topic do you want to explore?

- What seems most important about the question?

Given your responses to the above, what is a possible thesis?

Questions on approach

5. **How might you structure an answer to the question?**

   List the directive words and their meaning

   How many parts are there to the question?

   How will you structure your information?

   ----

6. **How will you acknowledge and examine your subjectivity?**

   To what extent will you include personal opinions? How will you acknowledge these?

   ----

7. **How much breadth or depth can this essay have?**

Directive words[10]

Analyse   Show the essence of something, by breaking it down into its component parts and examining each part in detail

Argue   Present the case for and/or against a particular proposition

Compare   Look for similarities and differences between propositions

Contrast   Explain differences

Criticise   Give your judgement about the merit of theories or opinions, about the truth of facts, and back your judgement by a discussion of the evidence

Critique   See Criticise

Define   Set down the precise meaning of a word or phrase. Show that the distinctions implied in the definition are necessary.

Describe   Give a detailed or graphic account

Discuss   Investigate or examine by argument, sift and debate, giving reasons for and against

Enumerate   List or specify and describe

Evaluate   Appraise and judge different perspectives; include your opinion

Examine   Present in depth and investigate the implications

Explain   Make plain, interpret, and account for in detail

Illustrate   Explain and make clear by the use of concrete examples or by the use of a figure or diagram

Interpret   Bring out the meaning of and make clear and explicit, usually also giving your own judgement

Justify   Show adequate grounds for decisions or conclusions

Outline   Give the main features or general principles of a subject, omitting minor details, and emphasising structure and relationship

Prove   Demonstrate truth or falsity by presenting evidence

Relate   Narrate/show how things are connected to each other, and to what extent they are alike or affect each other

Review   Make a survey of, examining the subject critically

State   Specify fully and clearly

Summarise   Give a concise account of the chief points or substance of a matter, omitting details and examples

Trace   Identify and describe the development or history of a topic from some point or origin

---

[10] Lorraine Marshall & Frances Rowland, 2006, pp. 98–99.

24.4

Initial analysis of your essay question

Activity 4

Outline as clearly as you can the argument and approach that you are considering for your essay. If you have not yet analysed your question precisely, write about the **possibilities** that you are investigating. Analysing your question carefully will help make your research and reading more efficient.

Question (exact wording): ....
....
....
....

Reword the question (in your own words):

This question ....
....
....
....
....
....

Thesis: ....
....
....
....
....
....

Supporting premises or reasons: ....
....
....
....
....
....

Approach (structure or organisation): _____

Provisional reading: (List reading and websites in the required citation format)

Questions and problems: _____

Before beginning to write your essay and after you have completed your research, repeat this process on the worksheet 'Revised analysis of the question' in Exercise 26, 'Writing the first draft'.

25. Researching information

Introduction:

Before beginning research for an essay or assignment, ensure that you have clearly analysed the essay question or assignment topic as outlined in Exercise 24. When researching you need to find out what others have written or said about the question or topic. Remember to be flexible in your approach to research and to use a variety of resources. In this exercise you are asked to frequently write down any thoughts or ideas about the question or topic.

This exercise encourages you

- to be systematic but flexible in your research;

- to value your previous experiences of research;

- to focus your research clearly on the essay question or topic;

- to use a variety of information sources, that is, to use resources other than books and journals.

Materials

25.1   Research skills
25.3   Critical thinking in the research process

25.2   Research methods for the essay

Approximate time

30 minutes

Reading:

Marshall & Rowland, 2006, pp. 101–112 and pp. 122–125.

Learning activities

Activity 1   Previous research situations

Consider a situation in which you had to gather information, for example, in school or everyday life or at work. Some examples might include a school project, a work report, information on starting a business, information on finance sources before borrowing money, information on a household item before purchasing it.

In your learning log, discuss the different research methods that you have used, differentiating between primary and secondary sources of information.

Activity 2   Primary and secondary sources

Read Marshall and Rowland, 2006, Chapter 7, pp. 101–112 and Chapter 8, pp. 122–125 before proceeding with this exercise.

Based on this reading, in your learning log define primary and secondary sources and explain the difference between them.

Activity 3   Research skills and methods

25.1   Read the attached material, 'Research skills'.

This material should help you complete the following worksheet.

25.2   Complete the attached worksheet 'Research methods for the essay', which is designed to help you think about the requirements for effective research.

If possible discuss your answers on the worksheet with another student or with your tutor.

Activity 4   Problems with research

In your learning log, list any issues or concerns that have arisen from completing the above activities.

Also, discuss these with your tutor

Activity 5   Critical thinking in the research process

25.3

The attached circular diagram, 'Critical thinking in the research process' illustrates the role of critical thinking in researching for an essay. This involves:

– researching the contemporary debate;
– considering relevant and opposing arguments;
– tentatively committing to a position;
– determining your thesis.

While researching it is important to tentatively commit to a thesis. However, further research may change your thinking on the question or topic and you may alter your thesis.

Refer to the circular diagram and map out how you plan to research your essay question.

Researching information

1. Previous research situations

Consider a situation in which you had to gather information, for example, in school or everyday life or at work. Discuss the different research methods that you have used, differentiating between primary and secondary sources of information.

2. Primary and secondary sources

Define primary and secondary sources and explain the difference between them.

3. Problems with research

List any issues or concerns that have arisen from the activities in this exercise.

Research skills

1. What technique will you use to locate useful references?

- Focus on the question or problem during the research process, and only look for material that relates to your analysis of the question.

- A starting point for relevant references is your unit study guide or materials which may have a list of references and recommended readings. Check the bibliography or references at the end of the main reference listed for the topic.

- Look under relevant subject headings in the library catalogue.

- Look in unit materials for lectures on, or relevant to, the topic. Check references mentioned in lecture(s) and if you cannot locate materials ask the lecturer for a list.

2. What types of secondary sources will you use?

- Use a variety of secondary sources; for example websites, books, journals, newspapers, lectures, television programmes, microfilm.

Secondary sources disseminate material which has already appeared in another form, and are interpretations of other sources. Textbooks are examples of secondary sources, as are abstracts, indexes, current awareness publications and popularisations. At the beginning of your studies, you will probably use mainly secondary sources for essays.[11]

3. If you plan to use primary sources, what are they?

- For many first year assignments the primary data is not mandatory.

- Primary sources might include data collected from an experiment, or from interviews or a survey, or from the Australian Bureau of Statistics.

- Primary sources are original manuscripts (books, letters, journals and so on) and contemporary records such as newspapers and reports. Primary publications contain original material, and often describe the results of research. You may use some primary sources in completing your essays.[12]

---

[11]   Trisha Cawley, 1989, Murdoch University library materials.
[12]   Trisha Cawley, 1989, Murdoch University library materials.

4. **How will you decide which references are useful and which are not?**
   - Keep the definition of the question in mind as you search for material.

   - Use effective reading skills such as previewing and skimming (Chapter 4).

5. **What problems do you expect in researching your question or topic?**
   Some of the problems might include:
   - books on the topic not in your library;
   - too much information on the topic;
   - not enough information available.

6. **How will you deal with these problems?**
   If locating information is difficult, you may need to select another question.

7. **Techniques for recording information so that it can be used later**
   - Always note full bibliographical details of all information. Provide references for all evidence you use in essays, including author, title, publication date and publication details. See Marshall and Rowland, 2006, pp. 249–257.

   - Keep your analysis of the question in mind and only make notes on material that is relevant. See Chapter 4, 'Reading', for techniques on note making.

   - Only photocopy material you will use. As you will eventually have to read all of the material, skim read it before you copy. Also, photocopying is expensive.

8. **Techniques for organising your information**
   - Develop a system for collecting and organising information before you begin.

   - The format for this system can be any one or a combination of the following:
     - notebooks
     - loose-leaf sheets in folders
     - loose-leaf sheets in ring binders
     - card system
     - computer data base

   - You can organise your information using:
     - separate page or card for each idea
     - by subject headings, or
     - by author or source.

Research methods for the essay

1. What techniques will you use to locate useful references?

----

2. What types of secondary sources will you use?

----

3. If you plan to use primary sources, what are they?

----

4. How will you decide which references are useful and which are not?

----

5. What problems do you expect in researching your question or topic?

----

6. How will you deal with these problems?

----

7. How will you record the information for use later?

----

8. How will you organise your information?

Critical thinking in the research process[13]

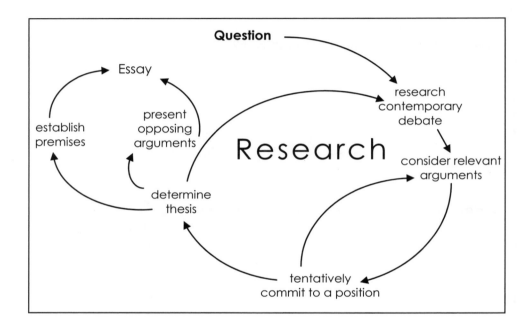

---

[13] Marshall, L., de Reuck, J., & Lake, D. 1996, *Critical thinking in context: A teacher's guide to the video*, Murdoch University, p.27.

26. Writing the first draft
Introduction

This exercise should be completed when you are ready to start writing your essay. The exercise emphasises that you can improve your writing if you:

- write often and about anything;
- verbalise the thoughts and ideas that you intend to write about;
- share what you write;
- separate the creative and editing writing stages (that is, don't edit as you create).

You can deal with this exercise in one of two ways.

- You can work through the exercise (and Exercise 27, 'Editing the rough draft') with another student who is studying the same unit and with whom you can meet or communicate with by telephone or email.

- You can work through this exercise and the next with a friend or a member of your family.

This exercise encourages you

- to write a number of rough drafts of your essay before you write the final version;

- to produce polished essays by working through the different stages in the writing process, including creating, revising and editing the rough draft(s);

- to develop strategies for generating a rough draft, including getting your thoughts down on paper, verbalising ideas, freewriting and sharing written work;

- to examine attitudes and approaches to writing generally, and to writing university essays specifically.

Materials

26.1   Revised analysis of your essay question

From Exercise 24:

 24.1   Essay writing process: circular model'

Approximate time

30–45 minutes

Reading

Marshall & Rowland, 2006, pp. 193–207.

Clanchy & Ballard, 1991, pp. 53–58.

Elbow, P. 1981, *Writing with power*, Oxford University Press, New York.

Learning activities

Activity 1   The essay writing process

Your essay writing process

In your learning log, explain how you go about writing essays. What process do you follow from when you look at the question to when you hand in the finished essay? Remember that there is no one correct way to write an essay.

Different approaches to essay writing

Read Marshall and Rowland, 2006, pp. 211–214 and 220–223 for information on various processes or approaches that students can use to write essays.

Note that there are differences between students who:

- write from a written plan;
- write from a mental plan;
- free write without a plan.

Note that there are also difference between students who:

- write out their essay only once, in what they consider to be the finished form (very few can write this well);
- write their essay roughly, then clean it up (edit) and then rewrite it neatly, (may work for short essays);
- write and re-write, do further research, add new points, and then write more (necessary for long essays).

When using the latter approach, computers enable you to easily re-write, add material and edit.

The creative and editing aspects of essay writing

This exercise explores the creative aspects of essay writing while the next exercise explores editing (refining or polishing) the essay. Although both exercised focus on essays, they can also be applied to other writing assignments.

The objectives of this exercise are to help you:

- to consider different ways to write the rough draft(s) of your essay;
- to verbalise your thoughts or ideas about your essay;
- to write down your thoughts and ideas about your essay.

Keep the following points in mind as you write your essays.

24.1

- An important part of the essay writing process involves writing down your thoughts or ideas even before you begin to write the essay. Refer back to the graphic 'Essay writing process: circular model' in Exercise 24 to refresh your memory.

- You should distinguish between and consciously separate the creative and editing stages of writing. Think about yourself as a creator and as an editor. In other words, you have two hats: one that you wear when creating and another that you wear when editing.

- You don't necessarily create the entire essay and then edit it. You can create a section and then edit it; then create another section and then edit, and so on. (You may find it useful to move backwards and forwards between this exercise and the next exercise.) When you have written the entire essay it is important to edit (or polish) the completed draft.

- When creating you don't have to start at the beginning of the essay. It is best to start a section with which you are familiar or which interests you the most.

- When creating, the creative process can flow more freely if you write for yourself – 'you' are the audience. When editing you then need to translate what you wrote for yourself to an audience. In university essays the tutor or marker is your audience.

- Aim to verbalise your ideas before writing them down. In particular, verbalise ideas that are difficult to write clearly. When editing, verbalise any sentences or ideas that are unclear and then rewrite them.

- Wherever possible, share your written work and accept constructive criticism. If you cannot share your work with another student taking the same unit, give the final draft to someone else (friend or family member) to proofread for you.

Activity 2   Assessing progress on the essay

24.1   Refer to the circular model, 'Essay writing process: circular model' in Exercise 24 and reflect on your progress with your essay.

In your learning log, discuss this progress.

Activity 3   The argument and structure of essays

Your argument and structure

Revise the questions listed in Exercise 24. Look at the completed worksheet and any comments that you received from another student or your tutor.

Remember that it is important to consider systematically the argument, content and structure of your essay.

26.1   Using the attached worksheet, 'Revised analysis of your essay topic', re-analyse your essay question or topic based on your research and reading.

Verbalising and structuring your argument

Explain to another person or talk aloud to yourself about the following aspects of your essay.

– the thesis or conclusion;
– the premises or reasons to be covered that support your thesis;
– the organisation/structure or order of your premises or reasons.

In your learning log write about your responses to these aspects.

Free writing your argument

Free writing is a technique that can help you express your ideas by allowing them to flow naturally.

Free write for 10 to 15 minutes outlining the argument of your essay.

If you find it difficult to outline your argument, free write for 10 to 15 minutes about the problems or concerns that you have with the essay.

When free writing:

- pretend that your brain is on the tip of your pencil;
- don't worry about neatness, don't erase anything;
- don't put your pen down;
- don't stop to edit or consider what you write.

Sharing your written work

First read Marshall and Rowland, 2006, pp. 203–206 for information on sharing your writing.

When you have finished writing, share your written work with another student or someone else. Meet them personally or chat over the telephone or by email.

Ask this person to comment on your work by:

- pointing out any positive aspects;
- providing constructive criticism, which involves suggesting improvements, focusing on content and avoiding comments on neatness, grammar and spelling (at this stage).

It can be helpful if you also comment on the other person's written work.

Activity 4   The importance of writing to you

Consider and discuss with another person (personally, by telephone or email) the following questions.

- Do you like to write? Why or why not?
- Does writing come easily to you? How often do you write?
- What do you write? (For example, poetry, emails, postcards, letters, essays)
- Who reads your writing?

In your learning log, explore your answers to these questions.

Read Marshall and Rowland, 2006, pp. 199–203 for further information.

Activity 5 Strategies to improve writing

Some strategies to improve writing include:

- to write often and about anything. Most university assessment is written, and as such writing is an essential skill that university students require and should be practiced regularly. You need to practise writing daily and in various ways. In other words, you need to exercise your writing muscles regularly.

- to verbalise (talk through) ideas with someone else (or yourself or to your cat or budgie) and write them down. Articulating ideas can help to clarify them.

- to share your writing. Have another person or several people read and provide constructive criticism on your written material. It is very important to find someone to do this.

- to separate the creative and editing aspects of the writing process. It is impossible to create and edit simultaneously. The creative aspect of writing requires that you create and develop, whereas the editing process requires that you critique your work.

What strategies do you need to develop or refine to improve your writing? In your learning log, write a paragraph or two about these strategies.

Activity 6 Using the free writing piece

Keep your free writing piece close by to refer to as you write the first draft of your essay.

Writing the first draft

1. The essay writing process

Explain how you go about writing essays. What process do you follow, from when you look at the question to when you hand in the finished essay?

2. Assessing progress

Reflect on and discuss your progress with your essay. (Refer to the circular model, 'Essay writing process: Circular model' to do this.)

3. The argument and structure of essays

Write about your responses to these aspects of your essay:

- – the thesis or conclusion;
- – the premises or reasons to be covered that support your thesis;
- – the organisation/structure or order of your premises or reasons.

4. The importance of writing to you

Explore your answers to these questions

- Do you like to write? Why or why not?

- Does writing come easily to you? How often do you write?

- What do you write? (For example, poetry, emails, postcards, letters, essays)

- Who reads your writing?

5. Strategies to improve writing

What strategies do you need to develop or refine to improve your writing? Write a paragraph or two about these strategies

Revised analysis of your essay question

26.1

Activity 3

Question: ....
....
....
....

Thesis: ....
....
....
....
....

Supporting premises or reasons (listed in order): ....
....
....
....
....
....
....
....
....
....

Approach: ....
....
....
....
....

27.   Editing the final draft
Introduction

The previous exercise was designed to help you create a first draft of your essay. This exercise will help you edit or polish the rough draft. When you have completed what you consider to be the final or penultimate draft of your essay, put it aside for several days (or longer if possible) before you start this exercise. Stop researching and don't add any new material. As in the previous exercise, you are urged to work with someone else, preferably with a student taking the same unit. In doing this, work through each other's essays, and apply the criteria outlined and comment on each other's essays.

When working with another person's writing remember:

- to begin with positive comments;
- to always consider the feelings of the writer;
- to reinforce the positive as people learn more from this than from negative criticism. Many people can be psychologically injured by the red pen mentality, so tread gently and be careful not to damage confidence.

This exercise encourages you

- to develop skills in editing or critically evaluating the final drafts of your essay to construct a polished piece of writing;

- to develop and apply specific criteria to your own and other written work;

- to develop strategies for examining various aspects of essays including:

    - the introduction;
    - the conclusion;
    - paragraph structure;
    - transitions between paragraphs;
    - referencing;
    - use of quotations;
    - sentence structure, spelling and punctuation.

Materials

For this exercise you need the final draft of your essay. If you work on this exercise with another student you will also need their essay.

27.1   Organising an argumentative essay
27.2   Transitional words and phrases
27.3   Referencing

From Exercise 21, 'Understanding the nature of university essays'

21.1   Essay structure: different pictorial representations
21.2   Essay structure: introduction, body and conclusion
21.3   Essay structure: functional stages
21.4   Example of a student essay
21.5   Essay outline: functional stages
21.6   Connecting the conclusion to the body of the essay
21.7   Essay marking guide

From Exercise 22, 'Understanding tutors' expectations and your purposes'

22.1   Expectations of university essays
22.2   Essay marking guide
22.3   Plagiarism and collusion: a caution to students.

Approximate time

60 minutes

Reading

Marshall & Rowland, 2006, Chapter 12, pp. 209–225 and Chapter 15, pp. 243–260.

Learning activities

Activity 1 The creative and editing aspects of essay writing

This exercise follows on from the previous exercise and considers the critical evaluation stage of editing your essay.

Activity 2 University essays

Expectations of your tutor

Refer to any information that details what is expected from you.

Revise Exercise 24, 'Understanding tutors' expectations and your objectives', and examine

22.1
22.2

- the information, 'Expectations of university essays', (Clanchy and Ballard) which outlines four expectations that tutors may have of your essay;

- the example marking criteria 'Essay marking guide' which you were asked to complete.

Your audience

It is a good idea to write your essays for someone who isn't familiar with the topic but who knows as much as other students taking the unit. It is important to show the reader (the tutor or marker) that you understand the terminology and concepts or ideas used in the essay. If you don't explain these, the reader will not automatically assume that you understand them.

Information on essays

21.1
21.2

Revise Exercise 21 and examine the graphics, 'Essay structure: different pictorial representations' and 'Essay structure: introduction, body and conclusion'. Reflect on what your essay should include.

Read Marshall and Rowland, 2006, pp. 209–225.

The following activities provide you with a **strategy for editing or critically evaluating** your own essay and other students' essays. Work through the activities in the order that they are presented.

Activity 3   A process for editing essays

If you are working with another student share your essays and follow the process outlined below. Ask him or her to read through your essay and do the same for your partner. If you are working alone follow the process using your own essay.

Re-read the essay question

Re-read the essay question and keep it in mind as you read.

Preview the essay

Preview the essay as outlined in Chapter 4, 'Reading'. Read the introduction and conclusion first. Don't read the essay in depth,

Note (write down) any positive aspects in the essay as you preview.

Read the essay for positive aspects

Remember that essays are constructed like a freight train. Re-read the quotation at the beginning of this chapter.)

Read through your essay noting positive aspects as you read.

Give first impressions

Outline your first general impression of the essay. Make sure that you give positive comments and be gentle with negative criticism. Move on quickly, and at this stage don't give an in depth analysis.

Activity 4   The introduction

What an introduction should contain

21.2

Refer back to Exercise 21, 'Understanding university essays' and examine the graphics 'Essay structure: introduction, body and conclusion'. Note the features of an introduction.

21.3 Refer to the graphic in 'Essay structure: Functional stages', and note that the introduction to university essays (depending on the essay question) usually contain the following stages:

- an introduction to the question or topic and background information;
- a summary of what you will cover in the essay;
- an outline of your argument or viewpoint presented or the conclusions reached.

The introduction[14] outlines **what you are going to say**. It should make clear your definition of the question and make the reader want to read on.

You should:

- outline your thesis or theme;
- indicate your main points;
- state how your essay is structured;
- outline your reasons for focusing on a specific aspect of a question;
- indicate the scope and limits of your essay.

To orient your reader to the topic you might:

- outline your theoretical perspective;
- explain the significance of the question; and/or
- provide a context for the essay.

Any terms or words that are central to the topic should be defined in the introduction or early in the body of the essay.

In a 1500 to 2000 word essay the introduction and the conclusion would comprise approximately 200 to 300 words each.

Examine and comment on the introduction

Alone or with a partner read the introduction to the essay and comment on:

---

[14]   Adapted from Marshall & Rowland, 2006, p. 214.

- the statement of the thesis;

- the premises or reasons used to support the thesis;

- a statement of the organisation of the essay (order of the points covered);

- the level of interest generated by the opening to the essay.

Answer the following questions.

- Does the introduction explain what the essay covers and how it is organised or structured?

- Is there a clear statement of the thesis or argument?

- How could the introduction be improved?

If the introduction does not explain the argument being presented and how it is organised, try to explain what you want to convey by speaking to another person or out loud to yourself. Then make any changes to the introduction.

Activity 5   The conclusion

What a conclusion should contain

 21.2   Refer to Exercise 21, and examine the graphic, 'Essay structure: Introduction, body and conclusion', and note the features of a conclusion.

 21.6   Examine the information, 'Connecting the conclusion to the body of the essay', and note how in the sample essay the conclusion relates to the introduction and the body of the essay. Note also that every sentence in the conclusion draws out major points by relating back to supporting premises.

The conclusion[15] draws together what you have said in the body of your essay. It should:

- sum up your argument;

- restate your thesis or theme;

---

[15]   Adapted from Marshall & Rowland, 2006, p. 220.

- draw together your main points;
- refer back to your introduction;
- round off your essay but not too abruptly – don't make it so abrupt that your reader is surprised the essay is finished.

Examine the conclusion

Read the conclusion of the essay and answer the following questions.

- Is the conclusion an effective one?

- Does the conclusion restate the argument, that is summarise the thesis and supporting premises presented?

- How could the conclusion be improved?

Make any changes.

Activity 6 The organisation of the essay

Examine the overall organisation of the essay

Read the entire essay and examine whether it has been ordered or structured in the best way.

 21.2 Refer to Exercise 21, and examine the graphic 'Essay structure: Introduction, body and conclusion', and note the features of the body of an essay.

Answer the following questions:

- Are the supporting premises developed logically in the body of the essay?

- Is the material presented relevant to the thesis?

- Are ideas and assertions adequately supported with evidence, examples and references?

- How can the logic or flow of ideas and evidence in the body of the paper be improved?

27.1 Refer to the attached material, 'Organising an argumentative essay', which provides one model for organising an argumentative essay. If it is an argumentative essay has it been organised in this way?

Examine paragraph structure

Remember that:

- each paragraph should contain only one main point;
- each sentence in a paragraph should relate clearly to the main point of the paragraph and the relationships should be obvious;
- paragraphs should (usually) be longer than one or two sentences;
- paragraphs should not be longer than half a typed page.

Read through each paragraph and answer the following questions.

- Is it a complete and unified paragraph?

- Does it contain only one main idea?

- Is the main idea easy or difficult to find?

- What is the main point of the paragraph?

- Does the main idea of the paragraph relate to the thesis of the essay?

Make the necessary changes to your paragraph structure.

Examine transitions or links

21.1 Refer to Exercise 21 and examine the graphic, 'Essay structure: Different pictorial representations' and note the importance of making links between the introduction and each major section of the essay, and between each major section and the conclusion. Also, note the importance of introducing and concluding each section or paragraph and leading on to the next.

27.2 Examine the attached table, 'Transitional words and phrases'. This table is also referred to in Exercise 18, 'Reading in depth'.

Examine the links or transitions between the paragraphs or sections and the supporting premises (and main points) presented in the essay.

Note whether each section in the essay has been concluded and the next one introduced.

Answer the following questions.

- Are there clear links (or transitions) between sentences, paragraphs, and sections in the essay?

- Does the essay indicate clearly where each section finishes and the next begins?

- Does each section link back to the introduction and does the conclusion link back to each section in the essay?

- How could the links between sentences, paragraphs and sections in the essay be improved?

Make any necessary changes to your essay.

Activity 7   Referencing

What is expected

Read Marshall and Rowland, 2006, pp. 243–257.

27.3
22.3

Also read the attached material, 'Referencing', and re-read 'Plagiarism and collusion' in Exercise 22.

Examine the referencing

Answer the following questions:

- Is the essay correctly referenced and are all sources of information acknowledged?

- Has the referencing (in-text citations and reference list) in the essay been checked?

- Is there evidence of inadvertent plagiarism of material?

Activity 8   The mechanics of the essay

What is expected

Read Marshall and Rowland, 2006, pp. 258–259.

Carefully read the essay and look for problems with:

– grammar;
– spelling;
– punctuation;
– presentation (layout including margins and spacing).

Examine the mechanics

Answer the following questions:

• Have the mechanics of the essay been checked?

• Has the essay been spell-checked?

Make any changes to the mechanics.

When you have a final copy of your essay ask someone to proofread it for the above. If you are working with another student ask them to do this for you.

Activity 9   Evaluate the essay overall

 22.2   Complete the 'Essay marking guide' from Exercise 22 'Understanding tutor's expectations and your purposes' to provide an overall evaluation of your essay.

If on the marking guide you receive a poor rating in any area, make the required changes to your essay.

Retain this marking guide and when you receive your tutor's comments compare the two.

Activity 10 Evaluate essay writing skills

In your learning log, discuss your essay writing strengths and weaknesses.

Explain any problems you have with essay writing. Explain if you would benefit from additional assistance.

Compile a list of questions to ask your tutor.

Editing the final draft

1. Evaluate essay writing skills

Discuss your essay writing strengths and weaknesses.

Explain any problems you have with essay writing. Explain if you would benefit from additional assistance.

Compile a list of questions to ask your tutor

Organising an argumentative essay[16]

27.1

Activity 6

An argumentative essay can be organised in an eight step process.

- First, *create interest in the topic* with a quote or anecdote.

- Second, state your thesis (that is, what claim or position is being conveyed in your essay).

- Third, state the *scope* of your thesis (that is, identify those related claims or positions you will not be defending).

- Fourth, state any *relevant background information* (that is, relevant facts).

- Fifth, *give your argument* (that is, your reasons for your thesis or conclusion).

- Sixth, state some possible *objections* to your argument (that is, reasons someone might disagrees with the premises you offer).

- Seventh, try to *defeat those objections* (that is, show why they are false or do not apply in your case).

- Lastly, summarise your position (argument) and try to give some 'food for thought' (that is the implications of your position for other issues).

---

[16] Marshall, L., et al, 1996, p. 27.

Transitional words and phrases[17]

Activity 6

Transitional words and phrases (connectives, conjunctions, or signalling words) connect ideas, concepts, observations or evidence. The list that follows is highly selective. Some of the common logical relationships used in academic contexts and the words and phrases that signal them are listed below.

Addition:
in addition, again, also, and, besides, finally, first, further, last, moreover, second, too, next

Cause and effect:
accordingly, as a result, consequently, hence, otherwise

Comparison:
similarly, likewise

Contrast:
in contrast, although, and yet, but, however, nevertheless, on the other hand, on the contrary

Examples or special features:
for example, for instance, in other words, in illustration, in this case, in particular, specifically

Summary:
in brief, in conclusion, in short, on the whole, to conclude, to summarise, to sum up

Connections in time:
after a short time, afterwards, as long as, as soon as, at last, at length, at that time, at the same time, before, earlier, of late, immediately, in the meantime, lately, later, meanwhile, presently, shortly, since, soon, temporarily, thereafter, until, when, while.

---

[17] Adapted from Marshall & Rowland, 2006, pp. 217.

Referencing

27.3

References are used to identify and acknowledge the sources you have used in your writing . You need to reference the authors whose works you have used whenever you:

- quote the exact words of another author
- closely summarise a passage from another author
- use an idea or material which is directly based on the work of another author (Clanchy and Ballard, 1981, p. 117).

This material should be used in conjunction with Marshall and Rowland (1993) where a number of different systems of referencing are described. You may use any of these provided you use it consistently and correctly. A commonly used system of referencing is the **Harvard System** in which all references are cited in the text of the assignment. The references are brief and include only the author's surname, date of publication, and page number (if a quote or specific detail is noted). Full details of this work then appear at the end of your assignment in the 'References' or 'Bibliography' section. For example, in the text of your assignment, you make reference to an author's work in the following way:

> Lederberg (1972) has outlined the concerns about the impact of science and technology on various systems.

If more than one paper by the same author is cited put the year in which each paper was published in brackets after the author's name. For example:

> More than thirty years later, Lang and Kohn (1970, 1973) performed detailed research using the same material.

When several references are cited together, both the authors' names and publication dates are placed in brackets. For example:

> In recent years, evidence has been found to ...(Weiner, Hulbert and Johnson, 1986; Chen and Smith, 1987).

If the same work by several authors is referred to more than once in the text of an assignment, the first time you cite these authors you need to mention each of these author's names (for example, Weiner, Hulbert and Johnson, 1986). In any subsequent references to this same work by these authors, you can use '*et al*'. For example, 'this research by Weiner *et al* (1986) has found similar results'. Other combinations are detailed in Marshall and Rowland (1993, table 15.2 pp.242-244).

At the end of your assignment, **in the Reference section**, all studies actually cited in the text of your assignment need to be listed. All authors are listed, by surname in alphabetical order. The name of all journals should be underlined, or in italics. When referencing **journal articles,** give the name(s) of the author(s), date of publication, title of the report, the journal in which it appeared, the volume number of the journal, and the page numbers of the article. For example:

> Hammond, K. R., and Adelman, L. (1987) 'Science, values and human judgement'. *Science*, 194, 386-396.

When referencing **books**, give the name(s) of the author(s), year of publication, the title of the book (underlined or in italics), the place of publication, and the publisher. For example:

> Kneller, G.F. (1978) *Science as human endeavour*, New York: Columbia University Press.

While different formats are acceptable if used consistently (that is, one format for the whole essay) all formats include basic information: author, title(s), publication details (year, publishing place) and page numbers.

Appendix

Numeracy answers

Apply the Five Step Framework to Table 1

'Estimated poverty rates and other characteristics of Australians, 1990 to 2000'.

20.5

Activity 5

Answers

Step 1: Getting started

Q1.1:   *The general topic being examined is poverty in Australia from 1999 to 2000.*

Q1.2:   *The characteristics used are the numbers of adults and children in poverty related to the half average and half median poverty lines, incomes of other groups and inflation.*

Q1.3:   *The table comes from the Smith family and NATSEM report. 'The Smith Family researches different forms of disadvantage to propose preventative responses to them, and to promote social change through research, advocacy and innovation'. NATSEM is the National Centre for Social and Economic Modelling based at the University of Canberra. You can expect these sources to be reliable. Note: To access the report from the web page go to the Education and Disadvantage link and locate the report under Publications.]*

Terms and footnotes

Q1.4:   *The average (mean) income is calculated by adding together all the incomes and dividing by the number of incomes.*

Q1.5:   *The 'half average poverty line' is set at half the national average (mean) income.*

Q1.6:   *A median is located in the middle of a set of numbers when they are arranged in order. (The median of an odd set of numbers is the middle number, the median of an even set of numbers is the mean of the two middle numbers.)*

Q1.7:   *The 'half median income poverty line' is set at half the national median income.*

Q1.8:   *Children are defined in the footnote to Figure 1 as: 'Dependent children means all of the children less than 15 and all 15 to 24 year olds engaged in full time study and living at home.'*

Q1.9:   *The inflation rate has been taken into account to make the incomes relative to the year 2000 incomes.*

Step 2: WHAT do the numbers mean?

A. 'Half average income poverty line'

Q2.1: *14.3 is the percentage of children in 1990 who were below the 'half average poverty line'. [Note that the Table does not refer to percentages directly. You need to assume that the use of percentage in Figure 2 is continued for the task]*

Q2.2: *743 tells us that 743 000 children were below the 'half average income poverty line' in 2000.*

Q2.3: *$723 is the median (middle) income per week in 2000. $832 is the average (mean) income per week in 2000.*

Q2.4: *2.76 tells us that in 2000 the middle (median) income was 2.76 times the income of people defined as poor. [Note 723 ÷ 262 = 2.76]*

3.18 tells us that the mean (average) income is 3.18 times the income of people defined as poor. [Note 832 ÷ 262 = 3.12]

B. 'Half median income poverty line'

Q2.5 *The 9.0 tells us that in 1990 9% of children in 1990 were below the 'half median poverty line'.*

Q2.6: *The 8.7 tells us that in 2000 8.7% of all Australians were under the median poverty line.*

Step 3: HOW do the numbers change?

A. 'Half average income poverty line'

Q3.1: *The least was in 1996. The most was in 2000.*

The poverty rate for children decreased to 1996 and then increased to 2000.

Q3.2: *The least was in 1900. The most was in 2000.*

The poverty rate for adults increased from 1990 to 2000

B. 'Half median income poverty line'

Q3.3: *The least was in 1995. The most was in 2000*

The poverty rate for children fluctuated between 1990 and 2000?

Q3.4: *The least was in 1990. The most was in 2000.*

The poverty rate for adults increased to 1996 and then declined and levelled off.

C. Numbers in poverty

Q3.5: *The least was in 1990. The most was in 2000.*

The number of children in poverty increased from 1990 to 2000.

Q3.6: *The least was in 1990. The most was in 2000.*

The number of adults in poverty increased from 1990 to 2000?

Step 4: WHERE are the differences?

Q4.1: *The numbers and rates increased for all categories from 1990 to 2000 except the rates for children that decreased to 13.1% in 1996 before increasing to 2000.*

Q4.2: *With the half median poverty line there is no consistency. However, there is an overall increase in all three categories from 1990 to 2000.*

Q4.3: *The main difference is that percentage values are all a lot higher for the half average poverty line than the half median poverty line. There are similar changes for both. [Note: refer to the fifth paragraph in the Introduction which makes it clear that the average refers to all people, including the most affluent.]*

Step 5: WHY do the numbers change?

Q5.1: *Factors which influenced the changes include:*

- *Increase in poverty of the unemployed in 1990's.*
- *Progress in early 1990's to fight against child poverty led to decrease in percentage.*
- *Minor rise in 1990's of child poverty due to increase in poverty of couples.*
- *Growth of part time work and casual employment increases family poverty.*
- *Increase in rents due to the housing boom.*
- *Increase in high earner's income in 1990's made the average higher.*

Apply Five Step Framework to the graph in Figure 3 'Trends in poor, middle average and top incomes, after adjustment for inflation, 1990 to 2000a'
Answers

20.6

Activity 6

Step 1: Getting started

Q1.1: *Changes in income per week.*

Q1.2: *(a) the money is adjusted to be directly related to the income in 2000.*

Q1.3: *Poor, middle (median), average (mean), 95%.*

Q1.4: *It comes from the Smith family and NATSEM report. 'The Smith Family researches different forms of disadvantage to propose preventative responses to them, and to promote social change through research, advocacy and innovation'. NATSEM is the Centre for Social and Economic Modelling based at the University of Canberra. You can expect these sources to be reliable. (To access the report from the web page go to the Education and Disadvantage link and locate the report under publications.)*

Terms and footnotes

Q1.5: *'Poor' is less than half the average family income for all Australians (after income tax and before housing costs).*

Q1.6: *The middle income if all incomes placed in order (50% below, 50% above).*

Q1.7: *Average (mean) is the sum of all incomes divided by the number of people receiving income.*

Q1.8: *95% of people receive an income below that amount.*

Q1.9: *The inflation rate has been taken into account to make the incomes relative to the year 2000 incomes.*

Q1.10: *By year*

Q1.11: *By dollars per week*

Step 2: WHAT do the numbers mean?

Firstly look at the legend to distinguish between the different lines.

Q2.1: *$200*

Q2.2: *$700*

Q2.3: *$800*

Q2.4: *$1650*

Step 3: HOW do they change?

Q3.1: *The least was in 1990/1996. The most was in 2000.*

The income for the top 5% fluctuated between 1990 and 2000?

Q3.2: *The least was in 1996. The most was in 2000.*

The income for the average people decreased to 1996 and then increased.

Q3.3: *The least was in 1996. The most was in 2000.*

The income for the middle people decreased to 1996 and then increased.

Q3.4: *The least was in 1990. The most was in 2000.*

The income for the poor people stayed about the same between 1990 and 2000?

Step 4: WHERE are the differences?

Q4.1: *The middle is the 50th percentile, half the people have incomes below it. The two graphs look very similar because they are 95% and 50% of the same total income.*

Q4.2: *The poor people's income is defined as half the average income so the graphs are similar in shape.*

Step 5: WHY do they change?

Q5.1: *Factors which influenced the changes include:*

- *Increase in poverty of the unemployed in 1990's.*

- *Progress in early 1990's to fight against child poverty led to decrease in percentage.*

- *Minor rise in 1990's of child poverty due to increase in poverty of couples.*

- *Growth of part time work and casual employment increases family poverty.*

- *Increase in rents due to the housing boom.*

- *Increase in high earner's income in 1990's made the average higher.*

References

Aukerman, R. C. 1972. *Reading in the secondary school classroom*. McGraw Hill, USA.

Barrett, Jill, Marshall, Lorraine, & Butcher, Linda. 1995. *From life to learning: transferable skills for independent learning, User's guide to the video*. Gripping Films Production, Academic Services Unit, Murdoch University.

Bertola, Pat, & Murphy, Eamon. 1994. *Tutoring in the social sciences and humanities: a beginner's practical guide*. Curtin University, Western Australia,

Boud, David. 1986 'Implementing student self-assessment'. *HERDSA Green Guide* No. 5, Higher Education Research and Development Society of Australasia, Campbelltown, New South Wales.

Buzan, Tony. 1993. *The mind map book*. BBC Books, London.

Buzan, Tony. 1974. *Use your head*. British Broadcasting Corporation. London.

Candy, P. C., Crebert, G., & O'Leary, J. 1994. *Developing lifelong learners through undergraduate education*. NBEET, AGPS, Canberra.

Chaffee, John. 1990. *Thinking critically*. Houghton Mifflin, Boston.

Clanchy, J. & Ballard, B. 1991. *Essay writing for students: a practical guide*. Longman Cheshire, Melbourne.

Clanchy, J. & Ballard, B. 1994. *Making the most of your arts degree: a guide for students in the Social Sciences*. Longman, Melbourne.

Elbow, P. 1981. *Writing with power: Techniques for mastering the writing process*. Oxford University Press, New York.

Gibbs, Graham. 1981. *Teaching students to learn: a student centred approach*. Open University Press, Milton Keynes.

Habeshaw, S. & Steeds, D. 1987. *53 interesting communication exercises for science students*. Technical Education Services Ltd, Bristol, UK.

Hardin, Garrett. 1968. 'The tragedy of the commons'. *Science*, Vol. 164, pp. 1243-1248.

Maddox, J. n.d. 'It's the good guess that counts'. *Science Diary*. source unknown.

Main, Alex. 1980. *Encouraging effective learning*. Scottish Academic Press, Scotland.

Marland, Michael. 1977. *Language across the curriculum*. Heinemann, London.

Marshall, Lorraine & Rowland, Frances. 2006. *A guide to learning independently*. 4th edn, Pearson Education, Sydney.

Marshall, Lorraine & Rowland, Frances. 1998. *A guide to learning independently*. 3rd edn, Addison Wesley Longman, Melbourne.

Marshall, Lorraine, de Reuck, John & Lake, David. 1996. *Critical thinking in context: a teacher's guide to the video*. Gripping Films Production, Academic Services Unit, Murdoch University.

McEvedy, M. R., Packham, G. & Smith, P. 1986. *Studying in Australia: speaking in academic settings*. Nelson, Melbourne.

Morgan, Frank. 1968. *Here and now: an approach to writing through perception*. Harcourt, Brace & World, New York.

Open University. 1980. *PME Mathematics across the curriculum*. The Open University Press, Milton Keynes, UK.

Sinclair, J. (ed.) 1987. *Collins Cobuild English language dictionary*. Collins, London, Glascow.

Stevens, M. 1987. *Improving your presentation skills: A complete action kit*. Kogan Page, London.

Sykes, J (ed.) 1982. *Concise Oxford Dictionary*. 7th edn. Clarendon Press, Oxford.

Taylor, Elizabeth, et al. 1980. *The orientations of students studying the social science foundation course*. Study Methods Group Report. No. 7. Institute of Educational Technology, The Open University, Walton Hall, Milton Keynes.

Tripp, David. 1993. *Critical incidents in teaching the development of professional judgement*. Routledge, London and New York.

Webb, Carolyn. (ed.) 1991. *Writing an essay in the Humanities and Social Sciences*. Learning Assistance Centre, University of Sydney.